'A Dutch Miracle'

To our teachers
Philippe Schmitter and Colin Crouch

'A Dutch Miracle'

Job Growth, Welfare Reform and Corporatism in the Netherlands

Jelle Visser & Anton Hemerijck

AMSTERDAM UNIVERSITY PRESS

Typesetting: Magenta, Amsterdam
Cover design: Kok Korpershoek, Amsterdam
Cover illustration: H.G. Pot, *Flora's mallewagen*, c. 1640. Panel, 61 x 83 cm. Coll. Frans Hals Museum, Haarlem.

ISBN: 90 5356 271 0

Contents

Preface

OVER THE PAST YEAR, the Dutch political economy has become the wonder and sometimes envy of foreign observers. The key to international acclaim has been the job miracle. In this book we explore the miraculous recovery from the severe unemployment crisis in the early 1980s to record job growth in the 1990s.

The original impetus for us to write this book came from Wolfgang Streeck, who invited us, independently from one another, to come to Cologne in the Fall of 1996 and give two seminars at the Max Planck Institute for the Study of Societies on recent changes in Dutch industrial relations and welfare reform. The trenchant questions by Wolfgang, and the institute's other directors, Renate Mayntz and Fritz Scharpf, during and after our presentations, reinvigorated our fascination with the puzzle of the miracle of job growth and welfare reform. Against the background of increased international praise for the Netherlands, our plan to combine our notes into a common paper turned into a full-scale project when, early in 1997, Saskia de vries, the publisher of Amsterdam University Press, approached us with her well-timed request to write a book on 'the Dutch miracle'. This speeded up our earlier plans and gave momentum to our desire to examine in greater detail the development of Dutch social and economic policy-making in recent times, covering the full width of industrial relations, social security and labour market policy.

With the encouragement of Saskia and her staff and the kind hospitality of the directors of the Max Planck Institute, we were able to get together in Cologne in the Spring and Summer of 1997. We are most grateful for their support, without which it would have taken us much longer to weave our ideas into a book. We also like to thank our colleagues at the University of Amsterdam and the Erasmus University in Rotterdam, for their endurance with our obsession of the past half year. We are especially thankful to Monika and Emke, for their enthusiasm and support for this riveting project.

In the attempt to link and relate the trials and tribulations of industrial relations, social security, and labour market policy in the Netherlands, we were immediately confronted with the complexities of Dutch corporatism. As this book embodies an argument about the proficiency of corporatism under increased international constraints, we decided to dedicate this book to our teachers, Phillippe Schmitter and Colin Crouch, now both at the European

7

University Institute in Florence. This dedication reflects our deep gratitude to Phillipe and Colin for introducing us to the fascinating diversity of modern European political economies.

The conceptual evolution of the project was greatly enhanced by the stimulating and critical comments from Fritz Scharpf, Wolfgang Streeck, Werner Eichhorst, Bernard Ebbinghaus, and continuing discussions with Phillipp Genschel at MPI. Among the Dutch scholars with whom we have in past years collaborated on many of the issues in this book, we would like to thank Ben van de Brande, Jan-Kees Helderman, Pieter-Jan Jongen, Kees van Kersbergen, Robert Kloosterman, Marc van der Meer, Maurice Rojer, Joris van Ruysseveldt, Jan-Peter van den Toren, and Romke van der Veen. It has been a pleasure to work with each of them.

Special thanks are due to Ellie van Kooten and Els Vogels, both at the Ministry of Social Affairs and Employment. In what may have been the hottest August of the century in this country, Els has been of unfailing help in providing us with essential information and inspired criticism. As always and sadly, the errors of fact and judgment are exclusively our own.

Jelle Visser and Anton Hemerijck
Amsterdam and Rotterdam, August 1997

Chapter One

How to Explain a Miracle?

IN 1986 SWEDISH SOCIOLOGIST GÖRAN THERBORN, in a book which he provocatively titled *Why Some People Are More Unemployed Than Others*, dubbed the country where he worked, the Netherlands, as 'perhaps the most spectacular employment failure in the advanced capitalist world'. Two years earlier unemployment had reached a record number of 800,000, nearly fourteen percent of the labour force. An almost equal number of workers had been eased out of the labour market through disability benefits and early retirement. According to calculations of the Organisation of Economic Co-operation and Development broad unemployment, which includes the registered unemployed who are unavailable for work, beneficiaries of disability pensions, people who have taken early retirement, or are on social assistance, workers in government-sponsored training schemes and in public labour pools, had soared to 27 percent of the labour force. The Netherlands was a prime example of Gøsta Esping-Andersen's pathology of *welfare without work* which in his view is typical for continental European welfare states. Foreign observers ridiculed the Dutch, in particular with respect to 'keeping more than a million people supported by the welfare state', as 'cloudy and lacking in realism'.[1] The expression *Dutch disease* made its appearance in economics textbooks as an example of expensive and unsustainable public welfare policies.

Ten years later, Dutch policies again draw international attention. While the international community, after the demise of the Swedish model, is on the lookout for new examples of capitalism with a human face, the Dutch 'miracle' occupies a prominent place in many commentaries. Central bankers and politicians praise the combination of welfare reform and fiscal conservatism with job creation and the maintenance of overall social security. They highlight the extraordinary proportion of Dutch people, male and female, who work in part-time jobs; the sustained policy of wage moderation; the successful approach of the Economic and Monetary Union convergence criteria; the absence of social unrest; and the consensual style of social policy reform. They cannot help to observe that the Netherlands is the only EU Member State that has succeeded in halving the unemployment rate during the past decade, from almost fourteen percent in 1983 to just over six percent in 1997[2], well below the dismal eleven percent average for the European Union.

9

Mr. Jean-Claude Trichet, president of the French Central Bank, recommends a 'Dutch miracle' of fiscal rectitude, welfare and labour market reform, social consensus and job growth to his compatriots.[3] Troubled with record unemployment, worsening public finances and reform stalemate at home, German policy advisors have turned to their 'big little neighbour' for inspiration.[4] Belgian politicians call upon trade unions and employers to follow the example of wage moderation and consensual policies of their Northern neighbour.[5] And even *The Economist* finds words of praise for 'the usual cosy Dutch consensus, epitomized by the country's odd-sounding government combination of left, right and centre (...) which expedited a significant departure from the weakened continental model of slackening economic growth, rising unemployment and (financial) predicament of the welfare state'.[6]

The words 'consensus' and 'departure' in the above quotation are well-chosen, for consensus is indeed a familiar property – however not to be exaggerated – of Dutch society and politics, and the employment performance of the Netherlands suggest a departure from the current unemployment malaise in the European Union and its own recent past. Where there are so few examples of strong job growth in Western Europe, and so few signs that it is possible to consensually adjust the institutional, social and mental pattern of a passive welfare state, the Dutch example does invite closer study.

RELATIVE SUCCESS AMIDST A EUROPEAN MALAISE AND A DISMAL PAST

Has there been a miracle? Our answer is that a remarkable change has taken place – away from the welfare without work society which the Netherlands was rapidly becoming during the 1980s. Table 1 compares the performance of the Netherlands with the European Union average using six broad indicators: real GDP growth, private consumption, investment, employment, unemployment, and net labour force participation. It is clear that over the past six years the Netherlands did better than its EU partners on each of these indicators. This has been achieved while bringing down the budget deficit to 2.2 percent of GDP in 1996, well within the 3 percent norm of the Economic and Monetary Union (the deficit was 3.8% in 1970, 7.2% in 1980). The collective expenditure quote has fallen for four years in a row and with it the GDP share of taxes and social charges. In 1996 this share was 44.4 percent (47.3% in 1970, 57.2% in 1980) which is still a respectable sixth place in the European Union, behind Denmark, Sweden, Belgium, Finland and France.[7] The total public debt has decreased to 78.5 percent in 1996. With inflation averaging under 2.5 percent for the last decade, there is no doubt that the Netherlands will join the EMU on the first occasion.

Table 1: Economic performance of the Netherlands in comparison with the European Union, 1991-96

	Netherlands	European Union
GDP	2.2%	1.5%
private consumption	2.3%	1.5%
investment	1.3%	−0.2%
employment	1.5%	−0.5%
unemployment level	6.2%	11.1%
employment/population ratio	64.2%	60.6%

Source: DNB (Dutch Central Bank), *Annual Report 1996*, Amsterdam, 1997, p. 24; and OECD, *Employment Outlook*, Paris, various years.

In Chapter Two we will examine the claim that there was an 'employment miracle' and discover that not all that glistens is gold. There was, and is, a remarkable rate of job growth: 1.6 percent per year on average since 1983. This is four times the average for the European Union and as good as the American 'jobs machine'. Compared to the latter, job growth is less associated with a sharp increase in earnings inequality. Inequality has increased but the Netherlands has been able to maintain a middle rank between Germany and Scandinavian countries on the one hand, Britain and the US on the other. Many of the new jobs, however, are part-time, sometimes for a very limited number of hours, irregular and with few career prospects; and they are still overwhelmingly held by women. Labour force participation, especially of women, has shown a remarkable increase, but participation rates of older males, between the age of 55 and 64, before legal retirement, has dropped to one of the lowest in Europe. Also the low employment chances of ethnic minorities and unskilled workers takes away some of the shine of the miracle and points to unresolved problems of social integration and economic efficiency.

Changes have been profound, even if incomplete. Welfare and labour market reforms have brought new chances but also new inequalities. Some groups lose out or have failed to benefit from recent economic success. Long-term unemployment has started to decrease, but still almost half of all the unemployed are one year or longer out of a job. Broad unemployment, although declining in absolute and relative terms, remains high at an estimated twenty percent of the current labour force. New jobs have gone predominantly to younger and better skilled recruits to the labour market. Unemployment remains a huge problem for unskilled and immigrant workers, with unemployment rates two to three times the national average. Youth unemployment, on the other hand, has fallen below the average, for the first time in two decades and is now 5.5 percent. In short, the success of the employment and labour market performance of the Netherlands is relative, to be put against the background of the dismal experience of the recent past, on the one hand, and the lacklustre performance of most European countries on the other.[8] There is no full employment yet and the present state of nearly full part-time employment may be judged a second-best solution only.

IN SEARCH OF AN EXPLANATION

How might we explain this relative success? The Netherlands shares the structural problems of other welfare states: the adjustment to the changing conditions of international competition, as well as the challenges of industrial change, an ageing population, longer life expectancy, rising health costs and health risks, changing family patterns and individualization of life styles (Flora, 1987). Moreover, the Netherlands shares the passive legacy of other continental welfare states, with a strong bias towards protection of steady employment, organized around a presumption of male breadwinners, combined with subsidized labour exclusion (Esping-Andersen, 1990). It is usually argued that welfare states are exceedingly hard to change (Esping-Andersen, 1996; Pierson, 1994). How could the politics of welfare reform in the Netherlands be successful?

On a theoretical level our answer has to be located in a combination of problem load, power shifts, institutions, politics and ideas. In Chapters Three and Four we will develop our theory of policy learning, which we will in later chapters apply to three core domains of the welfare state: industrial relations, social security, and labour market policy. In Chapter Three we argue that there are ways to overcome the forces of inertia and in Chapter Four we develop the hypothesis that the corporatist format of the Dutch economy might not only have helped the implementation of centrally agreed policies, but also facilitated a problem solving style of policy making and the adoption of 'other regarding' policies of interest groups, in particular of the trade unions. Our model allows, however, that learning is blocked and that corporatism stifles reform in one policy domain while organizing support for fundamental change in another policy domain. Policy changes are the result of *puzzling*, identifying and defining problems and solutions by state and societal actors, and of *powering*, authorizing and rallying support for the selection of particular problems and solutions.

Although it only attracted international attention in the mid 1990s, the 'Dutch miracle' has its basis in policy changes in the early 1980s. The 1981-83 recession was exceptionally severe, by international standards[9] and in the light of the post-war history of the Netherlands (van Zanden and Griffiths, 1989). National income declined during eight consecutive quarters[10] and the net investment rate, which had decreased from seven percent in the decade before the first oil crisis (1973) to 4.6 percent in the second half of the 1970s, slumped to a mere two percent. Many sectors suffered from overcapacity, firms ran into debts, and one of every 25 firms in manufacturing went bankrupt. Between 1981 and 1983 300,000 jobs were shed, mostly in industry, and nearly all full-time. Unemployment soared at a rate of 10,000 per month to a record 800,000 in 1984 and seemed unstoppable. The trade unions lost 17 percent of their members and of the remaining membership nearly one-quarter was out of work, on social benefits or in retirement. Union density plummeted and stood at a mere 25 percent by 1987, compared to 35 percent before 1980. The average disposable income of employed workers fell in three consecutive years (1981-83) by nearly ten percent; social benefits for people without employment fell even more.

In its recent reflections on the origins of the Dutch miracle, the Dutch Central Bank argues that in the light of the severity of the crisis

'it is no wonder that the government and the social partners reached the conclusion that "a limit was reached" and a change in policy and mentality was necessary'.[11]

In Chapter Three we will explore the theoretical meaning of this statement and argue that under particular circumstances a crisis does indeed create a 'sense of urgency' and works as a 'triggering device' for social learning and policy change. In the case of the Netherlands, the most important of these changes 'in policy and mentality' was the nation-wide recognition that for a higher level of investment, essential for the creation of more jobs and the struggle against mass unemployment, a higher level of profitability was required.[12]

This however was only the first lesson learnt in the Dutch political economy after a lengthy period of policy deadlock. Subsequent reform efforts concentrated on social security and most recently we have observed a policy change with respect to labour force participation and labour markets. The sequence of Dutch policy learning, we believe, has to be understood in terms of the intimate links between the policy domains of industrial relations, social security and the labour market.

THREE RELATED POLICY DOMAINS

In advanced welfare states the politics of economic and industrial adjustment, social protection, and labour market management appear as three institutionally separated policy domains. Although fundamentally engaged in the same task of meeting the material needs of citizens, different methods of provision apply in these domains. The diversity of the rights at issue – industrial rights, social rights, and the right to work – have a distinct history of advocacy and governance. The relationship with the formal employing organizations of the labour market is different in each case. Whereas industrial rights define the position of workers who are employed in organizations, social rights, following T.H. Marshall, are politically disengaged from the labour market. Social rights serve to protect the non-working population – the aged, the sick, and the unemployed – by providing them with sources of income, social security and public assistance, which helps them to make ends meet without necessarily relying on their labour power. The third policy domain entertains a tenuous position between those inside and outside the formal labour market. The right to work addresses the outsiders, asserts their right of participation and integration into society, and is extremely problematic (Elster, 1988).

Whereas industrial rights are established under labour law, collective bargaining and employee participation, social rights are institutionalized in social security entitlements and public assistance. The right to work may be anchored in a public commitment to uphold full employment and be underpinned by a so-called 'active labour market policy', but in a capitalist economy this right is crucially dependent for its implementation upon the voluntary cooperation of autonomous employing firms. The study of these domains has ended up at different places in the academic division of labour: industrial relations, social policy studies, and labour (market) economics. How problematic this division has become in practice was demonstrated in some of the major strikes of recent years, for instance, in November and December of 1995 in France, in the German metal industry and the Dutch construction industry earlier that same year. Each of these strikes went far beyond a classical industrial dispute and involved conflicts over welfare state retrenchment, economic development and labour market flexibility.

THE DOUBLE BIND OF MODERN WELFARE STATES

The measure of public protection from market forces offered by modern welfare states has been aptly coined 'decommodification' by Esping-Andersen. With this concept he refers to 'the degree to which individuals, or families, can uphold an acceptable standard of living independent from market participation' (1990: 37). The degree and forms of decommodification are, in his view, fundamental to the understanding of the cross-national diversity in welfare state development. Decommodification, however, tends to obscure that social development is critically dependent upon private economic activity to create wealth, employment and a tax-base for welfare programs. There are obvious limits to disengaging the policy domain of social rights from that of economic adjustment and labour market efficiency.[13]

The comparative study of industrial relations has been more attentive to the impact of changes in world markets on domestic actors and their collective strategies for advancing and defending social and industrial rights. Students of corporatism have explicitly dealt with the type of bargained cooperation between government and organized interests over the definition and execution of export-led growth strategies in response to changes in world markets (Streeck, 1992). In his richly documented study of industrial policy making in seven small European nations during the 1960s and 1970s, Peter Katzenstein (1985) has demonstrated how these corporatist political economies have come to employ a sophisticated, stable and highly institutionalized strategy of 'flexible adjustment' to changing external conditions. Flexible adjustment in this context features two commitments: first, a dedication to international trade liberalization; and second, a commitment to domestic compensation, or the development of a variety of welfare programs aimed at an acceptable distribution of social costs associated with economic change. Following Katzenstein, it is the 'double bind' of foreign economic exposure and domestic social compensation that historically compelled the small European nations to expand as welfare states. As a matter of fact, Esping-Andersen's quantitative assessment of the levels of decommodification across eighteen OECD countries corroborates the argument that small and open economies have developed extensive welfare programs, as they were the largest decommodifiers in the world (Esping-Andersen, 1990: 52).

Katzenstein's rather benign assessment of patterns of democratic corporatism in Austria, Belgium, Denmark, the Netherlands, Norway, Sweden and Switzerland, based on the more fortuitous experience of the 1960s and some part of the 1970s, ignores the kinds of policy feedback mechanisms from the domain of established social rights on the evolution of strategies of external adjustment. He accords little autonomous effect to substantive and administrative differences in compensatory social policies. By contrast, Esping-Andersen is very attentive to the idea that social rights and attendant welfare programs, once they are institutionalized, are hard to change and evolve rather independently, or with considerable time-lags, from fundamental changes in the world economy. If wages are sticky, like economists argue, than social wages, enshrined in laws and statutes, are probably even more so. Welfare state retrenchment or downward adjustment of welfare programs, requires cumbersome re-negotiations over established social rights.

The national diversity in the programs and politics of welfare states is very large, but this should not be confounded with unrestricted national sovereignty in choosing the direction of reform. It is therefore that we believe that the problem of external adjustment, with its links to foreign trade, wage costs, collective bargaining and industrial rights, should be systematically studied together with the problem of renegotiating internal compensation or established social rights. In our study of the Dutch case we try to bridge the gap which divides the study of industrial relations and welfare state development, and show how the problems and solutions in the three policy domains – wage formation, social policy, and labour market policy – are related.

WAGE MODERATION, WELFARE REFORM, AND ACTIVATING THE LABOUR MARKET

For an explanation of the 'Dutch miracle' we must go back at least fifteen years. In these fifteen years there were three major policy reversals in the three domains just mentioned. The return to wage moderation took place in the early 1980s and was above all an adjustment to changing conditions in world markets. This was followed by a series of adjustments in the area of domestic social compensation and a major overhaul of social security in the early 1990s. From the mid-1990s, finally, the adoption of an active labour market policy stance, in order to enhance overall efficiency and create a new domestic balance between wages and social benefits, gained political currency. We will present the story of these policy changes – what happened, how it happened and what it meant – in three different chapters. We shall try to demonstrate that these three policy shifts, although embedded in different institutional surroundings and involving different actors, were inter-related: they created the conditions and the demand for one another, and neither of these policies could have been successful on its own.

Wage moderation is the subject of Chapter Five. Its implementation was crucial in adjusting the Dutch economy to changing external conditions – to put it in one phrase, to adapt to much tougher international competition in foreign and domestic markets. With one of the most open economies in the world[14], the Dutch must earn a substantial part of their prosperity abroad. Inaugurated by the Central Accord, concluded between central union and employers federations in 1982, the sustained policy of wage moderation helped to lower the real exchange rate and improve price competitiveness of Dutch firms and products.

The wage moderation strategy must be seen against the background of the transformation towards a service economy, with productivity rates consistently below those in manufacturing. As a matter of fact, wage moderation entailed two political exchanges which followed each other in time and importance: one between workers and employers, the other with the government. In the first exchange wage moderation was traded against a modest reduction in annual and weekly working hours. In the second exchange, which became more important with the passage of time, wage restraint was compensated by lower taxes and social charges, made possible by improved public finances and a broader tax base through the creation of more jobs in domestic services. This helped to maintain spending power and boosted domestic demand, especially in services. Since 1982, central agreements and wage co-ordination between trade unions and employers associations have been instrumental in setting annual targets. Success – in essence the strong job growth rate, the recovery of profitability of Dutch firms and strong union membership growth after a decade of decline – has created greater confidence and contributed to the continuity of the policy of wage moderation. Redistribution of work through a general reduction of labour time has played a comparatively small role, more important has been the extraordinary growth of part-time jobs, the massive entry of women in the labour force, and the replacement of older workers by younger, cheaper and possibly more flexible and skilled workers. With some delay, the Dutch trade unions have come round to support these changes and have taken a positive attitude towards part-time employment and flexibility, despite its apparent adverse effects on union organizing.

Our analysis of this domain reveals both continuity and change. While little or no change was noticed in the institutional framework of industrial relations – its organization, bargaining practice, legal rule or public support – there was a sharp shift in power relations, in ideas and in the policies that were adopted. The biggest policy lesson, we argue, had to be learnt by the unions and was provoked by the deep crisis of the early 1980s. Weakened but in a political environment of unquestioned institutional security and semi-public status, they returned to the consensual policy style which had characterized Dutch corporatism in the early post-war years (Windmuller 1969). It was helpful that the institutional framework of a concertation economy was still there and did not have to be invented.

The second policy shift concerns the *reform of social security* and is the topic of Chapter Six. Beginning with a freezing of benefits in 1983 and an overhaul of unemployment insurance in 1987, the major reforms took place in the early 1990s with the tightening of the two main exit routes from the labour market: disability insurance, and sickness leave. These exit routes had become very popular and were a major factor in the low labour market participation rates. The labour force participation rate of older males, in the age between 60 and 65, dropped from 70 to 22 percent between 1973 and 1991.[15] Generous social security programs helped firms and workers to adjust to novel work patterns and competitive conditions, but at the same time these programs caused a rise of non-wage costs and contributed to the vicious circle of high productivity growth and job decline. The social security budget of the Netherlands is already among the highest in the world; if expenditure rises and is financed out of earnings-related contributions or taxation, then the tax and contribution wedge, or the difference between gross and net pay, increases. This adds to labour costs, threatens the price competitiveness of firms and undermines the support of unions and workers for wage moderation. Rising social security costs, needed to finance the exit of less productive workers from the labour market, tend to block the second exchange referred to above, the one between tax relief and wage restraint. Without this exchange voluntary wage moderation needs other carrots, for instance a general reduction in working time without loss of pay, or indeed easy exit routes for older workers who have been made redundant.

Initially wage moderation was seen and presented by the unions as a solidarity measure between employed workers and people depending on benefits, and as a way to defend the comparatively high level of entitlements. With the passing of time the causal connection is reversed. In the late 1980s the continuation of wage moderation became dependent on lower charges and taxes, and upon a cost-containment of social security. The initial measures, including a freeze of social benefits, tightening of eligibility to social security programs, a reduction in the duration of benefits and the lowering of maximum entitlements of earnings-related benefits from 80 to 70 percent, did bring cost-savings but were partly undone through collective bargaining and could not stop the rising number of claimants. By 1989, the number of people receiving disability benefits threatened to reach the staggering figure of one million, one-sixth of the employed labour force. This crisis of inactivity served as a triggering device for policy learning on the part of state actors. In a dramatic *cri de coeur*, prime-minister Lubbers proclaimed that the Netherlands had become a 'sick' country in 1990. Shortly after, his Centre-Left government announced a policy package of financial incentives aimed to discourage the use of the sick leave and disability schemes. Beneficiaries already enrolled in the scheme were to be re-examined on the basis of more stringent eligibility rules, and for many people benefits were lowered or taken away. These harsh measures provoked widespread protests and nearly wiped out the two political parties – the Christian Democrats and the Social Democrats – who took responsibility for them. The Social Democrats, having joined the third Lubbers government following the 1989 elections, lost one-third of their members in only a few years. The party lost one-quarter of its electoral support in the 1994 general elections. Since the Christian Democrats lost even more support, the Social Democrats surprisingly became the 'victors' of these dramatic elections, having become the largest party. Subsequently, Mr. Wim Kok, the party's leader, was able to forge a new coalition government with the Liberals of the right and the centre, condemning the Christian Democrats to an opposition role for the first time since 1918.

Unlike wage moderation, welfare reform was a policy against the unions. In 1983, a coalition of public sector unions had tried to stop the first Lubbers government from executing its intended lowering of government employee salaries and social benefits, without success. In 1991 the unions staged what was probably the largest postwar demonstration in The Hague, against the government's plan to curtail the disability program, to no avail. The government, joined by most of the opposition, now sought the exclusion of the trade unions, and employers association, from the administration of the social security program and break the century-old corporatist legacy of bipartite rule in this policy area. One can only speculate how much larger the union opposition against welfare reform would have been, had the policy of wage moderation failed to produce more jobs.

Like many other continental welfare states, the Dutch social security system features a considerable organizational involvement of employers' associations and trade unions in the administration of social policy. While levels and duration of benefits are established by law, social policy administration and implementation has historically been the affair of the social partners. In 1993, a heavy-weight parliamentary inquiry into the functioning of the organization and administration of social security in the Netherlands established what essentially everybody knew, namely that the Dutch social security system had been abused by claimants and mismanaged by the social partners. These conclusions initiated a series of reforms, intended to increase the control of the public purse and limit the direct administrative involvement of unions and employers. Financial incentives to elicit desired behaviour and competition between private and public providers have been introduced in a bid to improve efficiency. Summing up, and in contrast to industrial relations, we observe in the social security field considerable institutional discontinuity and disagreement, between unions and employers, and between the two of them and the government. The initiative and consensus, in this case, were political. It is not insignificant that in the past fifteen years all major political parties, from right to left, shared at some stage in the government responsibility for welfare retrenchment.

The third policy shift and the subject of Chapter Seven, concerns the innovation of *labour market policies* and the emphasis on activating measures of various kinds, particularly targeted at the core of the younger long-term unemployed. Hard won social security reform, initially opposed by the unions, and the revived confidence in corporatist adjustment, embraced by unions and employers, slowly but surely concurred with a shift in the problem definition of the alleged crisis of the Dutch welfare state. Policy-makers came to realize that the low level of labour market participation was the Achilles' heel of the extensive but passive Dutch system of social protection. In 1990, the *Netherlands' Scientific Council for Government Policy*, an academic advisory board with a mandate to carry out future studies in areas it sees fit, proposed to break with the past and advocated a policy of maximizing the rate of labour market participation as the single most important policy goal of any sustainable welfare state.[16] Gradually, this lesson, though not the specific policy recommendations, which included a lowering of the statutory minimum wage, were embraced by the government.

The current government has placed 'jobs, jobs, and more jobs' in the centre of its social and economic policies. A series of special programs, geared toward the reintegration of unskilled and low-paid workers into the labour market, has been moved in since 1994 and appears to have had a modest success in bringing down youth and long-duration unemployment. Another element of these policies is the use of the lowest wage scales in collective agreements in the expectation that more jobs for unskilled workers will be retained or created. The possibility for the government to destabilize collective bargaining by refusing to make sector agreements binding on non-organized firms, has been used as a bribe to elicit 'good behaviour' from unions and employers. The public employment service has been reformed twice in recent years but is not yet a 'one counter service' combining social security and job placement services. Private employment agencies have gained a considerable market in recent years and are increasingly involved in the management of subsidies and job placement for unemployed workers. In our understanding, the biggest change in policy thinking and practice, still incomplete, lies in this policy field, breaking a long tradition of passive, or absent, labour market policies. It is in this policy field also that interest groups, private sector organizations, local government, opinion leaders and scientists outside the usual corporatist inner circle of unions and employers, and social security experts, have been invited in.

QUESTIONS

What lessons can we draw? The 'Dutch miracle' represents a departure from the pessimistic forecasts of jobless growth, welfare without work and the end of full employment. At the same time it constitutes a break with the traditional picture of full employment on the basis of full-time working hours and open-ended employment contracts. Can the emergent one-and-a-half jobs model create a new social optimum in a post-industrial society? Can the 'Dutch miracle' be taken as a model for policy learning in countries with high structural unemployment and rising social security outlays? These two questions will occupy us throughout this book. The answers will be again discussed in the final and concluding chapter.

Notes

1   *The Economist*, 30 January 1982

2   The 1983 figure is taken from the old unemployment statistics, based on the number of registered unemployed (OECD, *Economic Survey of the Netherlands 1986*, Paris 1986: 44, Table 18). From 1988 unemployment statistics have been based on labour force sample surveys. The old and new figures are not comparable (this is further discussed in Chapter Two)

3   *Le Monde* of 23 January 1997; see also 'Le modèle hollandais', in *Le Monde* of 2 December 1996; 'Le bonheur est dans les tulipes…', the title story of *Le Nouvel Observateur*, 3 October 1996; and more critical 'Miracle our Mirage aux Pays-Bas', in: *Le Monde Diplomatiqe* of July 1997.

4   The expression 'Großer kleiner Nachbar' was used by the Cologne-based *Institut der Deutschen Wirtschaft* in its weekly bulletin of 25 July 1996; see also Bernhard Jagoda, the president of the Federal Labour Market Board, 'Modell Niederlande – Ein Vorbild für Deutschland?', in *Wirtschaftsdienst*.

Zeitschrift für Wirschaftspolitik, Hamburg, Institut für Wirtschaftsforschung, vol. 77, no. 4 (April 1997). A detailed Dutch-German comparison of labour market developments and policies is presented by Günther Schmid, one of the directors of the Wissenschaftszentrum in Berlin, in his 'Beschäftigungswunder Niederlande. Ein Vergleich der Beschäftigungssysteme in den Niederlanden und in Deutschland', Berlin: Wissenschaftszentrum, discussion paper FS I 96 – 206 (also in English as 'The Dutch Employment Miracle', discussion paper FS I 97–202)

5   Interviews with Flemish Economics Minister, Mr. Eric van Rompuy: "We must mirror ourselves to Holland", and with Belgian Employment Minister Mrs. Miep Smit, 'Follow the Dutch example, but not blindly', *De Standaard* of 11 October 1996. See also the discussion in *Samenleving en Politiek. Tijdschrift voor een democratisch socialisme*, which devoted its issue of March 1997 to a comparison between Belgium and the Netherlands.

6   'Too good to be true?', in *The Economist* of 12 October 1996.

7   OECD, *National Account Statistics*, OECD, various years.

8   The *Wall Street Journal* (27 December 1997) underscores the inversion of the country's poor image in the past and writes that there now seems to be 'a new Netherlands that, surprisingly, appears to be working'. *The European*: 'Dutch find miraculous cure for unemployment' (10 April 1997) puts its emphasis on the difference with the sluggish performance of other European economies.

9   In its introduction of the *Economic Survey for the Netherlands 1984/1985* (Paris, February 1985, p.7), the OECD writes that 'the deterioration in its growth and employment performance was indeed worse than that of other countries. Since the mid-1970s real GDP has grown at a rate below the OECD average and the unemployment rate has shot up to one of the highest in the OECD region'.

10   A common definition of a recession is a decline of national income during at least two consecutive quarters. By this definition the 1981-83 recession was exceptionally severe and the 1992-94 recession was none, since national income declined only during one quarter.

11   'Zo kon het niet langer', *Jaarverslag 1996*, De Nederlandsche Bank (DNB), Amsterdam 1997, p. 24.

12   This later became the best-known aspect of 'the Dutch miracle' or Dutch approach to job growth and was first discovered by Mr. Jacques Delors who gave it a central place in his call to create in Europe a more 'employment intensive' growth pattern; see the White Paper on *Growth, Competitiveness, and Employment*, Brussels: European Commission, 1993.

13   Sherwin Rosen (*Journal of Economic Literature*, 1996: 734-5) suggests, against Esping-Andersen, that this is what caused the downfall of the 'Swedish model' in which 'a large fraction of women take care of the children of women who work in the public sector to care for the parents of women who are looking after their children'.

14   Exports and imports of goods and services amounted to 89.2% of GDP in 1994, compared with 74.8% in 1970 and 70.9% in 1950. For 1994 the comparable figure for the United Kingdom is 41.8%, for Germany 39.3%, for France 34.2%, for the United States 17.8% and for Japan 14.6% (Kleinknecht, 1996).

15   It should be added that, possibly thanks to early retirement, a much larger proportion survived until the legal retirement age, as much fewer workers died while in employment.

16   Wetenschappelijke Raad voor het Regeringsbeleid (WRR), *Een werkend perspectief, Arbeidsparticipatie in de jaren '90*, The Hague: SDU, 1990, reports to the government no. 38.

Chapter Two

Miracle or Mirage?
Job Growth and Labour Market Developments

E MPLOYMENT is the key indicator by which the success of Dutch policies is to be judged. Admirers draw attention to the high rate of job
growth, the apparent willingness of the Dutch to work part-time and
accept flexible jobs and working hours.[1] Critics, on the other hand, express
doubts and highlight the precarious nature of many of the new jobs, the persistence of long-term unemployment, inactivity, and the increase in social inequality and low pay. They point out that the employment miracle is 'fragile',
possibly only a 'mirage'.[2]

In this chapter we set out to examine these contrasting claims and present
the available information on employment, working hours, part-time work,
flexible jobs, unemployment, social inequality and low pay. In Chapter One
we argued that the Dutch miracle is relative – the Netherlands receives better
marks than its European class mates, and better marks than some years ago.
In this chapter our aim is to illustrate this claim with facts and figures. Hence,
our approach is historical and comparative; current performance is compared with the recent past and with developments in other European countries.

EMPLOYMENT, LABOUR FORCE GROWTH AND
UNEMPLOYMENT

At first sight, the figures on job growth are impressive. In 1996 6,8 million
people have paid work, an increase of 25 percent compared to the 5,5 million
people in employment in 1982. In these fifteen years the average rate of job
growth was 1.6 percent per year, which is as good as the American 'jobs machine' and four times better than the 0.4 percent average for the European
Union.[3] If employment is expressed in hours rather than jobs, the picture
does not change significantly; the Netherlands still out-performs the rest of
Europe by a large margin.

Table 2: Employment growth in the Netherlands, the EU and selected OECD countries

	1983-93	1994	1995	1996	1997*
Netherlands	1.8	0.8	2.4	1.9	2.0
EU	0.4	− 0.7	0.5	0.1	0.4
Belgium	0.5	− 0.7	0.3	0.1	0.5
Germany**	0.7	− 1.8	− 0.3	− 1.2	− 0.9
France	0.1	− 0.4	0.9	− 0.2	0.2
DK	0.2	1.2	1.6	1.0	1.3
SW	− 0.6	− 0.7	1.6	− 0.6	− 0.4
UK	0.6	1.2	0.8	0.5	1.3
US	1.8	3.2	1.5	1.4	2.3

Source: OECD, *Employment Outlook*, issues of July 1994 and July 1997, Paris: Organisation of Economic Cooperation and Development

* Projection   ** Until 1993 West Germany only

Employment growth is driven by strong labour force growth, 1.4 percent per year between 1982 and 1995, compared with 0.5 percent in the European Union. This reflects relatively rapid population growth (the birth rate declined later than in other European countries) and a catching-up of the low female participation rate to European averages.

Unemployment has decreased, but only slowly. The standardized unemployment rate, measured in an internationally comparable manner as the number of people without jobs who actively look for paid work and are available within two weeks, has dropped to 6.5 percent, which is near the current rate in the United States and much lower than the European average (see Table 3). Accurate comparisons over time are somewhat impaired because of changes in the definition. Older workers, aged over 57 $\frac{1}{2}$ need no longer register and the registration data on which statistics before 1987 were based did include people who were unavailable for jobs. These problems aside, unemployment, at eleven or fourteen percent of the labour force in 1983, was much higher than in other countries and much higher than today.

Our final comparative indicator is the employment/population ratio. In 1983 the Netherlands had the lowest ratio of all OECD countries, 52.0, seven points below the EU average. In 1996, the employment population ratio has risen to 66.0, the largest leap in the whole OECD area and seven points above the EU average (see Table 4). The catching up of women is clear from

Table 3: Unemployment in the Netherlands, the EU and selected OECD countries

	1983	1990	1993	1994	1995	1996
Netherlands	9.7	6.2	6.6	7.1	6.9	6.3
EU**	9.2	8.5	10.6	11.4	11.1	11.5
Belgium	11.1	6.7	8.9	10.1	9.9	9.8
Germany*	7.7	4.8	7.9	8.4	8.2	9.0
France	8.1	9.0	11.7	12.3	11.7	12.4
DK	..	7.7	10.1	8.2	7.1	6.0
SW	3.9	1.8	9.5	9.8	9.2	10.0
UK	11.1	7.1	10.5	9.6	8.8	8.2
US	9.6	5.6	6.9	6.1	5.6	5.4

Source: OECD, *Employment Outlook*, issues of July 1996 and July 1997, Paris: Organisation of Economic Cooperation and Development, Table A

* Until 1993 West Germany only

** Not standardised (commonly used definition), see *Employment Outlook 1997*, Table B

Table 4: Employment/population ratio's by sex in Netherlands, the EU and selected OECD countries

	men			women		
	1983	1990	1996	1983	1990	1996
Netherlands	69.1	76.2	76.6	34.7	47.0	55.0
EU**	75.8	74.2	69.8	42.9	46.7	48.4
Belgium	70.4	67.3	67.3	36.6	41.0	45.8
Germany*	76.6	76.4	73.4	47.8	52.8	54.3
France	74.4	70.4	67.2	49.7	50.6	52.1
DK	78.4	82.5	81.4	65.2	71.5	67.8
SW	84.7	86.9	74.7	75.5	81.8	70.6
UK	78.7	83.7	77.7	55.3	63.7	64.1
US	78.9	83.1	82.3	57.7	65.8	68.1

Source: OECD, *Employment Outlook*, issues of July 1996 and July 1997, Paris: Organisation of Economic Cooperation and Development, Table B and C

* Until 1993 West Germany only

** Not standardised (commonly used definition), see *Employment Outlook 1997*, Table B these figures, but it is also relevant to note that the decline in net participation rates among men has stopped.

A Job-intensive Growth Path

Job growth started at the end of 1983 when the country recovered from a deep recession, was particularly pronounced in the second half of the 1980s, continued through to 1992, faltered during the shallow 1993 recession and stagnated in 1994 (see Figure 1). There has been a strong recovery, especially in labour market terms, in 1995 and since; job growth was stronger than expected at nearly two percent per year between 1995 and 1997. Job intensive growth reflects three main factors: moderate wage increases, development of labour intensive services and job redistribution.

Figure 1: Employment Growth, 1970-1996

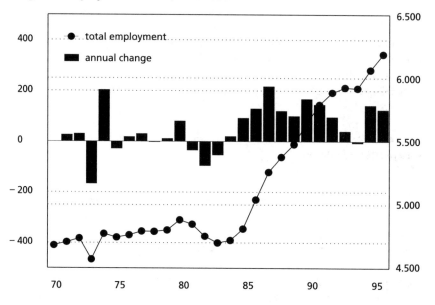

Wage Moderation

According to the Central Planning Bureau (CPB, *Centraal Planbureau*), the government's official economic forecasting office, wage moderation has been 'Holland's single most important weapon in international competition'.[4] CPB estimates that the effect of lower labour costs has dominated the effect of lower aggregate demand. For the second half of the 1980s the Bureau estimates that two-thirds of job growth can be attributed to wage moderation and one-third to the expansion of the world economy. The Dutch Central Bank (DNB, *De Nederlandsche Bank*) points out that whereas unit labour costs in manufacturing rose by 2 percent in France and 2.6 percent in Germany between 1983 and 1995, the rise was zero in the Netherlands. During this period the number of persons holding jobs increased with 0.1 percent per year in France, 0.4 percent in Germany, and 1.5 percent in the Netherlands.[5] Table 5 summarizes the development in absolute and relative labour costs and unit labour costs since 1980. The relative advantage of the Netherlands is clearly shown.

Table 5: Labour costs in manufacturing in the Netherlands and in selected OECD Countries, changes from 1980 to 1994, and levels of 1994

	% change in labour costs*			level	indirect costs **	labour costs ***	unit labour costs ****
	1980-89	1989-94	1980-94	1994			
Netherlands	31.3	19.8	57.5	DM 34,87	80%	79	89
Belgium	24.3	28.1	59.2	DM 37,35	94%	85	90
Germany	54.9	30.6	102.4	DM 43,97	82%	100	100
Denmark	40.9	19.5	68.4	DM 34,41	22%	78	93
Sweden							
	43.9	– 6.8	34.1	DM 31,00	70%	71	94
UK	61.4	13.4	63.1	DM 22,06	40%	50	106
US	59.1	5.8	68.3	DM 27,97	43%	64	99

Sources: Department of Social Affairs and Employment (SZW), *De Nederlandse verzorgingsstaat in internationaal en economisch perspectief*, Den Haag: SDU, 1996, tables 2.1-2.3

*   Per hour worked in manufacturing, in Deutsch mark
**   Indirect labour costs as a percentage of direct labour costs
***   Index total labour costs per hour worked in manufacturing (see column 4), Germany = 100
**** Index of total labour costs per unit produced in manufacturing, Germany = 100

We will discuss the politics of external adjustment, wage moderation, the role of trade unions and institutions in Chapter Five. Here we simply note that wage moderation contributed to job intensive growth in three ways. First it helped investment by restoring the profitability of business and thus created a necessary condition for job growth. The share of labour income in net enterprise income dropped from over 90,5 percent in 1980 to 83.5 percent in 1985 and has hovered around 83 or 84 percent since. Second, it contributed to the sale of manufactured goods and tradable services in foreign markets, raising net exports and growth in the open sector of the economy (see Table 6). Third, it helped to keep more people on the payroll. As a corollary, labour productivity per hour, although very high by European and American standards (see also Schmid 1996), increased less than in other countries.

Table 6: GDP, per capita and per hour, 1982-95, the Netherlands compared with the EU average

	Netherlands	EU
GDP / per capita	2.02	1.85
GDP / per hours worked	2.60	3.77
hours per worker	− 1.06	− 1.79
employment/Population ratio	0.60	− 0.06

Source: CPB, L. Bovenberg, 1997, Table 1
Annual percentage changes

The average number of hours worked per job decreased and is now the lowest in the OECD (see below). But due to the strong increase in the number of jobs the total volume of hours worked between 1983 and 1995 increased much more than in the European Union. As a consequence and in spite of the lower growth in productivity per hour worked, GDP per capita has grown faster than in other countries (see Table 6). Measured by its GDP per head (expressed in purchasing power parities) the Netherlands had since the early 1970s steadily fallen from 5th to 11th place in 1988, but has since climbed up to a 7th position. Wage moderation seems to work – it does spread around more jobs and does not, on average, make people poorer.

The Shift to Services
Measured by the size of its industrial sector, the Netherlands has never been a classical industrial country. At the end of the 19th century around one-quarter of the labour force was employed in industry. At its maximum, around 1960, manufacturing industry, including mining and utilities, employed one-third of the labour force, much less than in Germany, France, Britain or Belgium. Restructuring, labour shedding and relocation of labour intensive manufacturing industries to low wage countries, combined with divestment and contracting out of activities to services, have reduced the size of the manufacturing sector (including gas and oil mining and utilities) to only 18.2 percent of total employment in 1996. Services have leaped to 74 percent. In the past ten years growth has been strongest in commercial services (i.e. commerce and

retailing, hotels and restaurants, financial and business services, and communication), from 20 to 30 percent of total employment between 1960 and 1987 and on to 37 percent in 1996. The share of non-tradeable services (i.e., government, social and community services, and personal services) rose from 21 to 30 percent to 1987 and has since stagnated.[6]

These developments – less hours worked per job, and more jobs in services – show up in productivity statistics as a decreasing trend.[7] The shift to services cannot explain all of the decline, because in industry productivity per hour is also decreasing, in spite of contracting out. These are apparently world-wide trends and have provoked Robert Solow to observe that 'computers are everywhere, except in the productivity statistics'.[8]

The service sector has particularly attracted women into the labour market. Almost half of the women who found a job since 1975 did so in the health sector, education, community and social services, and retailing. The strongest rise occurred among married women. Although the absolute number of married women in the working population at working age (15-64) decreased with around 100,000, the number of women in the labour force increased with 800,000, and the participation rate of married women jumped from 15 percent in 1975 to 42 percent in 1994. Among unmarried women the rise was less pronounced, from 43 percent to 55 percent, contributing an extra 600,000 to the labour force.[9] The proportion of women who expected their first child and had no paid employment dropped from 33 to 19 percent between 1980 and 1992; the share of women who did work but stopped fell from 55 to 35 percent; the share of women who continued with a reduced number of hours rose from 5 to 28 percent; and the share of women who continued with unchanged hours increased from 6 to 19 percent.[10]

The increase in the labour participation of women with children has enhanced the need and created the extra income for family orientated services, jobs that are mostly jobs taken up by women. Since these services are in the Netherlands historically undeveloped in the public and communal sector, low cost commercial services in these areas have become more important. Increased flexibility, through part-time and temporary employment, has supported this dynamic.

Job Redistribution, Part-time Jobs and Flexibility
Redistribution of employment to involve more people has been a key element in the return to a job intensive growth pattern. Average annual working time per employee is lower than in any other country: 1,372 hours per year in 1996, around 31-32 hours per week. This is 350 hours less than in 1973, 160 less than in 1983 (see Table 7). Comparison across countries is problematic, since the average combines full-time and part-time jobs.[11] In the Netherlands the average annual working time of full-time employees was 1,741 hours in 1995, which is 5-6 percent less than in 1979, but considerably longer than in Germany where collective reduction of the average working week has played a much larger role.

Table 7: Average annual working hours per employee in the Netherlands and in selected OECD countries

	1973	1979	1983	1990	1996*
Netherlands	1724	1591	1530	1433	1372
West Germany	1804	1699	1686	1562	1508
France	1771	1667	1558	1539	1529
SW*	1557	1451	1453	1480	1554
UK*	1929	1821	1719	1773	1732
US	1896	1884	1866	1936	1951

Source: OECD, *Employment Outlook 1997*, Paris: Organisation of Economic Cooperation and Development, July 1997, Table G
* Total employment

Part-time and flexible jobs account for three-quarters of the job growth since 1983. Sixty percent of all new jobs since 1987 were part-time jobs of less than 35 hours per week. The incidence of part-time jobs has risen by a staggering 20 percentage points, from 16.6 percent in 1979 to 36.5 percent in 1996. This is an absolute record in the OECD (see Table 8); the only countries with percentages of part-time workers near the Dutch ones are Iceland (27.9%), Switzerland (27.4%), Norway (26.5%), Sweden (23.6), the United Kingdom (22.1%) and Denmark (21.5%), countries which deviate in one way or the other from the continental model of welfare state and industrial relations.[12]

Part-time work is largely women's work, with nearly three out of four part-time jobs held by women, and two out of three women with paid employment working in part-time jobs. But the incidence of part-time work among male workers has increased as well, and currently one out of six male workers has a part-time job. This is, again, a record in the industrialized world and stands in sharp contrast to the low incidence of part-time work among men in Belgium (3%), France (5.3%), Germany (3,6% in 1995), and the United Kingdom (5.4%).

Table 9 shows that there are two concentrations of part-time jobs—one around 20 hours per week, the typical half-day job, and one in the category of 30-35 hours per week, the typical four days a week jobs. Also noticeable is that women work more often in small part-time jobs of less than 20 hours per week. Three out of four small part-time jobs are found in only three sectors: in personal services, in particular cleaning, in hotel, restaurants and catering, and in retail.[13]

Table 8: Incidence of part-time employment in selected OECD countries, by sex, 1973-1996

	men			women		
	1983	1990	1996	1983	1990	1996
Netherlands	6.8	14.8	16.1	22.0	36.4	38.0
Belgium	2.0	2.0	3.0	19.7	25.9	30.5
West Germany	1.7	2.6	3.6*	30.0	33.8	33.8*
France	2.5	3.3	5.3	20.1	23.6	29.5
DK	6.5	10.4	10.8	43.7	38.4	34.5
SW	6.2	7.4	9.3	45.9	40.4	39.0
UK	3.3	5.2	5.6	41.3	44.3	42.7
US	10.8	10.1	10.9	28.1	25.2	26.9

Source: OECD, *Employment Outlook 1997*, Paris: Organisation of Economic Cooperation and Development, July 1997, Table E
*   1995

Table 9: Weekly working hours of men and women, 1994

weekly working hours	women	men	all
< 12 hours	378	176	554
	17%	5%	10%
12 - <20 hours	281	69	350
	13%	2%	6%
20 - <30 hours	440	92	532
	20%	3%	10%
30 - <35 hours	255	132	387
	12%	4%	7%
35 hours and more	822	2,838	3,660
	38%	86%	67%
total	2,176	3,307	5,483
	100%	100%	100%

Source: CBS, *Arbeid en lonen van werknemers*, The Hague, 1996, 121-3 (based on enterprise surveys

Until 1993 most job growth came from part-time employment, but in recent years flexible contracts are growing faster. Of the 300,000 new jobs created in 1994, 1995 and the first half of 1996 roughly half were flexible, forty percent were part-time and ten percent full-time. A flexible contract features a limited duration (or fixed term), sometimes for a variable number of hours per month, week or day. In total, eleven percent of all jobs were temporary in 1994, which is not very different from the European average (see Table 10). The incidence of temporary work is especially high among young people.

The use of temporary work agencies to gain employment has risen significantly and on a wider scale than in other European countries. Temporary work agencies specialize in buffering fluctuations, matching product demand changes and labour supply, for instance in the case of seasonal fluctuation, but they are also used by employers to avoid dismissal protection requirements and as a screening device. Over the past fifteen years, this kind of flexible work increased from 1,5 percent in the 1970s to 2,5 percent around 1990 and 3.5 percent in 1995. There is a also a typical cyclical pattern: in the upswing product demand is first met with extra effort of existing employees as hoarding is reduced, followed by extra agency work; if growth continues, agency work tends to stabilize.

Table 10: Incidence of temporary jobs in the Netherlands and major OECD countries, 1983-1994, in percentage of all employees in paid jobs

	1983	1990	1994
Netherlands	5.8	7.6	10.9
Belgium	5.4	5.3	5.1
Germany	..	10.5	10.3
France	3.3	10.5	21.0
DK	..	10.8	12.0
SW	..	9.7	13.5
UK	5.5	5.2	6.5

Source: OECD, *Employment Outlook 1996*, Paris: Organisation of Economic Cooperation and Development, July 1996

WOMEN ENTER THE LABOUR FORCE

The rapid increase in part-time employment and the entry of women into the labour force are two sides of the same coin. Twenty-five years ago, the Netherlands had the lowest labour force participation rate of women within the OECD: 29.2 percent, lower than in Ireland, Greece, Spain or Italy, each with rates in the low thirties. Within its own region the low female participation rate was an anomaly: Germany and the United Kingdom each had rates of 50 percent or higher, Belgium of 40 percent, the Nordic countries were already in a class apart.[14] Since 1973, the labour force participation rate of women has surged from 29 to 60 percent, which is the strongest rise in any OECD country. The current rate is still lower than in the Nordic countries, the United Kingdom or the United States, but is now level with the rate in Germany and France, and six points ahead of Belgium.[15]

Various developments have contributed to increased female participation, foremost among these are the higher level of education of women, declining fertility rates, and emancipation. Combining aggregate labour market trends (Maassen van den Brink, 1995) and Kea Tijdens' (1996) study of staffing policies in the banking sector, we can draw the following picture of alternating pressures of supply and demand explaining the part-time phenomenon.

In the 1960s labour markets were very tight, unemployment for male workers fell below 1 percent in some years and manufacturing firms started to recruit unskilled workers in Mediterranean countries (see Chapter Seven). Women's work, for wages, was girl's work. The overwhelming majority of families consisted of a male breadwinner and a full-time housewife. Women tended to marry in their early twenties and the average age at which they give birth to their first child is 23. According to the census of 1960 only 0.6 percent of all women with children under the age of four had paid employment (Moree 1991: 102-3). In services and in the public sector employment contracts terminated at the day of marriage.[16] A law forbidding employers to dismiss women for reasons of marriage or pregnancy was only introduced as late as 1973. Tax disincentives were considerable; earnings of spouses were added to those of her husband; in 1973 this became optional but the view that women's wages are supplementary was only fully removed in 1990 with the introduction of individual fiscal treatment.

In response to tight labour markets, a condition which in the expanding service sector continues until the mid 1970s, employers began to see married women as a possible labour reservoir and a way to escape from high wage pressures. In banking, for instance, they set up data-entry pools in which married women, with older children, were recruited in half-day (five days, four hours) jobs under temporary contracts. Married women were encouraged to stay until they had their first child, at reduced hours (five days, six hours; or four full days). Due to longer education, women entered the labour market later and the average age at which they have their first child went up.

After the mid 1970s labour markets became slack again and from 1976 un-employment rates for women tended to be higher than for men. In particular, women with higher levels of education decided to stay in the labour market. Withdrawal from the labour market became more costly in terms of income and careers foregone. The uncertainty of obtaining a (good) job when leaving and re-entering the labour force at later age, made women think twice. The participation rate of married women increased (see Figure 2). In banking, eighty percent of all women kept on working after marriage, but this propor-tion dropped to 25 percent after child birth. Increasing numbers of women sought to re-enter the labour market and they did so at a younger age of their youngest child. Requests for reduced hours increased and staff surveys showed that women wanted part-time jobs far more than men. Unemploy-ment reduced their chances of re-entering and increased the chance of having an unemployed husband or partner. More women decided to continue work-ing whilst raising young children (Hartog and Theeuwes, 1983).

Figure 2: Participation rates in the Netherlands, by sex, 1960 and 1993

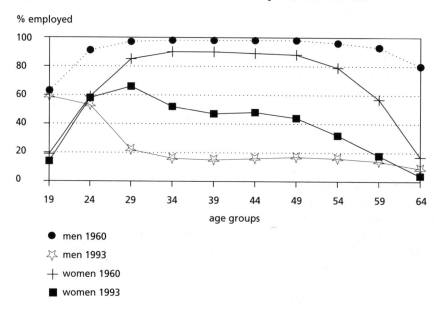

In the early 1980s, employers discovered part-time as an alternative for col-lective working time reduction and countered union demands for a collective reduction of the working week (see Chapter Five). For employers, part-time employment was the ideal alternative because it is an individual choice and allows differentiation across groups of workers, disconnects operating hours from working hours, brings actual and contractual working hours nearer as part-time workers tend to be sick in their own time, and is reversible. Higher overhead and co-ordination costs are recaptured by lower absentee rates and fringe benefits for part-time workers.[17] From 1983 full-time jobs are increasingly transformed into part-time jobs.

Supply pressures continued. The social norm with regard to work outside the home of women with young children is changing. The majority opinion against women who combine the care for young children with paid work is rapidly evaporating. In 1982 57 percent of all women between 18 and 37 years held the view that the care for children under the age of six and paid employment could not be combined; in 1993 the share of women holding this view had declined to 26 percent.[18] In survey after survey reduced hours gains it as preference from withdrawal from employment or full-time jobs. More women want to retain their job and the pressure for child care, leave arrangements and 'come back rights' increase. Most child care is still arranged informally, through family relations, neighbours, and friends. Day-care centres for young children were, and still are, in short supply[19], and provision has historically been a matter for Church-related welfare institutions targeted towards the poor (van Rijswijck-Clerkx, 1981). This is a characteristic heritage of the 'continental Christian Democratic welfare state' (van Kersbergen, 1995). Family-orientated services tend to be underdeveloped and

> 'typically shaped by the Church, and hence strongly committed to the preservation of traditional familihood. Social insurance typically excludes non-working wives, and family benefits encourage motherhood. Day-care and similar family services are conspicuously underdeveloped: the principle of "subsidiarity" serves to emphasize that the state will only interfere when the familiy's capacity to service its members is exhausted (Esping-Andersen 1990:27).

Ultimately, the absence of day-care facilities and a communal or public infrastructure for family-orientated services in the Netherlands has made part-time work the dominant coping strategy for women. An important side-effect is that it has created a strong demand for commercial family-orientated services and flexible work.

LONG-TERM UNEMPLOYMENT AND VULNERABLE GROUPS

In terms of employment patterns, job tenure, flexibility and service employment, the Dutch labour market may have moved in the American direction, except that wage differentials have increased less. Statistics on long-term unemployment show, however, that the Netherlands still shares the problem of continental European labour markets (see Table 11). Like most EU countries, the Netherlands has a severe problem of long-term unemployment (Layard et al., 1991). Unlike the US, the biggest risk is not to become unemployed when holding a job, but to stay unemployed once a job is lost. In 1992, when the unemployment rate (6.7%) was marginally lower than in the US (7.3%), this reflected quite different realities. In the US, on a monthly basis, about two percent of all workers lost their job, in the Netherlands less than half a per cent. In the US forty percent of the unemployed found a new job within a month, against five to six percent in the Netherlands.[20]

Between 1977 and 1990 the average length of (uncompleted) unemployment spells has increased by a factor of three (de Beer, 1996: 95). The combination of employer selection, lack of (re-)training and lack of incentives to leave social security produces severe inefficiencies and inequality of opportunity in the Dutch labour market, the overall improvement of its performance notwithstanding. Since 1984, the proportion of unemployed being out of a job for one year or longer has been fifty per cent or more. This is 'the most significant downside of the Dutch employment miracle' (de Beer, 1996: 328). A large number of people who were laid off in the 1980-1983 slump never found their way back into a paid job. Most new jobs have been taken by young entrants and women (re-)entering the labour force. For example, of the 700,000 additional jobs created between 1984 and 1990 only about 100,000 went to people on benefits (van Wijnbergen, 1995).

Table 11: Long-term unemployment in the Netherlands and in selected OECD countries, percentage unemployed longer than 12 months

	1983	1990	1996
Netherlands	48.8	49.3	49.0
Belgium	64.8	68.7	61.3
West Germany	41.6	46.8	48.3*
France	42.2	38.0	39.5
DK	44.3	30.0	26.5
SW	10.3	4.7	17.1
UK	45.6	34.4	39.8
US	13.3	5.5	9.5

Source: OECD, *Employment Outlook 1996*, Paris: Organisation of Economic Cooperation and Development, July 1996

*   1995

OLDER WORKERS

A large part of the problem of long-term unemployment does not show up in the statistics. First, since 1984 the requirement to register for job search has been lifted for older workers. Second, there appears to be a considerable group of people who do register for unemployment benefits without being engaged, in any significant way, in seeking employment or being available for work. In the mid-1980s estimates of the non-available component in registered unemployment data varied from 30-50 percent; recent surveys show that this may not be much better today.[21] Third, in the Netherlands disability pensions have been used on a larger scale than elsewhere in Europe as a 'velvet exit' for older and less productive workers from the labour market, and as a means for employers to increase productivity (see Chapter Six). How much this became an escape route for older workers is shown by a comparison with Germany and Belgium, where other routes (early retirement, continued unemployment until legal retirement) have been more commonly available. Per 10,000 wage earners between the age of 55 and 64, there were in 1987 434 disablement pensions in Belgium, 262 in West Germany, and 980 in the Netherlands (Prins, 1991: 65). The unemployment component in disability has been estimated at between 10 and 50 percent.[22]

Fourth, early retirement has become a regular feature of collective bargaining since 1983. The legal retirement age in the Netherlands is 65, but actual retirement is closer to 60. Most collective agreements allow workers to pre-retire and fifty percent of the eligible workers actually use their option to leave. Indemnification is generally at ninety percent of last earned wages, in net terms, and pension rights are retained. Social pressure on older workers to take part in an exchange of 'young for old' has been considerable, especially in the 1980s, when a large number of young workers entered the labour market and youth unemployment was twice the national average. At the time, the most favoured policy choice aimed at preventing the development of long-term youth unemployment by asking older workers to make room for school-leavers and fresh entrants in the labour force. Figures for the mid-1980s indicate that only 35 percent of the vacated jobs did actually lead to new recruitment and that the other 65 percent were used to reduce overcapacity. As late as 1987, the government issued an 'administrative order' to the directors of the regional public employment offices, allowing them to grant dismissal, under certain conditions, to workers above the age of 55. In recent years the government has tried ways to increase the participation of older workers and counter blatant forms of age discrimination in hiring decisions. Employers, on their part, are trying to find alternatives to financing existing forms of collective early retirement which turn out to be very expensive (up to eight percent of the wage bill in some cases). All this reflects a shift in thinking on the costs of inactivity and a growing awareness of the new policy problem of financing an ageing welfare state. This will be a prominent theme in Chapter Six.

To sum up, the true indicator of the problematic side of the Dutch labour market for older workers is not the unemployment rate but the low employment/population ratio. The ratio for women between the age of 55 and 64 the ratio was, and still is, low (19.4% in 1996 against 12.5% in 1983), the ratio for men in the same age group has declined to 41 percent, five points below the EU average and nine points below the average for the OECD (see Table 12).

Table 12: The unemployment and employment/population ration for men between the age of 55 and 64

	employment/population ratio			unemployment		
	1983	1990	1996	1983	1990	1996
Netherlands	50.5	44.5	40.7	6.7	2.8	3.5
EU	58.5	53.2	46.4	6.9	6.2	9.8
Belgium	47.7	34.3	32.2	5.8	3.1	4.7
West Germany	57.4	52.0	47.2*	9.0	9.9	15.2
France	50.4	43.0	38.6	6.0	7.3	8.6
DK	63.1	65.6	58.4	6.2	5.2	6.0
SW	73.9	74.4	66.0	4.0	1.3	8.6
UK	62.6	62.4	57.0	10.6	8.4	9.5
US	65.2	65.2	64.7	6.1	3.8	3.3

Source: OECD, *Employment Outlook 1996*, Paris: Organisation of Economic Cooperation and Development, July 1996

DISCOURAGED WORKERS

The unemployment rate does not reflect the true state of slack in the Dutch labour market. One might even argue that the low unemployment rate, based on the criteria of 'actively seeking work' and 'availability to take the job within two weeks' is a sign of failure, rather than an indicator of success, because it reveals the large distance of many vulnerable groups from the formal labour market. One possible indicator, the OECD's U7 rate which attempts to measure the degree of 'discouragement' as a consequence of labour market slack, suggests that in 1993 unemployment stood at 10.6 percent, compared to 13.3 percent ten years earlier.[23]

In its 1996 survey of the Netherlands the OECD praises part-time work as an example of flexibility, but also notes that it is unclear to what extent part-time employment reflects part-time unemployment. A survey in 1993, when unemployment was on the rise, showed that fifteen per cent of all part-time workers were unable to find full-time jobs, but a similar proportion of full-time workers, hence a much larger number of people, preferred a four-day working week.[24] The 1996 labour force sample survey showed that ten per-cent of all employees with a job of twelve hours per week or more wanted to work less, and seven or eight percent more hours. The preference for shorter hours is strongest among older workers and among women who work full-time; the preference for longer hours is found among young people and among women who work less than two days. Most content are women who work between 17 and 25 hours per week. Men find it more difficult to ask for less hours because they believe that employers see it as lack of ambition.[25]

Unemployment, and more in particular long-term unemployment, is con-centrated among the low-skilled and has an ethnic dimension (Salverda, 1997). Unemployment among workers with only eight years of education is twice the national average, among non-native workers three times the aver-age. The problem appears to have become larger rather than smaller; jobs with only elementary or basic vocational training are disappearing and most new jobs require longer schooling.

LOW PAY AND EARNINGS INEQUALITY

According to some authors structural effects, in particular the replacement of older workers by young people, with higher skills and less seniority, are a ma-jor part of the Dutch wage moderation story. They argue that the exit of old-er workers via the social security system and the creation of flexible, part-time and low paid jobs helped to circumvent the 'downward wage rigidity of those in employment' (Kloosterman and Elfring, 1990: 115). Low pay is most relevant in two sectors: cleaning and retail, possibly also in agriculture (Roor-da and Vogels, 1993). There appears to be a partial overlap with other aspects of 'bad jobs': few employment rights, and low qualifications. A fairly large proportion of workers improve their employment position, but chances are poor for people without skills, and for ethnic minorities (de Beer, 1996; Salverda, 1997).

The comparison with the United States is interesting. As in many coun-tries, the halt in wage growth in the 1980s and 1990s reflected the change from a seller's to a buyers' market, especially with respect to unskilled and semi-skilled labour. Unemployment in the early 1980s was high in both countries, and over the 1983-93 period average unemployment is only one

percentage higher in the Netherlands (7.7 percent) than in the U.S. (6.8 percent). Both countries also shared sustained labour force growth, 1.5 percent
per year on average in the decade between 1983 and 1993, which is nearly
three times the influx of new recruits to the labour market in the European
Union (0.6%). In the United States wage restraint appears to have been dic-
tated by the market and has affected mainly, if not exclusively, workers at the
lower end of the wage distribution. Real wages of unskilled workers in the
U.S. have declined during the past two decades with one percent per year.
Wage inequality indicators, such as the D5/D1 ratio or the Gini-index, show
a sharp rise in inequality (Freeman and Katz, 1994; OECD *Employment Outlook 1996*, Ch. 3)

**Figure 3: The incidence of low pay and earnings Inequality in the Netherlands
and selected OECD Countries in 1994**

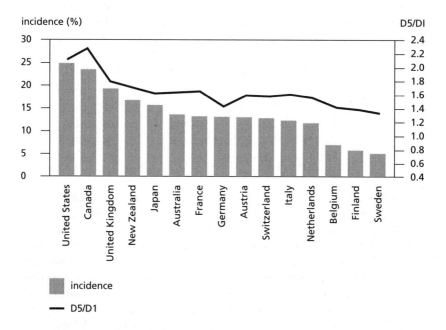

Figure 3 compares the incidence of low pay and earnings inequality in 1994 in
a number of OECD countries. The Netherlands is located between the highly unionized Scandinavian countries and Belgium on the one hand, and the
United States, the United Kingdom and New Zealand, countries in which the
unions are weak or have been weakened in the past decade, on the other.
Earnings inequality has increased in the Netherlands in the past decade, as it
did in nearly all countries except West Germany and Belgium, but the increase has been fairly modest. The picture in Figure 4 suggests that there is no

strong relationship between earnings inequality and employment growth. The Dutch employment miracle shows that success can be achieved without a sharp rise in earnings inequality[26]; in Chapter Five we will argue that this is in fact a condition for continued wage moderation.

Figure 4: Employment Growth and Changes in Earnings Inequality in the Netherlands and Selected OECD Countries, 1982-95

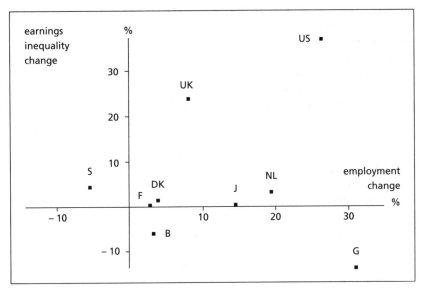

Source: Roorda and Vogels, 1997.

Unlike wage developments in the US, wage moderation in the Netherlands has been part of a concerted policy by the trade unions during the past fifteen years. It is an essential element of that policy that they have put the brakes on the growth of higher earnings as well. Moreover, the statutory minimum wage, although relevant for only a small percentage of the adult workforce, reduces earnings differentials between men and women, between firms and sectors, and reduces exploitation of unskilled workers in the sweat trades (Roorda and Vogels, 1997). The enduring freezing of an already low statutory minimum wage in the Unites States, for example, explains one-third of the increase in wage differentials between firms. In the Netherlands the statutory minimum wage used to be very high by international standards, since it had to provide for a family with a full-time housewife and two children. The minimum wage has since 1982 been lowered and frozen until 1990 and again between 1993 and 1996, and its current value, expressed as percentage of the average wage, has declined to 51.1 percent, compared to 64.4 percent in

1980 and 54.6 percent in 1990. In real terms (purchasing parities), the adult minimum wage in the Netherlands in 1995 was lower than in Belgium but higher than the SMIC in France and almost twice as high as in the United States (Roorda and Vogels, 1997: 22).

POVERTY

In recent years, surveys show that around one million of the 6,6 million households, or sixteen percent, find it difficult to make ends meet and see themselves as poor. The incidence of poverty, thus defined, is largest among single parent households with young children, and single person households, in particular women in old age.[27] Among these two groups poverty is also most persistent. Of all people with a low income, at or just above the social minimum of seventy percent of the statutory minimum wage in the case of a single person, forty percent had been in the same situation during the past three years. Research on the basis of panel data from the United States, West Germany and the Netherlands, suggests that in the late 1980s, on the basis of objective criteria (defining poverty as an household income of below fifty percent of the median), only three percent of all households in the Netherlands were poor, against eight percent in West Germany and 18 percent income in the United States (Hagenaars, 1991). In the Netherlands and in Germany the transfer-out ratio, from poverty to something more, is much higher than in the United States, and spells of poverty are shorter, but in the U.S. the escape from poverty is more often through the labour market, rather than through social security.

POLICIES

In this chapter we have demonstrated that the labour market performance of the Netherlands shows strong and weak elements: strong job growth, a fall in the unemployment rate to almost half the current level in the EU; but also a high level of structural unemployment and sharp disadvantages for unskilled and non-native workers. That most newly created jobs are part-time may be seen as a *second-best outcome*: the expansion of part-time work has helped to attenuate the social division between fully employed and fully unemployed people.

In 1975 about 85 percent of all married men between 15-64 were sole breadwinners; in 1994 this proportion has dropped to one half. The one-and-a-half jobs model per household is gaining ground. In most cases this means that the man works full-time; income statistics suggest that, on average, women earn 30-35 percent of the household income. Time budget data show that there is no equal balance of paid and unpaid work between the sexes. In two-earner households with young children, men tend to spend on average 10 hours, women 28 hours per week on household chores and child care, whereas men tend to spend 18 hours more on paid work.[28] Liberating the family from those welfare burdens that impede women's labour supply is important. Two-earner families run a much lower risk of poverty, and there is an employment dividend in the demand for family-orientated services. In other words, a 'win-win' solution. Two-earner families (with children) suffer from lack of time (not money) and spend more on services in the market (Esping-Andersen, 1997).

The development towards the one-and-a-half jobs model is an example of *fortuna*, policies which prosper because they accord with the circumstances (Macchiavelli, 1970).[29] The extraordinary increase of part-time jobs was not the outcome of government policy; 'It just came our way', to cite one of the top aides of Mr. Ad Melkert, the current Social Affairs and Employment Minister. In the job crises developing after the recessions of the 1970s there had been attempts by his predecessors to promote the image of part-time work, but the stereotype was to see part-time jobs as either a 'dead end' – the proverbial cleaning lady – or as a 'luxury' – like a small city car for the professor's wife. In the 1980s attempts to hire government employees and youths in part-time jobs had figured among the various measures to combat rising youth unemployment, but these measures had been undone by the priority given to reducing public spending and public employment. Until 1982 employers and unions showed little interest in part-time jobs, and in most collective agreements employment rights and benefits favoured full-time workers (Leijnse 1985).[30]

This has changed, under influence of pressures of demand and supply, in particular through the increased presence of women who combine paid work and care. Recent collective agreements do acknowledge this development and try to improve on facilities and rights, for instance through extensive leave provisions and 'come back rights'. It appears that in 1996 eighty percent of all collective agreements have established pro rata wages and fringe benefits. After eight years of hesitation, the government heeded joint advice from employers and unions and decided in 1993 to abolish the statutory exemption of jobs of less than one-third of the normal working week from application of the legal minimum wage and related social security entitlements. This discrimination against small part-timers has been in force for a quarter of a century, in fact since the introduction of the statutory minimum wage in 1969. Currently, most taxes are neutral and social security benefits are usually pro rata. It appears that the part-time/full-time wage gap has narrowed to five percent, which helps to explain the popularity of part-time jobs among male workers. Since 1993, the central organizations of unions and employers have recommended that employers grant workers' requests to work part-time unless there are compelling business reasons for rejection. A right to part-time work is currently under parliamentary review.

In 1995 unions and employers signed the first proper collective agreements for temporary workers, introducing a right of continued employment and pension insurance after 24 months of service. This agreement formed part of a major agreement between the central organizations of trade unions and employers on 'Flexibility and Security', concluded in May 1996. This central agreement paved the way for an overhaul of Dutch dismissal protection law, now also under parliamentary review. The agreement is a compromise, not just between employers and employees, but also within the unions between workers with and without stable jobs. A relaxation of statutory dismissal protection for regular employment contracts (i.e., a longer probation period, more possibilities for negotiated termination-of-employment, but with the possibility of legal appeal) is exchanged for an improvement of the rights of temporary workers (e.g., continued employment after two years, pension contributions and social security rights).

The 'biscuit agreement' offers another example of the social pragmatism with which Dutch unions currently approach the flexibility issue. In order to address the overcapacity in the biscuit industry (11,000 workers), redundant workers will not be put on the external labour market but be hired by *Randstad*, the largest temporary work agency, who will train workers and try to find new employment, preferably in the same industry. This agreement is seen as a 'win-win' solution and as a model for other restructuring firms and industry. It goes hand-in-hand with a trend in Dutch firms to increase mobility across employers and industries, and avoid lay-offs, which have become more expensive, now that various escape routes using collective funds have been closed off.

New legislation removing constraints on shop opening hours, business licenses, temporary job agencies, working time, dismissal law and so on, consolidate this development towards flexibility. In 1996 a new law on working hours, replacing the 1919 Labour Act, permitted longer working hours and work during the weekend and evening hours, if agreed between employers and workers. The consultation requirement which pertains to firms of 10 and more workers under the relevant Dutch legislation on works councils and employee consultation, has been extended to firms with 3-9 workers. Through the individualization of social security and tax legislation the breadwinners model is further undermined. Old age pension, national assistance and survivors' assistance laws have been individualized (see Chapter Six).

But not all is well. The problems of pricing unskilled workers back into jobs, reversing the dependency on social security, and re-inventing ways back into the labour market for vulnerable groups, continue to pose formidable challenges to current policy makers.

Notes

1   This is especially true for the reception of the 'Dutch model' in Germany. See, among many other recent reviews in the German press: 'Abbau der Arbeitslosigkeit nach dem "Holländischen Modell"' in *Wirtschaftsdienst. Zeitschrift für Wirtschaftspolitik*, Hamburg, Institut für Wirtschaftsforschung, vol. 77, no. 4 (April 1997); 'Genesung auf holländisch. Mehr Beschäftigung, niedriches Defizit: Die Wirtschaftsreformen schlagen an', *Die Zeit* (10 January 1997); 'Die flinke Nachbar', *Die Wirtschaftswoche* (20 February 1997); the Deutsches Institut für Wirtschaftsforschung, 'Die Niederlande: Beschäftigungspolitisches Vorbild', Berlin: Wochenbericht 1997, no. 16 (April 1997); and Günther Smid, 'Beschäftigungswunder Niederlande', o.c.

2   L. Delsen and E. de Jong, 'Het wankele mirakel', *Economisch-Statistische berichten*, 23 April 1997, 324-7; 'Miracle ou mirage aux Pays-Bas', *Le Monde Diplomatique*, July 1997.

3   Time-series data of 'persons in paid employment' are based on the *Arbeidsrekeningen* (labour accounts) of the Central Bureau for Statistics (CBS, *Centraal Bureau voor de Statistiek*), which combine survey data on households and enterprises and offer the most complete information and the only continuing time series on the development of the labour market. All jobs, including those of between 1 and 12 hours weekly are included in these accounts; such jobs are, however, excluded from the quarterly Labour Force Sample Surveys (*Enquête Beroepsbevolking*) of the CBS. EU figures (current membership) are based on the OECD, *Employment Outlook* 1994, 1995, 1996, 1997, published in Paris by the Organisation for Economic Cooperation and Development, July each year.

4   CPB, *Centraal Economisch Plan 1995*, The Hague: SDU, 1995: 268.

5   DNB, *Jaarverslag 1996*, Amsterdam, 1997, p. 25.

6   In occupational terms the shift is even larger. The share of manual and technical occupations in industry and transport in total employment nearly halved from 43 percent in 1960 to 23 percent in 1994; the share of servicing, administrative and commercial occupations increased from 30 to 38 percent; and the share of specialist, scientific and managerial occupations doubled from 12 to 25 percent. The latter figure suggests strong within-sector shifts; for instance, within manufacturing the share of administrative, commercial, professional and managerial jobs increased from 35.5 percent in 1977 to 46.5 percent in 1993. All figures based on CBS data (see note 3).

7   CPB, *Centraal Economisch Plan 1996*, The Hague, 1996: 106.

8   'Anatomy of a miracle', *Financial Times*, 20 June 1997.

9   Survey data based on the Manpower Survey (*Arbeidskrachtentelling*) of 1975 and the Labour Force Sample Survey of 1994, both published by the CBS. In 1975: jobs of 15 hours per week and more; in 1994 of 12 hours and more.

10   Ministry of Social Affairs and Employment (SZW, *Ministerie van Sociale Zaken en Werkgelegenheid*) and CBS, *Emancipatie in cijfers*, The Hague, 37, table 4.3.

11   The grand average of 1,383 for all employees in 1995 is calculated as 61.6% full-time workers times 1,741 hours per year plus 26.8% part-time workers times 880 hours plus 10.6% flexible workers times 780 hours. Source: CBS, *Arbeidsrekeningen*, o.c.

12 OECD *Employment Outlook 1997,* o.c., 177, Table E. A part-time job is a job of less than a full working week, with a minimum of one hour per week. Definitions and methods of calculation vary between countries. If part-time work is defined in a more restrictive and internationally comparative way as a job of less than 30 hours per week, the Netherlands still outranks other countries, though by a lesser margin (Table F). In the Dutch figure, temporary shorter working hours due to economic adversity, *Kurzarbeit* or part-time lay-offs, has since 1973-74 not been widely used and is not reflected in these figures on 'voluntary' part-time employment. The difference with Germany in this respect is large and reflects a different institutional mix of commitment and flexibility in the two countries (den Broeder 1996).

13 CBS , *Werken en leren in Nederland in 1996,* The Hague, 1996: 126, Table 3.5.

14 OECD *Employment Outlook 1996,* Paris, 1996: 197, Table K.

15 OECD, *Employment Outlook 1997,* Paris 1997: 165, Table C.

16 Relevant legislation, preventing married women from continuing employment in the civil service, dates from the 1930s and was followed by employers in the private services.

17 Council of Central Business Associations (RCO, *Raad van Centrale Ondernemingsorganisaties*), *De arbeidsduur,* October 1980; and RCO, *De arbeidsduur nader bekeken,* April 1983. Surveys confirm the idea that part-time workers are less absent due to illness; see CBS, *Sociaal-Economische Maandstatistiek,* April 1997.

18 Among men there was a similar change of opinion, but it is also true to say that a majority still expects women to do the combination. *Emancipatie in cijfers,* o.c., 39, Table 4.4; and Sociaal-Cultureel Planbureau (SCP), *Sociaal en Cultureel Rapport 1996,* Rijswijk: VUGA, 1997.

19 Only two percent of children under the age of four and 3.7 percent of children under the age of six have access to organized day-care centres during working hours (Maassen van de Brink e.a.,1995: 24). Waiting list for public day-care centres are long and increasing. Firms provide only a small proportion of private centres and most day-care is a matter of private arrangements. Many elementary schools, however, offer stay-over facilities during regular (9-5) working hours.

20 OECD, *Employment Outlook 1993,* Paris 1993, Table 3.3.

21 J. Thijssen, 'Kijk op werkloosheid', *Economisch-Statistische Berichten,* 28 May 1997, 430-2

22 OECD, *Economic Survey of the Netherlands 1996,* Paris, 1996, 46

23 The 'U7' rate for labour slack was developed by the US Bureau of Labour Statistics and is an additive measure of the number of unemployed, discouraged workers and (half of the) involuntary part-time workers, expressed as a percentage of the labour force. In 1993 the three rates for the Netherlands were estimated at 7.2%, 0.6% and 5.6%/2, adding up to 10.6% (For men the rates were 5.5%+0.2%+2.2%/2=6.8%; for women 9.8%+1.3%+10.8%/2=16.2%). Note that discouraged worker is a subjective concept, indicating people who would like to work but are not seeking work because they feel that no suitable job is available. Comparability across countries can be problematic, since survey questions asking people to express their 'distance' from the labour market differ. Involuntary part-

time work relates to 'underemployment' as defined by the International Labour Organisation and refers to people who usually work full-time but are working part-time because of economic slack, persons who usually work part-time but would prefer to work more hours or a full-time job. See: OECD, *Employment Outlook 1995*, Paris, July 1995, Chapter Two; and C. Sorrentino, 'International Comparison of Unemployment Indicators', *Monthly Labor Review*, March 1993

24   Organisatie voor Strategisch Arbeidsmarktbeleid (OSA), *Aanbod van arbeid*, The Hague: SDU, 1993: 16-9.

25   A.M.S. Boelens, 'Meer en minder uren willen werken', *Sociaal Economische Maandstatistiek*, CBS, May 1997.

26   Entry wages have been lowered in some sectors, for instance in education and universities, and youth minimum wages have fallen sharply relative to adult wages (Salverda 1996). Yet, it is hard to overlook the contrast with the U.S.; Beaudry and Dinardo (1991: 665-688) calculate that in the United States one percent more unemployment lowers the relative wages of newcomers, compared to workers in employment, by three percent. Hartog et al. (1994: 528) have estimated that a similar rise in unemployment in the Netherlands is associated with a relative decline in newcomers wages of less than one percent.

27   See H.J. Dirven, 'Moeilijk rondkomen met het inkomen', *Sociaal-Economische Maandstatistiek*, CBS, January 1997; and H. Bos, 'Lage inkomens 1995', *Sociaal-Economische Maandstatistiek*, CBS, February 1997.

28   J.de Hart, *Tijdopnamen*, Rijswijk: Social-Cultural Planning Bureau, 1995: 58.

29   '(On the other hand) he is likely to make fewer mistakes and to prosper in his fortune when circumstances accord with his conduct…' (N. Macchiavelli, *Discourses*, Third Book, Chapter Nine, in the translation of L.J. Walker, edition of 1970 by Bernard Crick, Harmondsworth: Penguin, 430. In the translation of Ch.E. Detmold the same sentence reads: '(But) he errs least and will be most favoured by fortune who suits his proceedings to the times…' (ed. Max Lerner, New York: The Modern Library, 1950: 441).

30   This appears to have been the general case in continental European welfare states. See: Casey, 1983.

Chapter Three

Welfare Reform, Institutional Theory and Social Learning

L IKE ALL EUROPEAN WELFARE STATES, the Netherlands is confronted with a number of changes which fundamentally challenge the basic
assumptions upon which the welfare state in the period of industrialization and since has operated (Flora, 1987). Five structural challenges can be
distinguished. These are: (1) the intensification of international competition;
(2) the changing role of domestic macroeconomic policy; (3) the transformation of the world of work; (4) the demographic changes related to ageing and
decreasing fertility, and, finally, (5) changing family relations. Together these
changes have produced a wholly novel social risk profile for the citizens of advanced welfare states. The institutions and programs of the welfare state reflect to a large degree the institutional frozen world of Fordist mass production, stable employment relations, full employment for male breadwinners,
and traditional family relations. For this world the original passive transfer-
based system of social protection may have been adequate. Today it no
longer is and this in a nutshell is the crisis of the welfare state.

Welfare reform is a hazardous undertaking; we need only to refer to the recent elections in France, lost by Mr. Chirac and his Centre-Right coalition, to
demonstrate the scant rewards social security reform can gain, politically. We
recall that in the Netherlands, the parties of Christian Democrats and Social
Democrats, that were historically the political driving forces of the development of the welfare state and in recent times the main managers of its retrenchment, respectively lost one-third and one-quarter of their electoral
support in the 1994 general elections. Welfare state reform is extremely risky;
yet, it happens. Major cutbacks in social security programs together with administrative changes have been introduced in many European countries.
While cross-national diversity in generosity, administration, and normative
orientations remain, the basic trend over the past decade has been to make
social policies more restrictive.

Comparative studies of the reform of the welfare state tend to feature political inertia rather than policy change. In spite of the impressive challenges
of structural change, the welfare state is believed to be remarkably immune to
change. This portrait is exemplified in two important recent publications:
Gøsta Esping-Andersen's edited comparative collection on *Welfare States in
Transition* (1996a) and Paul Pierson's study *Dismantling the Welfare State?*
(1994) on welfare retrenchment in the United States and Britain in the days of

Reagan and Thatcher. Both studies argue that, despite serious external challenges and major domestic pressures, the institutional landscape of the contemporary welfare state has largely remained in tact. If the environment of
the welfare state has changed, the welfare state itself has not. In the words of
one of them: 'the contemporary politics of the welfare state is a politics of the
status quo' (Esping-Andersen 1996b: 266-7). Pierson contends that 'the welfare state remains the most resilient aspect of the postwar political economy'
(Pierson 1996: 179). Apparently, the sheer size and the complexity of the
problems facing national welfare states put institutional conservatism at a
premium. Both authors highlight different aspects and levels of political inertia; whereas Pierson concentrates on meso-level programmatic obstacles to
reform, Esping-Andersen emphasises the resilience of macro-level characteristics and policy legacies of the different welfare state regimes.

It is indeed a characteristic feature of the postwar welfare state that spe-
Although Pierson presents his study as an argument about institutional
change, it is essentially a study in political inertia. *Dismantling the Welfare
State* offers many important insights for the comparative study of social policy reform, all resting on the political predicament that 'frontal assaults on the
welfare state carry tremendous electoral risks' (Pierson 1996: 178). Pierson
maintains, rightly, that processes of retrenchment should not be misunder-
stood as the mirror image of the development of the welfare state. He de-
ploys this contrast to underline that welfare expansion usually generated a
popular politics of credit-claiming for extending social rights and raising
benefits to an increasing number of citizens, while austerity policies affront
voters and networks of organized interests. The post-1945 welfare state has
produced an entirely novel institutional context. Once welfare programs, like
social housing and health care, have become solidly established, they have
created their own program-specific constituencies of clients and professional
interests. As a consequence, Pierson argues, 'the emergence of powerful
groups surrounding social programs may make the welfare state less dependent on the political parties, social movements, and labour organizations that
expanded social programs in the first place' (Pierson 1996: 147).

It is indeed a characteristic feature of the postwar welfare state that specialized social programs in the policy areas of social housing, health care, education, public assistance, social security, and labour market management
have developed into institutionally separate and functionally differentiated
policy domains. Therefore, a general weakening of the Social Democratic
and Christian Democratic parties and the trade union movement, the main
historical supporters of welfare state expansion, need not translate into a
commensurate weakening of social policy. Supported by strong popular at-
tachments to specific policies, professional policy networks are today able to
muster substantial veto powers against reform efforts. Moreover, given the
political salience and popularity of social policy, it is not easy to turn a political preference of 'dismantling the welfare state' into an attractive electoral
proposition. Shifting the goals from expansion to retrenchment imposes

'tangible losses on concentrated groups of voters in return for diffuse and uncertain gains' (Pierson 1996: 145). On average, 'retrenchment advocates thus confront a clash between their policy preferences and their electoral ambitions' (Pierson 1996: 146).

Esping-Andersen's analysis of *Welfare States in Transition* underscores the institutional rigidity of advanced welfare states even more strongly than Pierson does. In Esping-Andersen's understanding, the problems confronting different welfare state regimes can be transcribed from their historically developed institutional characteristics. While social actors, particularly left-wing parties and trade unions, were once able to design and develop social policy by mobilizing important political and ideological power resources, today's policy makers operate under path-dependent regime characteristics, not of their own choosing, which extremely narrow their policy options and leave them with almost no support.

Welfare States in Transition, refurbishes and extends Esping-Andersen's 1990 landmark study of *The Three Worlds of Welfare Capitalism* on the divergence of welfare state development in Western Europe and North America. The new study considers the three welfare state regimes in terms of their aptitude to respond to a number of major challenges of structural change. Esping-Andersen distinguishes three 'path-dependent' post-industrial trajectories, each with their own regime-conforming trials and tribulations. The residual 'Liberal' or 'Anglo-Saxon' welfare state, of which the Unites States and increasingly Britain are exemplary cases, is haunted by a persistent downward pressure on low-skill wage levels, which is likely to create profound poverty traps. The universal 'Social Democratic' Scandinavian welfare state, with its historically strong commitment to equality and employment, will most likely suffer from an under-supply of skilled and educated workers because of serious disincentives to work extra hours as a consequence of the extremely high levels of general taxation, in spite of its historically strong commitment to active labour market policies. Most worrying, however, is the future of the 'compensatory', transfer and breadwinner-based, welfare state of the European continent. The welfare states of France, Germany, Belgium, Italy, Spain and the Netherlands are trapped in a vicious cycle of 'welfare without work', as they have embarked on a strategy of large-scale labour-shedding in response to industrial restructuring in the 1980s. More than the universal Scandinavian and the residual Anglo-Saxon regimes, the welfare states of the European continent are particularly ill-suited to the post-industrial and post-Fordist challenges, because they are orientated towards passive income compensation, creating a new class of excluded citizens: the non-employed low-skilled inactive citizens, who are unable to gain access to the labour market because of the prohibitively high gross labour costs that are a direct consequence of the need to finance the system through social security contributions.

In the accounts of Pierson and Esping-Andersen, the role of vested interests, especially of networks of trade unions, professionals pressure groups, street-level bureaucrats, is mainly conservative. There is not much room in these accounts for negotiated reform, for compromises between political reformers and the representatives of organized interest groups. Both Pierson and Esping-Andersen describe the role of interest groups essentially in negative, rent-seeking terms: in pursuing their pre-defined self-interest, these groups will most likely employ their acquired privileged status in the various social policy areas to veto any change that might harm them or their clients. Implicitly, Pierson and Esping-Andersen adhere to the Olsonian perspective on organized interest groups as 'distributive coalitions' which do not care about the negative externalities and aggregate welfare losses they cause (Olson, 1982). The possibility that some 'encompassing actor' may care about externalities and develop a broader view or strategy, is not taken into consideration. By urging students of comparative social policy to study retrenchment in a disaggregated manner, concentrating on particular policy programs, Pierson appears to fall victim to the liberal-pluralist bias of his Anglo-Saxon case material. Similarly, in Esping-Andersen's analysis of the pathology of welfare without work, there is no room for the possibility that the organized 'insiders' in the labour market include the interest of 'outsiders' in their strategies of collective action. Trade unions, in this view, are nearly always on the wrong side of the battle – against reform. The strong emphasis on the forces of political inertia really is the strength and the weakness of institutional theory.

STRENGTH AND WEAKNESS OF INSTITUTIONAL ANALYSIS

The standard portrayal of institutional change revolves around two conditions. First, as institutions grow old they tend to become trapped in a performance crisis, which cannot continue indefinitely. Second, a political crisis will eventually ensue to bring about a shift in the balance of power, which will most likely produce a new political coalition bent on a radical overhaul of the prevailing rules-of-the-game (Krasner, 1984; 1988). In our view, this revolutionary-episodic image of institutional change in terms of crisis and catharsis is unsatisfactory. It suggests that the policy-making elite in advanced industrial societies is unwilling and unable to generate institutional change in a more proactive, adaptive, planned, gradual and reformist manner, before a severe performance crisis creates a revolutionary vacuum. Before we formulate our alternative, a brief summary of the main features of institutional analysis is necessary.

In recent decades there has been a resurgence of political institutionalism in comparative political studies and policy analysis. March and Olsen were the first to rediscover and emancipate institutions as the key independent variables in structuring decision-making and policy outcomes (March and

Olsen, 1989). The experience of different national responses to the economic turbulence after 1973 was a fruitful ground for the establishment of a comprehensive research program with a focus on political institutions as key variables for the explanation of this divergence (see: Berger and Dore, 1996; Hall and Taylor, 1996; Scharpf, 1991). The central question became whether different policy outcomes across countries are systematically related to identifiable institutions.

Rather than explaining the interaction between political inputs and policy outputs in terms of economizing on scarce resources, political institutionalists interpret the interrelation between politics, institutions and policies from the vantage point of the relatively stable rules-of-the-game of decision-making in order to bring out the independent effect of institutional arrangements on policy-making. Their contribution to comparative policy analysis lies in demonstrating how policy demands and policy outcomes are linked together in different ways in dissimilar political systems. Institutions are however not viewed as having a direct effect on policy outputs, but rather as important intervening variables. Policy choices are prompted, shaped, structured or constrained, but certainly not invented by the prevailing rules-of-the-game.

There are essentially three ways in which distinctive institutional logics leave their imprint on policy processes and outcomes. First, by distributing power and access to the decision-making process, the rules-of-the-game affect the degree of influence and power that any one set of policy actors can bring to bear on the policy process (Immergut, 1992). This element of the institutional 'mobilization of bias' (Schattschneider 1960) carries enormous weight for the policy capacities of elected governments in different political systems. Westminster or 'the-winner-takes-all' electoral systems tend to concentrate policy-making power in the hands of single parties, while consociational democracies tend to diffuse power among coalition parties. In the first case the active participation in policy formation of minority parties is discouraged, in the latter case participation is instead encouraged (Lijphart, Rogowski and Weaver, 1993).

Second, through the establishment of responsibilities and relationships to other actors in designated policy arenas, the rules-of-the-game structure the competencies of collective action and shape the definition of self-interested strategies of collective action of the relevant policy actors and thereby critically influence the character or policy-style of decision-making processes. As we will show in Chapter Four, corporatist patterns of interest representation favour comprehensive organization, stability, orientation towards common interests, and a consensual or problem-solving style of decision-making. This contrasts with the prevailing self-interested and ad hoc bargaining style of decision-making in pluralist systems of interest representation. However, the unanimity decision-making rule which dominates corporatist systems tends to create a 'joint decision trap' and 'policy immobilism', if a consensus over objectives or values is lacking (Hemerijck, 1995; Scharpf, 1988, 1989).

Third, the rules-of-the-game prescribe the range of substantive policy goals and sanctions that actors are allowed to bring to the policy making agenda. A tidy separation between institutional rules and policy content is difficult to make, since many actors care about the rules as much as about the content, precisely because they believe the rules to constrain the range of appropriate or legitimate policies (March and Olsen, 1989). It is best to understand the relationship between structure, decision style and policy content in terms of 'elective affinities' (Weber, 1985): substantive policy ideals only become effective in institutional environments which are able to translate them into concrete decisions and feasible strategies of implementation. Summing up, the rules-of-the-game structure the distribution of power and influence of different policy actors, delineate appropriate styles of decision-making, create incentives for 'exit' and 'voice' (Hirschmann, 1970), and inform and shape the substantive goals of policy actors.

The methodological hallmark of political institutionalism, needless to say, is comparative. By highlighting the particular and varying institutional features of different political systems, the comparative method helps to elucidate the differential effect of institutions on policy-making; how they came into being, how they establish or underwrite authority relations, how they are maintained, and to what consequence. Most contributions concentrate on the institutional characteristics of the nation-state, which is essentially considered the most tenacious institutional domain within which collective action and public policy making takes place (Scharpf, 1991). It is the enduring nature of domestic institutions, as opposed to the fluidity of historical events, that allows a meaningful comparison of national policy experiences.

In agreement with rational choice reasoning, students inspired by political institutionalism do recognize that the interests of different policy actors are strategically informed and pursue their interests as rationally as they can with the institutional incentives, constraints and resources at their disposal. However, by subscribing to a more inductive methodology, they seek to identify the identity and interests of these actors through comparative-historical research, rather than through deductively driven but empirically empty models. A decade of political institutional analysis has produced a wealth of studies on how 'state traditions' and 'policy legacies' impact on subsequent policy choices within single countries (Skocpol, 1984; Skowronek, 1982) together with more comparative accounts of cross-national differences in policy responses to common external pressures (Katzenstein, 1978; Hall, 1986; Scharpf 1991).

Students of political institutionalism tend to emphasize the 'path-dependent' consequences or 'lock-in' effects of policy legacies, which limit the range of subsequent policy choices. The emphasis on institutional inertia is aptly captured by Stephen Krasner:

> The range of options available to policy-makers at any given point in time is a function of institutional capabilities that were put in place at some earlier period, possibly in response to very different environmental pressures (Krasner, 1988: 67).

Institutions and their consequential effects for policy development cannot be adequately appreciated without an understanding of the historical process. However, not all political institutionalists agree with Krasner that policy changes, if they take place, should be explained, not so much in terms of current policy priorities of power relations, but rather in terms of the prevailing effects of 'path dependency', which critically constrain the available repertoire of contemporary policy reform. The emphasis on isomorphism, path-dependency and inertia is both the strength and the weakness of this approach.

The central message that 'history matters' is highly relevant; it provides for a compelling understanding of the 'lock-in' effect of policy continuity. Institutions, to be sure, are enduring entities which cannot be changed at will and at once. However, policy continuity over time and space should not be exaggerated. There is often a 'crypto-deterministic bias' in studies in the tradition of political institutionalism (Mayntz and Scharpf, 1995: 45). This bias has led many students to downplay elements of intentionality, voluntarism, misjudgement and erratic behaviour of policy actors. Moreover, it leaves us with a rather problematic underdevelopment of theories of policy change. Institutional change is believed to be episodic; after long periods of stability, change may occur as a result of the accumulated maladjustment of existing institutions to changes in external or internal conditions. Krasner argues that institutions are subject to change at so-called 'critical junctures', periods of transition, when external challenges are fairly substantial. At such moments existing policy routines are called into question and a struggle over a significant change of the rules-of-the game is likely to surface (Krasner, 1988: 67-9). Under stable conditions, on the other hand, policy makers lean heavily on the existing institutional arrangements and make incremental adjustments only at the margin in order to accommodate changes in the world around them. In short, only at rare moments of revolutionary crisis can politics overrule institutions rather than the other way around.

Institutions or rules-of-the-game delineate the opportunity set for policy makers, the 'repertoire of legitimate and routinized policy responses' at their disposal (Scharpf, 1987). How well they are able to solve policy problems and determine the course of policies, depends as much on these repertoires as upon the motivations, preferences, strategic goals, power resources, positional interests, collective identities, and cognitive frameworks that enable them to make sense of the complexity of the situation in which they find themselves. The question of how policy choices effect policy performance cannot be answered by merely focusing on institutional characteristics. Because it is implausible that a particular set of institutions would always favour a particular policy outcome, regardless of the preferences and motivations of the participant policy actors and the exogenous changes in their environment, Mayntz and Scharpf (1995) advocate a more intentional perspective, which they coined an 'actor-centred institutionalism':

> This framework of an actor-centred institutionalism is characterized by its giving equal weight to the strategic actions and interactions of purposeful and resourceful individual and corporate actors and to the enabling, constraining, and shaping effects of giving (but variable) institutional structures and institutionalized norms (Scharpf, 1997).

From the vantage point of an 'actor centered institutionalism', institutional change is thus constrained by two factors: (1) preferred policy choices of intentional actors; and (2) existing institutions delineating the available room for feasible institutional change in the direction chosen by strategic actors. While the origins of today's rules-of-the-game are historically separated from current policy makers, in order to understand and explain the institutional effects of past institutions on contemporary policy processes and policy outcomes, scholars should concentrate more on the kind of incentives, risks, opportunities, and constraints that these rules supply for participant policy makers.

Within the perspective of an 'actor centred institutionalism' one can see three main reasons why actors with a privileged position wish to stick to given rules and oppose institutional reforms: sunk costs, uncertainty, and political conflict (Genschel, 1997). There are usually considerable set-up costs; institution-specific investments, made at formative moments in the past, render change for actors costly. Moreover, such changes are fraught with uncertainty; actors know how to play the rules within which they have historically evolved and often defend these rules even if they have become associated with sub-optimal policy outcomes (Crouch, 1995). With the passing of time, a particular institutional arrangement, associated with a specific 'decision styles', may become, not so much an independent precondition for achieving particular policy goals, but a desired product of policy in its own right. In some respects, Crouch infers, policy actors may give more priority to a favoured means of achieving substantive goals than to these goals themselves, precisely because the latter are inherently uncertain. Genschel maintains that in the face of high levels of risk and uncertainty, policy actors will more likely stick to their old institution, even when there are conceivably better behavioural alternatives. In other words, things have to get much worse before they get better and purposeful change becomes a feasible option. Finally, given the distributive bias of institutions, institutional change is prone to political conflict. When the political stakes are high, it is most likely that a risk averse policy elite, together with its clientele, will strongly resist institutional reform. As we saw before, this idea of institutions as 'immovable movers' (Genschel 1997: 44) is particularly prevalent in the studies of welfare state reform.

INSTITUTIONAL CHANGE AND POLICY LEARNING

Path-dependency is about historical contingency, not necessarily about policy inertia. Undoubtedly, sunken costs, uncertainty and political conflict contribute to institutional inertia, but we agree with Genschel that this does not imply that no adaptation is possible without destruction. He identifies two sources of change which essentially leave the prevailing rules-of-the-game in tact: patching up and transposition. In the first case, exogenous pressures are diverted by supplementing established institutions with additional rules and procedures, designed to relieve bottlenecks in the existing institutional format. In the second case, an institution which is initially established to cope with particular environmental conditions is put to very different uses. Originally created as a means for a specific purpose, institutions can gradually transform into more general rules of procedure for a larger set of emerging policy problems. New problems are likened to old problems, and institutions that worked adequately for old problems are transposed to attack new policy problems.

In the history of the Netherlands we find an example in the Accommodation of 1917 (Lijphart, 1968). The importance of this settlement of the divisive school issue lies in its consequence of sharing sovereignty over policies as a general rule of procedure in various other policy domains. Major public policies in the areas of education, health care and public housing, came to be compartmentalized and subsequently farmed out to the subcultural pillars that made up Dutch society. Once formalized and made into a routine, consociational politics and societal pillarization facilitated a spill-over process from the political arena to the sphere of social and economic policy-making.

Similarly, changes in the balance of power can create a situation in which prevailing institutions are put to the service of newly emerging interests who find it possible to creatively exploit the existing rules-of-the-game. We will encounter some examples of such patching up in our case studies. In general terms, our hypothesis is that rather than confronting the extremely uncertain event of a complete institutional overhaul, policy actors will choose to patch up institutions with new structures or transpose them to new functions as long as possible, because these two strategies of institutional change are less costly, less risky, and less politically divisive. Surely, these strategies of institutional adaptation may in the longer run be associated with unsatisfactory performance and not take away the desire for more fundamental institutional changes.

A particularly subtle understanding of institutional change has recently been put forward by Peter Hall. Although Hall agrees with Krasner that institutional change typically follows uneven trajectories, he underscores the degree to which reform is accompanied by processes of social learning, which means that in addition to 'the contest for power' there is also 'the play of ideas' (Hall; 1989; 1992; 1993). Hall borrows the notion of policy learning, of 'puzzling' and 'powering' of knowledge bearing policy actors from Hugh Heclo. In Heclo's much quoted formulation:

> Politics find its sources not only in power but also in uncertainty – men collectively wondering what to do. Finding a feasible course of action includes, but is more than, locating which way the vectors of political pressure are pushing. Governments not only 'power' (or whatever the verb for that approach might be); they also puzzle. Policy-making is a form of collective puzzlement on society's behalf; it entails both deciding and knowing. Much political interaction has constituted a process of social learning expressed through policy (Heclo, 1974: 305-6).

According to Heclo and Hall, many accounts of institutional change fail to develop an overarching image of the way in which ideas fit into policy processes. Moreover, Hall departs from the dominant 'state-centred' perspective in political institutionalism and includes in his analysis societal developments, outside the state, in an attempt to link the flow of ideas between the spheres of the state and civil society, in what he calls 'social learning'. He defines learning as:

> A deliberate attempt to adjust the goals or techniques of policy in response to past experiences and new information. Learning is indicated when policy changes is the result of such a process (Hall, 1993: 278).

Learning ensues when policy-makers adapt their cognitive understanding of policy development and adjust policy practices on the basis of the knowledge gained from past policy experience. In general, any conception of learning presumes, on the one hand, a cognitive interpretation of experiences, mostly in terms of success and failure. On the other hand, and in practical terms, learning is directed towards increasing performance. Hall's concept of policy learning is critically informed by policy failures, and the extent to which such failures create a window of opportunity for new political coalitions to place alternative policy ideas on the agenda. In agreement with Heclo, he highlights that policy development entails both intellectual puzzling over what to do under conditions of uncertainty and bounded rationality, and political powering between competing interests.

Hall's understanding of policy-making involves three central variables: the principal goals that guide policy in a particular field; the techniques or policy instruments used to attain those goals; and the precise setting of these instruments. Together these three elements define what he calls a policy paradigm. In Hall's view, the ideas embodied in a policy paradigm have a status somewhat independent of institutions. He believes that a policy-making process can be structured by a particular set of ideas, just as it can be structured by a set of institutions. Ideas in this context refer to a programmatic set of statements of cause and effect concerning specific policy problems together with a policy theory or method for influencing these causal relationships with an eye on solving policy problems. When the principal policy goals and assumptions about causes and effects are taken for granted, a policy paradigm is solidly anchored in accepted practices that link priorities, content, the institutions and the instruments of policy.

Just as there is much institutional inertia in the world of policy-making, intellectual inertia is also widespread. Policy actors – individuals – are notoriously reluctant to give up their cognitive understanding of the world. Ideas in agreement with current policy practices and accepted political doctrine enjoy a considerable comparative advantage over untried proposals based on unconventional ideas. Even when new policy ideas receive strong theoretical backing, they inevitably lack empirical support.

Hall's question is whether processes of social learning proceed incrementally, or are instead marked by the kind of 'punctuated equilibrium' that informs most institutionalist conceptions of political change. Inspired by the work of Thomas Kuhn, Hall analytically distinguishes between three levels of policy learning, which he numbers first, second, and third order changes. First and second order change are likened to the period of 'normal science', when the prevailing policy paradigm explains what it purports to and allows policy processes to proceed 'as a largely technical manner'. Third order change, when the whole basis, goals, and ends of policy are reformulated, is likened to a Kuhnian 'scientific revolution'.

First order changes are no more than minor adjustments in the precise settings of the policy instruments at hand. Purely technical adjustments are undertaken in order to keep policy development on track. The overall normative legitimacy of the central policy goals and cognitive appropriateness of the prevailing policy theory are not in the least questioned. As a consequence, policy development concerns an incremental process of change in the setting of the instruments. When minor adjustments fail, the policy instruments themselves are up for grabs. Periods of second order change are characterized by a kind of retooling and the introduction of new policy techniques. Third order change is the most radical step in Hall's understanding of social learning. It concerns a radical shift in 'the hierarchy of goals and set of instruments employed to guide policy' (Hall, 1993: 284). In agreement with Kuhn, Hall maintains that a paradigm shift is usually associated with an increasing frequency and intensity of anomalies within the existing policy paradigm. Policy actors will inevitably become engaged in a highly politicized, open-ended struggle over appropriate policy goals and instruments. At such periods of radical change, new and untested ideas compete for attention and power.

Hall maintains that first and second order changes usually take place within relatively closed policy networks. Third order change, since it concerns a truly significant deviation from earlier policy trajectories in favour of an untried alternative, is a rare event and probably accompanied with a significant 'shift in the locus of authority over policy'. Central to Hall's argument is that processes leading to third order changes are never confined to the policy communities of the incumbent political elite.

Hall characterizes the shift from Keynesianism to monetarist macroeconomic policy in Great Britain in the 1970s as an example of third order change. He traces the fight between these two competing economic policy paradigms, each deeply rooted in very different understanding about how the economy operates. Ultimately, the rejection of Keynesianism and the adoption of monetarism was based on increasing evidence that fiscal activism intensified the crisis of stagflation. Broader social forces, particularly the media who were themselves deeply involved in the electoral competition between Labour and the Conservatives, expanded the range of policy discourse beyond the state and the political parties. The wave of strikes in the infamous 'Winter of Discontent' of 1978 gave the debate over policy change the needed 'sense of urgency'. The outcome of the elections of 1979, finally, enabled Mrs. Thatcher to bring about a full-scale paradigm shift in macroeconomic policy-making.

Hall's contribution to the understanding of the dynamic of institutional change renders an attractive conceptual framework for our empirical case. In the Netherlands the unemployment crisis of 1982, the 'no-nonsense' approach of the new Centre-Right coalition under Mr. Lubbers, and the Central Accord of that year in which central union and employers organizations agreed to give priority to a recovery of profits as a condition for investment and jobs, have rightly been described as a major 'change in policy and mentality' (see Chapter One) and as the start of a new era in Dutch social and economic policy-making. This was almost a third order change by Hall's standards, a shift in 'the hierarchy of goals', but not in the set of instruments employed to guide policy. It did not come from outside the relatively closed policy network of the elite of union leaders, employers, government officials, and their advisors. It did revive rather than destroy or reorganize the joint institutions of concertation – in particular the bipartite Foundation of Labour in which unions and employers meet since 1945 and negotiated the 1982 Accord, which was later rediscovered as the hallmark of a new era of consensual corporatism at its best.

Our case, we believe, shows the limitations of two – empirically related – dimensions of Hall's analytical framework. His understanding of the move from a second to a third order change still shows signs of Krasner's punctuated and crude logic of 'institutions determine policy' until 'politics determines institutions' (Thelen and Steinmo, 1992). Paradigmatic social learning is advanced from outside an intellectually inert policy elite and is only likely to gain political authority in the case of a radical shift in the balance of political power (Hall, 1993: 280-1). This generalization, derived from his splendid analysis of the Thatcherite revolution, is premature, because it may not fit political-institutional contexts different from the pluralist and 'winner-takes-all' British system.

Second, while Hall rightly cautions against making too rigid a distinction between the state and society for understanding the dynamic of social learning, especially with respect to the shift from second to third order learning, empirically his analysis remains very state-centred. This is no surprise, for under the Westminster political system, where two parties compete for an absolute majority in parliament, a severe performance crisis will inevitably reach its climax in partisan political competition (Lijphart, 1984). Once elected into office, the concentration and high degree of executive power and administrative autonomy available to British governments, enable incoming governments, if they so wish, to bring about a major departure from the policy legacy of their predecessors. A truly radical policy overhaul is far more difficult to accomplish in political systems which operate under the electoral rules of proportional representation and require multi-party coalition governments.

The likelihood of path-breaking reform in institutional theory is sometimes equated with the number of veto-points in the chain of decision-making where policy decisions require consent from various actors, like parliaments, organized interest groups, sub-national governments and the public at large through referenda (Tsebelis, 1990; Immergut, 1992). According to this line of thinking centralized hierarchies are in a favourable position to launch path-breaking institutional change. The more solid and durable the majority, the greater the concentration of executive authority, the greater autonomy of an elected government, and, consequently the greater the likelihood of comprehensive reform. By contrast, consociational democracies, based on low electoral thresholds, relying on less stable coalition governments, are confronted with a multitude of veto-points in the decision chain, and should thus be considered to have serious difficulty in achieving policy reform. Given these opportunities to block policy change, institutional change in a country like the Netherlands, should be considered all the more surprising. Especially when, in addition to the consociational rules-of-the-game, coalition governments rely on consensus building with organized interest groups in various policy areas, adding to the already larger number of veto points in the decision chain.

We surely must consider the particular status and role that organized interest groups play inside and outside policy-making process. The interplay of interest groups and government has been the key concern of the students of pluralism, corporatism, policy networks and communities. We saw, especially in the study of Pierson, that the fate of welfare reform in a liberal democracy is to a large part in the hands of pressure groups which can veto reform proposals. The possibility that under specific institutional preconditions, comprehensive interest groups might have learned from failure and feel themselves under a sense of urgency 'to make things better' and support reforms against the short-term interests of some of their constituency, is lacking. In Hall's empirical account of the U-turn in British economic policy, the input of organized interests like trade unions and employers organizations to social learning is merely restricted to inspiring and animating the policy debate in the periphery of decision-making arenas; their capacity to learn and bring about third-order change is ignored. This is probably correct in the empirical case that Hall purports to analyze, but is it in the Dutch case – packed with comprehensive, quasi-monopolistic interest organizations and corporatist institutions?

Like Hugh Heclo and Peter Hall we believe that puzzling and powering are important dimensions of social learning and policy change. For the analysis of our Dutch case it is therefore important to analytically specify the interplay of puzzling and powering in policy settings where organized interest groups share in public policy responsibilities. This implies for the theoretical analysis of social learning in a corporatist polity, that the institutional variable of the division of labour and responsibilities between state actors and organized interests in particular policy areas must be incorporated into our analysis of institutional change and policy learning. In the next chapter we develop a framework of how this might be done.

Chapter Four

Policy Learning under Corporatism

THE CORPORATIST LITERATURE OF THE 1970S AND 1980S has made an important early contribution to the revival of the study of the institutions between state and markets in capitalist democracies. In the midst of the allegedly ungovernable 1970s, there was empirical support for the hypothesis that modern market economies, if they were capable of integrating business and labour interests into the formation and implementation of public policies, were better able to manage the social, political, and economic shocks which occurred from the late 1960s through the late 1970s (see the collections of Schmitter and Lehmbruch, 1979; Lehmbruch and Schmitter, 1982; and Goldthorpe 1984, also the contribution of Streeck, 1984). The ability of advanced industrial society to manage social conflict and improve economic performance, these authors claimed, is contingent on an institutional infrastructure which incorporates the societal interest of organized capital and labour into nation-wide economic policy making. During the 1970s, in particular, tripartite incomes policies were seen as an almost indispensable tool of crisis management. In the 1980s, however, with the rise of neo-liberalism after the second oil crisis, corporatism appeared to lose its rationale, when many of its finest examples ran into serious employment, fiscal and monetary difficulties.

A number of arguments have been put forward to explain the sudden demise of corporatism in the 1980s. By the end of the decade of the 1970s, centralized incomes policies were in trouble nearly everywhere in Europe (Flanagan, Soskice, and Ulman, 1983; Visser 1990). Some authors were ready to predict the 'the end of organized capitalism' (Lash and Urry, 1987). Students of industrial relations discovered the 'challenge of flexibility' (Baglioni and Crouch, 1990) and found the pressures towards decentralization and liberalization hard to reconcile with the corporatist approach (Locke, Kochan, and Piore, 1995). A new generation of scholarship in economic sociology and industrial organization gave much weight to the fundamental changes in the organization of production, away from the Fordist, high volume and standardized mass production, and towards a high value added, flexible, craft-based and diversified method of production, based on micro-electronic technologies and increased subcontracting (Boyer, 1988; Piore and Sabel, 1984;

Sorge and Streeck, 1988). Focusing on changes in domestic labour markets, Esping-Andersen (1993), among others, has argued that the structural growth of atypical patterns of employment following the secular transformation of the traditional family and individualization of life-styles within the welfare state, has created a far too heterogeneous labour force for effective corporatist representation and collective bargaining. In highlighting the historical corollary of corporatist success and Keynesian macro-economic intervention, finally, political scientists have suggested that the thoroughgoing liberalization of international capital markets in the 1980s has sharply curtailed the political capacities of national governments to deliver full employment in exchange for societal wage restraint through the use of fiscal and monetary policy measures (Scharpf, 1991).

Corporatism is dead, long live corporatism! (Schmitter, 1989). Corporatism remains important, even under conditions of intensified international competition and decreased national leverage over economic policies ('globalization'), but, as we show in our Dutch case-study, in novel ways not anticipated by the authors who tended to equate corporatism with Keynesianism. To be sure, the scope of supply-side corporatism is narrower and more predicated on generalized trust and consensus, deep within the firms, networks and interest organizations which make up the economy, than the Keynesian strategies of wage moderation, demand management and redistributive social policy. These could be negotiated and directed from above by a small elite of leaders, politicians and technocrats, even at the risk of tensions with the rank-and-file. In the economies of the 1990s, corporatism has to work, if it works at all, in the micro-world of thousands of little negotiations in firms, unions, employers organizations, and public agencies (Regini, 1995, and our Chapter Five).

Moreover, it appears that the European project has been an important contributing factor in reviving the corporatist approach at the national level. The negotiation of bipartite and tripartite social contracts on wage moderation, labour market flexibility and employment in a number of member states, notably in Austria, Ireland, Italy, the Netherlands, Portugal and most recently in Spain, together with the failed attempts to reach such pacts in Belgium and Germany, appears to have been prompted by the Maastricht Treaty and the decision that states must meet a number of convergence criteria in 1997 if they wish to qualify for membership in the Economic and Monetary Union and a common European currency early in the next century. While the new social pacts all focus on the fight against unemployment, they also, and perhaps more surprisingly, aim at participation in the EMU. The budgetary convergence criteria, which require savings on welfare expenditure and put a brake on the aspirations and claims of many *droits acquis* represented by the trade unions, appear to have rekindled the need of European states to try and find cooperative positive-sum solutions in order to gain the consent of the key interest group capable of derailing the austerity and adjustment policies on which they have staked their future. In the 1980s European trade unions were taught the bitter lesson of the Thatcherite revolution and discovered that a policy of non-cooperation may waste away union power. In the 1990s, however, European governments could not fail to notice that a politics of imposition, as tried by Mr. Silvio Berlusconi and his centre-right coalition in Italy in 1994, and a year later by President Jacques Chirac and Prime Minister Alain Juppé in France, was likely to run into massive social unrest which could wreck the reform effort and promising electoral fortunes.

CORPORATISM, STATE AND SOCIETY

Corporatist researchers have centred their institutional arguments around two key variables. These are the administrative structures of the state, on the one hand, and the organizational attributes and power resources of organized interests, on the other. Corporatist governance presupposes that state officials are able and willing to share political authority with functionally organized interest groups in society, and that these interest groups are willing and capable of mobilizing the support of their constituent membership in exchange for political influence. In the 1980s a great deal of research effort concentrated on the 'society-centred' characteristics of the functional interests of organized labour and capital. In particular, the so-called 'encompassing organizations', i.e. comprehensive, centralized, and concentrated organizations, were believed to be inherently oriented towards responsible strategies of collective action, corresponding with the public goals of full employment and price stability (Bruno and Sachs, 1985; Calmfors and Driffill, 1988; Lange and Garrett, 1985; Olson, 1982; Visser, 1990).

In recent studies a 'state-centred' perspective on corporatism has reemerged and insisted on the importance and variety of state and administrative traditions in Europe (Crouch, 1993; Lehmbruch, 1992). Colin Crouch, in particular, argues that historical contingencies of state traditions have had important consequences for the evolving character of (self)organization in civil society and for the shaping of domestic patterns of interest intermediation. As the process of state formation in Europe has historically preceded the development and mobilization of many social cleavages, in particular the class conflict which took shape in the latter half of the nineteenth and the beginning of the twentieth centuries, state traditions did shape the political and legal context for the representation and mobilization of organized interests such as unions and employers. They created or denied the avenues for access to and co-management of public policy making. This, in turn, had momentous consequences for the definition of interests and choice of strategies of interest groups.

Corporatism revolves around a rather distinctive interplay of state traditions and cleavage mobilization. Neither state capacity nor the power of interest organizations are the sole determinants of corporatist governance. Crouch's notion of 'shared public space' aptly captures the proximity of and reciprocity between organized interests and state actors. By way of sharing public space, the state devolves part of its most distinctive resource – legitimate coercion and the capacity to make and enforce binding agreements – to organized groups which it does not control (Crouch, 1986). In the words of Claus Offe (1981), the state may endow a limited number of private organized interest groups with a 'semi-public status' in the policy process. As such, the corporatist state is best conceptualized as an 'enabling' state; a state which actively sponsors voluntary associations emergent from civil society in helping them to organize themselves and acquire discipline in what they stand for and do (Streeck and Schmitter, 1985).

Through the systematic engagement in decision-making processes over public policies, organized interests may become *staatstragende Kräfte* (state-bearing forces) (Crouch,1993). The gain for private interests is preferential access to public policy formation. The democratic state may expect, in return, that the effectiveness of its policies is improved when the responsibility of policy delivery is placed, in part or in full, in the hands of the interest groups whose members are the target of the policy. By bringing private interests into to the administrative levels of the state, the state is able to widen its sources of information and professional expertise, resolve problems of public policy implementation and overcome dilemmas of coordination across policy agencies (Hanf and Scharpf, 1978). By promoting and protecting a comprehensive organization of interest organization, it is hoped that these organizations 'will have reasons to be somewhat less restrictive' in the pursuit of their own group interest and 'internalize' some of the harmful effects on others which their policies would otherwise produce (Olson, 1982).

In this study we define corporatist governance as:

> The extra-parliamentary political practice of ongoing negotiations between the formal representatives of the organized interests of capital and labour, facilitated by the state and conditional upon substantive outcomes, over issues of social and economic policy-making under the primacy of the democratic constitutional state.

Some authors have restricted corporatism to a particular pattern of industrial relations. We hold that such a conception is too narrow. As we will show in Chapters Six and Seven, corporatist governance applies to a much wider range of issues and policies, extending into the spheres of social security and labour market management.[1] This said, it should also be stressed that corporatist governance does not exemplify an all-inclusive system of political regulation. It concerns the 'partial' political practice of negotiated social and economic policy regulation (Panitch, 1986: 161). With respect to the participating corporate actors, these include, next to the democratic state, the organized interests of capital and labour at national or industrial-branch levels, sometimes extending into the regions.

We wish to emphasize that corporatist practices, while taking place outside the parliamentary channel of representation, remain subject to parliamentary scrutiny and the rule of law. The tendency to view corporatist governance as a non-democratic political practice, reminiscent of Fascism, is understandable for historical reasons but nevertheless misleading. In the absence of direct state coercion, corporatist governance in a democratic polity is to be understood as a form of 'generalized political exchange' between the democratically elected government and the organized functional interests (Cawson, 1986; Crouch, 1993; Marin, 1990; Pizzorno, 1978). The term 'exchange' presupposes a fundamental degree of choice and self-interest of each of the parties in the process, whether private or public. Ideally, in a corporatist exchange private interest groups such as unions or employers associations forego the use of their political and economic power for self-seeking purposes in exchange for participation in or control over the policies of others, including those of the state. By defining such adjustment processes as 'ongoing' and 'negotiated' we want to draw attention to the fact that – in correspondence with the maxims of 'actor centred institutionalism' – each side has a degree of autonomy but that in corporatist exchanges exit costs tend to be high.

CORPORATISM AND POLICY-MAKING STYLE

The institutional format of corporatist governance entails a number of positive effects on learning. These are institutional stability, lengthy time limits, 'pacta-sunt-servanda', shared understandings, and a problem-solving style of joint decision-making. The corporatist response to policy failure is founded, in Hirschman's typology, in the deployment of 'voice' (Hirschman, 1970). Participants are obliged to explain, give reasons and take responsibility for their decisions and strategies to each other and to the rank and file, but at times also with respect to the public at large; to deliberate a wider range of policy issues; and to take consideration of alternative policy avenues. Corporatism restrains participants to go it alone or 'exit'. This creates a pressure to compromise, which over time may produce a sense of mutual debt and become an element of 'loyalty', which in turn serves as a normative break on 'exit' and 'free riding'.

Corporatist institutions of interest intermediation tend to stabilize participation and give negotiations a longer time horizon. Iterate gaming and the 'shadow of the future' help to install patience, generate trust and the search for 'win-win' solutions (see Axelrod, 1984). Following Philippe Schmitter (1983), a corporatist bargaining system lies in the fuzzy zone between an 'accommodation of interests' in which contracting parties 'agree to some specific distribution of initial contributions and subsequent outcomes', and a 'reconciliation of purposes' in which they 'learn to interpret reality in broadly the same way and to value generally the same thing'. This may be likened to a 'problem solving' style of policy making based on steady commitment and trust (Scharpf, 1989: 261). In economic terms the gains of such a system lie in the saving of transaction costs, as a consequence of the increased stability and predictability of behaviour, and the avoidance of damaging conflicts.

The most interesting property of a corporatist system of interest intermediation, from our point of view, lies in the possibility that interest groups redefine the content of their self-interested strategies in a 'public-regarding' way. In our understanding, this is not a matter of voluntarism or good-spirited action in which 'rent-seeking' interest groups miraculously transform themselves to become 'public-regarding' altruists. 'Public-regarding' behaviour relies on mutual trust, a notion of duty and a sense of fairness. Following Robert Putnam (1993) mutual trust is enhanced through a 'norm of reciprocity' or:

> '(...) a continuing relationship of exchange, that is at any given time unrequited or imbalanced, but that involves mutual expectations that a benefit granted now should be repaid in the the future' (172).

To sustain 'a norm of reciprocity', Putnam maintains, actors should partake in 'networks of civic engagement', which allow them on an organizational footing to meet on a regular basis and to renew their pacts and pledges. There are many moments in ongoing industrial relations that employers or trade unionists dodge their part of the deal. The strength of corporatism, according to Phillippe Schmitter, is that through frequent, protracted and multiple exchanges, participant actors become:

> '(...) better informed about each other's intentions, respectful of each other's capabilities, and willing to trust each other's commitments' (Schmitter, 1983).

Through their participation in 'networks of civic engagement', actors do feel and can be held responsible for policy outcomes, defined in terms of public goods, like jobs for all, more work for minorities, etc. This entails a significant shift in the definition and interpretation of what is in a group's best interest. Negotiators can be persuaded to include the interests of outsiders in the labour market in their concertation with each other and the state. This requires *Ordnungspolitik* of interest intermediation, a sanctioned structure, contingent on substantive policy-outcomes, and a shared responsibility, in which private interest groups are constantly reminded and encouraged to rethink and re-define their interests in terms of what that means for other groups and for the future. In Putnam's terminology, the denser the networks of civic engagement, the more likely trust and 'public regarding' behaviour will be forthcoming. The reasons for this are straightforward: networks of civic engagement increase the costs of defection; they nurture robust norms of reciprocity; they facilitate communication and improve the flow of trustworthy information and important knowledge; and, finally, they embody the past success of 'public regarding' cooperation, thereby encouraging future collaboration (Putnam, 1993: 173-4)

In terms of 'puzzling', corporatist actors can indeed rely on more and longer memories and are better equipped to learn from past policy experiences. Crouch argues that by operating in lengthy chains of articulated encounters, state officials and the social partners accumulate knowledge of policy failure and success, gain the ability to detect systematic errors at the macro level and diffuse the new information towards the meso- and micro-levels of policy implementation. In terms of 'powering', corporatist actors have more resources to quell resistance and overcome the perverse effects of 'free riding' behaviour. The formal institutions of corporatism, by relying on large measures of political support, professional expertise, and societal commitment, couple problem-solving styles of decision-making at the macro-level with effective processes of policy implementation, by building on organization resources at meso- and micro-levels.

There is an interesting parallel between corporatist and pluralist bargaining on the one hand and tight and loosely coupled organizations on the other (Weick, 1976). The heavy overlay with institutions in corporatist governance makes decision-making processes presumably more sluggish and sticky than is the case in institutionally thin and disaggregated pluralist bargaining. Pluralist bargaining systems, like loosely coupled organizations, are well positioned to maximize the returns of flexibility and grass-root originality. In the face of a permanent performance crisis, such systems are typically unable to take advantage of a learning curve and to mobilize resources to attack the crisis at hand. In addition, they invite overcrowding of policy agenda's with a multitude of demands and disjointed localized solutions. In terms of 'puzzling', pluralist systems of interest representation are better equipped to detect and solve local errors, but they seem unable to encourage a more general awareness of problems, because of the absence of the means of communication and the incentives for developing shared beliefs and common solutions. In terms of 'powerering' pluralism is inclined to substitute 'exit' for 'voice', which is often associated with a loss of efficiency at the system level (Freeman and Medoff, 1984). Essentially, the relative proficiency of corporatism or pluralism revolves around the empirical questions of when and where local pluralist solutions are sufficient and under what conditions more collective solutions are indispensable.

THE INSTITUTIONAL LOGIC OF CORPORATIST GOVERNANCE

While in our view corporatism inspires a number of positive learning effects, it also harbours disadvantages and contingent political risks. Virtuous cycles can turn into vicious cycles, while organized trust can induce both upward and downward spirals. By incorporating functional organized interests into the administrative structures of the state, organized interests are indeed able to frustrate public policy and stifle change. The reliance on the organizational capacities of societal interests can, in case of fundamental disagreement over policy alternatives, enable privileged interests to slow down and foil effective decision-making, causing a certain degree of 'policy inertia' or 'institutional sclerosis'. In the Dutch case-study we will encounter examples of this, especially in the area of social policy discussed in Chapter Six.

While granting a comprehensive and stable institutional format for generalized exchange between a democratic government, or its agencies, and functionally organized interests, corporatist governance is not static. Corporatist practices are dynamic, their constituent parts are in constant motion, and participant actors react to changing pressures and changing perceptions of their environment. In order to map, in a theoretically meaningful way, the dynamic of corporatist governance and social learning, we suggest a fairly simple and parsimonious conceptual framework (see Hemerijck, 1995).

Corporatist governance has two, analytically distinct properties: the degree of *institutional integration* of organized interests into the framework of public policy formation; and the degree of *societal support* for corporatist policies offered by organized interests. Institutional integration and societal support represent the key canons of corporatist theory. Corporatism embraces a strong belief in the advantages that derive from integrating voluntary associations in policy-making and administration. Societal support alludes to the corporatist proposition that responsive policy-making is contingent on consensual intermediation among comprehensively organized interest associations, together with their respective abilities to maintain rank and file compliance with agreed policies.

The dimension of institutional integration of corporatist governance underscores the relative importance of the state as a core institutional structure. It corresponds with Crouch's notion of 'shared public space', and can be viewed as the combined indicator of the objective capacity and strategic willingness of the state to share regulatory authority with organizations of civil society, which it does not administratively control (Crouch, 1986). Institutional integration requires *Ordnungspolitik*, designed to demarcate the authority span and policy scope of corporatist governance (Streeck and Schmitter, 1985). Institutional integration, firstly, revolves around the extension of authority which is devolved to private interest organizations and to bipartite or tripartite structures in public policy formation. This may vary from mere informal and ad hoc advice to officially partaking in decision-making and policy implementation on a more permanent basis. Secondly, institutional integration demarcates the policy scope of corporatist governance, i.e. the range of policy domain in which organized interests are permitted a say. As a matter of course, the selective incorporation of some interest groups into public policy implies the disenfranchment or marginalization of other societal interests.

Corporatist political exchange requires state actors not merely to create and maintain a framework for political exchange, but also to develop a certain minimal steering capacity to guide its outcomes in the direction of public goods. The particular role of the state in corporatist governance corresponds with Scharpf's notion of the 'shadow of hierarchy' in strategic games (Scharpf, 1993). The ultimate availability of hierarchical intervention and state ratification of the agreements reached between private interests, helps to curb distributive conflict and limits opportunism among bargainers. The state's authority to approve and ratify implies the power to disapprove and nullify, and hence the possibility to insist on *bonafide* negotiation processes, whose outcomes are never beyond public criticism. A well-functioning corporatist governance system may, paradoxically, require a strong state which is capable of disapproval if need be. In Chapter Five on industrial relations – the domain where since the early 1980s the autonomy of unions and employers became a highly treasured good – we come across some interesting examples of how the state may use its authority to change the outcomes of bargaining between autonomous private interest organizations.

The postulated 'relative autonomy' of the state does not suggest that state actors can change the level of integration as if they were operating a lever. State actors both shape the corporatist institutions and operate within them. Corporatist institutions and policies contain a self-reinforcing element, but they cannot by themselves sustain the benign economic and social outcomes, proposed in corporatist theory. By guaranteeing and facilitating the necessary infrastructure and policy scope of corporatist governance, the democratic state can only prompt, perhaps bribe, but not coerce, private actors to adopt 'public regarding' views and strategies. For corporatism to work, consent and support must be given freely.

The dimension of societal support denotes a combined indicator for the objective capacity and strategic willingness on the part of organized interests to engage in corporatist political exchange. Corporatist political exchange can only develop if corporate actors are sufficiently comprehensive and united. The key 'society-centred' corporatist argument is that the success of corporatist political exchange depends largely on the strategic capacity of comprehensively organized or 'encompassing' societal interests. Encompassiveness relates to the two main functions of interest group representation, their capacity to represent members' demands in negotiations with others, and the ability to lead their members and ensure members' compliance with the agreements they conclude.

It is self-evident that the degree of societal support is a great deal more fluid than the extent of institutional integration. The need to represent membership and the need to ensure their loyalty are in a constant tension. When this tension between what Schmitter and Streeck (1981) call the 'logic of influence' and the 'logic of membership' is not successfully articulated by the leaders of organizations, a 'representation crisis' may ensue and put the corporatist exchange in jeopardy. Societal support may also be threatened from without, by the mobilization of new interests. There is no direct relationship between the level of institutional integration and the degree of societal support. We have no reasons to assume that the more organized interests are integrated into public policy-making processes, the more supportive they will be. There is a difference in the dynamics of change, however. While societal support may dwindle at surprising speed, institutional change requires complex renegotiations, including time-consuming legislative and administrative procedures to change the law. Institutional inertia is a kind of slack resource for organizations whose membership base is rapidly declining. A case in point are the Dutch trade unions, which in a few years in the early 1980s lost scores of members. Yet, their presence in bi- and tripartite policy making institutions, such as the *Foundation of Labour*, the *Social-Economic Council*, social insurance boards and many more, or their capacity to negotiate collective agreements on behalf of 75 percent of the Dutch workforce was not questioned, not, that is, until much later.

For the purpose of analyzing the changes in corporatist governance in the Netherlands, we propose a two-by-two model in which societal support and institutional integration are placed along two independent axes (see Figure 5). Applying a simple dichotomy, we distinguish between high and low degrees of institutional integration on the vertical axis, and between high and low levels of societal support on the horizontal axis. Three different patterns of corporatist governance can thus be distinguished. We call them 'innovative', 'responsive' and 'immobile'. We also identify one non-corporatist formation, which we dub 'corporatist disengagement'. By tracing the relationship between institutional integration and societal support over time, the typology allows for a dynamic interpretation of corporatist institutional change.

The analytic construct of *innovative corporatism* pertains to corporatist institution-building under conditions of high societal support for national policy co-ordination and low levels of institutional integration. Exceptional circumstances together with favourable state traditions and legacies of comprehensive cleavage mobilization allow the democratic state and societal interests to set up corporatist policy structures. Corporatist innovation concerns a formative period wherein bi- and tripartite structures are built as a stable set of institutional arrangements for the mutual advantage of public goals and private interests. National policy-makers, historically able and willing to share political space, take the initiative in setting up institutional structures

Figure 5: Corporatist institutional change

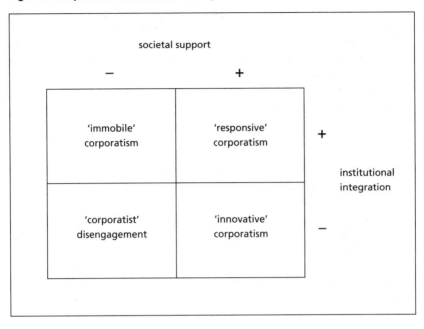

for public status attribution with the important assistance of functional organized interests, which are organizationally and ideologically prepared to engage in political exchange. Dutch corporatism experienced its 'innovative' phase after the liberation, when the acclaimed bipartite *Foundation of Labour* (1945) and the tripartite *Social and Economic Council* (1950) were set up. More recently, the demonopolization and tripartization of the Dutch Public Employment Service in 1991 is another example of corporatist innovation (see Chapter Seven). In terms of policy learning, innovative corporatism always involves a form of 'paradigmatic change', a formative moment of the establishment of a new policy paradigm, a novel institutional order together with appropriate policy techniques and instruments.

Once in operation, original institutions and policies come to define the administrative routines and standard operating procedures of corporatist governance. They create a 'path dependency' by limiting the future adoption of alternative policies and institutional arrangements. The analytic construct of *responsive corporatism* concerns a pattern of governance in which corporatist structures of interest intermediation have become solidly ingrained and organized interests are involved in public policy formation as a matter of routine. It combines high levels of societal support, carried over from the innovative period, and high levels of institutional integration. Under these conditions, the institutional structure of corporatist governance contains a high degree of decisional capacity to encourage a coherent domestic strategy of flexible adjustment to external challenges under a shadow of undisputed state hierarchy. A broad consensus over central policy goals, justifying the hierarchy of ends and means, renders policy elites sufficiently autonomous from partisan pressures to enable executive agencies to formulate and implement policies based upon efficiency, expertise, and professional rationality rather than political expediency. In its responsive format, corporatist governance is largely self-enforcing and most successful in achieving economic prosperity and social stability.

In the postwar period the Dutch political economy experienced two periods of responsive corporatism, the first between 1950 and 1962 and the second after 1982, both revolving around consensual policies of external adjustment (see Chapter Five). Positive demonstration effects, moreover, are likely to reinforce mutual trust among functional organized interests and bolster the legitimacy of corporatist governance in the overall democratic polity. Success can allow for a spill-over of corporatist practices in terms of authority span and policy scope. In agreement over general rules of distributive justice, responsive corporatist systems can produce a high capacity for joint problem-solving over substantive policy issues ('nothing works like success'). Responsive corporatism facilitates policy learning, by relying on a larger degree of a 'goodness of fit' between policy problems, institutional structure, decision style, and policy solutions.

We have argued above that corporatism is likely to facilitate negotiated adjustment on the basis of policy learning among the participant actors in their search for win-win solutions. But we have also shown that there is no straightforward implication of social efficacy and economic efficiency. Institutions define the opportunity set of public policy formation, not its success. Problem-solving continues to be a fragile decision-style, as Scharpf (1989) has observed, which is critically dependent upon commitments to a common understanding of long-term policy goals and the preservation of high-trust relationships. Next to the benign variant of responsive corporatism, our typology allows for a degenerated and malignant version of corporatist governance. We coin this variant: *immobile corporatism*. This is a situation of 'concertation without consensus' and 'institutional sclerosis', phrases which increasingly made their appearance in the Dutch discussion over the pros and contras of corporatism during the 1970s and early 1980s (see for an early registration of anti-corporatist sentiments: Geelhoed, 1983). Corporatist immobilism over external adjustment ended with the bipartite Accord of Wassenaar in 1982 (see Chapter Five). In contrast, Dutch social security administration and implementation moved in the 1980s into a crisis of governability (see Chapter Six).

While corporatist structures are present, fundamental agreement over policy goals and over the nature and cause of the policy problem is lacking, not just among the representatives of the democratic state and the organized interests at the decision centres, but also within the rank and file. Organized interests, most likely, employ their semi-public status and membership support as veto-powers in the negotiations, frustrating the attempts to reach a new consensus or to accept public-regarding decisions over substantive policy issues (Mayntz and Scharpf, 1975). Under such circumstances the unanimity rule of decision-making which dominates corporatist systems is likely to create a true 'joint decision trap' (Scharpf, 1988). This situation of stalemated problem-solving under high-conflict constellations, frustrates coherent responses to internal and external challenges, which, in turn, will increase the level of economic maladjustment, social conflict and political protest. Under such conditions, corporatist institutions and policies are a barrier rather than a help to the formation and implementation of effective public policies.

The condition of immobile corporatism lays bare the fact that political exchange is driven by a paradoxical trade-off, which we first try to understand by looking at it from the point of view of the democratic state. When state policy-makers engage in corporatist governance, they make themselves dependent upon organized interests. By integrating these interests into the public policy process, state actors want to gain more control over policy formation and policy outcomes. When societal support wanes, as in immobile corporatism, the state discovers that it has been sucked into an institutional setting from which it derives little or no rewards, but can nevertheless not easily free itself. The state may feel itself imprisoned by its corporatist engagements. This does not imply that purposeful change is ruled out. A period of immobile corporatism is typically characterized by a significant politicization of policy-making, a style in which interest groups and state officials will try to put the blame on each other, be they 'stubborn' trade unionists, 'untrustworthy' cabinet ministers, or 'free riding' industrialist. Each side will entertain the idea of exit, but participation in unfruitful encounters is usually continued in an attempt at 'blame avoidance' (Weaver, 1986), a distinctive political strategy of 'passing the buck', blaming others for policy immobilism (see also Wassenberg, 1982). This strategy of scapegoating is rather common when policy failures are discovered in a corporatist setting.

Corporatist immobility may be overcome under conditions in which state actors regain unequivocal power over organized interests (Scharpf, 1986). Our typology suggests that state actors can choose among two options. They can try to reinvigorate societal support in an attempt to move back to a form of responsive corporatism. Or they can try to end the corporatist engagement so as to self-assuredly change the prevailing policy paradigm, in an attempt to extricate the state from its dependence on societal support. Usually, the first strategy is associated with enlarging the scope of shared public space to reinvigorate societal support, whereas the second strategy is based on a denial of shared public space.

The analytical construct of *corporatist disengagement* postulates that state actors will choose the second response and after a longer or shorter period of immobility will fundamentally revise their propensity to share public space with functionally organized interest groups. In the Netherlands, the traumatic experience of a spiraling crisis of inactivity in the late 1980s and early 1990s, revealing the growing inadequacy of the bipartite institutional format and the passive policy concern for income replacement, rather than activation, provoked the government to fundamentally change the rules-of-the-game of the Dutch system of social security after 1993. The process of corporatist disengagement underscores the importance of concentration of power in the hands of political actors as well as the role of agency in critical periods of immobile corporatism when continued failure cries for action. Delay is more probable since disengagement is combined with high costs, serious political risks and uncertainty. The option of disengagement is constrained by administrative routines, previous policy choices and accumulated veto positions of organized interests. If the state has the autonomy to deal with policy problems in an authoritative fashion, government officials involved in corporatist practices will believe themselves to be in need of overall consensus when societal support starts to erode. Organized interest, too, will be reluctant to break out of the stagnant corporatist policy framework in favour of untried alternatives. Employers may fear more conflict, unions a loss of influence over national policies.

Immobile corporatism creates a complex game situation. For the state the choice may be between committing itself even more, or pulling out. For employers and unions there is the additional option 'to get the state out' and regain autonomy by strengthening their mutual alliance. This option requires trust in each other, or full confidence in one's unilateral power. Many of these games are asymmetrical: forcing the weakest party to give up its still existing ability to veto change and create disturbances, while convincing the strongest party not to give up on its institutional commitments and demand changes which cannot (yet) be accepted by the other. In other words, asymmetrical exchanges of this kind continue to require a high degree of trust between participant actors (Regini, 1995).

Immobile corporatism, thus, points to a critical balance between the institutional and normative exit barrier, shifting power balances between the actors, and the capacities of the state to maintain autonomous strength vis-à-vis societal interests, and defend a sense of distributional fairness. The possibility of innovation and the return to a responsive type of corporatism are critically dependent upon the trust between the social partners and upon the expectation that state actors will not accept opportunistic strategies in the face of unresolved conflict and have the hierarchical authority to make this view stick. All this has to be found out through experience and it is therefore that in a protracted situation of immobility, under the guise of scapegoating and blame avoidance, the participant actors may actually learn and prepare the steps for negotiated institutional reform.

HYPOTHESIZING CORPORATIST POLICY LEARNING

In Chapter Three we have argued that welfare state reform is difficult, but we have also shown ways in which it happens, through patching up institutions, transposing their use, and processes of policy learning. We have furthermore argued that processes of learning are institutionally nested. This means that in a consociational democracy and corporatist economy like the Netherlands paradigmatic changes in ideas and policies may happen slower and less visible than in a majoritarian democracy and pluralist economy like Britain. In brief, the transition from Keynesianism to monetarism did also occur in the Netherlands, but it took longer, was less celebrated by its victors and less hard on its victims.

Like Peter Hall's, our concept of social learning is informed by policy failures and anomalies, and by the extent to which new information and insights into the relationships of cause and effect in various policy domains, generate intellectual focusing events and political windows of opportunity for reform. We also distinguish between a number of narrowly defined dimensions of change, however we hypothesize that these dimensions are not per se related to each other in some kind of fixed sequencing of events. We distinguish between: instrumental adjustment; institutional reform; and paradigmatic change. Our understanding of instrumental adjustment, combines both fine-tuning in the setting of policy instruments (Hall's first order change) and changes in the techniques of the policy instruments themselves (Hall's second order change). Empirically, instrumental fine-tuning and changing policy techniques are difficult to distinguish. Moreover, in political terms, a change in the setting of instruments, like a significant cut in the level of social insurance benefits, can provoke far greater opposition than a less visible selective change in eligibility. In essence, instrumental adjustment concerns all those technical and instrumental changes which are undertaken to keep policy development on track. The overall intellectual and normative legitimacy of the programmatic set of policy ideas, ideals, principles and central goals are not contested. Under the politically stable conditions of periods of instrumental adjustment, policy development proceeds in a routinized and incremental manner. Policy makers lean heavily on existing institutional arrangements within which political demands are mediated and environmental changes are channelled.

When instrumental adjustments fail to keep policy development on course, more politically demanding changes will be ventured. In the case of accumulated anomalies and policy failures, doubts will be raised about the adequacy of the institutional set-up, the rules-of-the-game and the division of responsibilities between the state and the organized interests. Under conditions of immobile corporatism, policy makers are likely to become the target of political criticism from within and without. In the case of political

stalemate, the attempt to put the blame on others becomes a dominant political tactic. Policy immobilism may, however, give way to a reordering of responsibilities and tasks short of a complete breakdown. This we coin institutional reform.

We agree with Hall that paradigmatic change involves a substantial departure from the prevalent policy priorities in terms of content, on the basis of a
wholly different understanding of the policy problems at hand. Changes in
the problem definition of policy are most likely a matter of social and political
debate. Such changes will probably first be ventured outside the existing corporatist policy elites. The question of whether the successful establishment
of a new policy paradigm requires a state-led strategy of corporatist disengagement is an empirical one. The alternative route is one of patching up the
prevailing corporatist institutional framework, in order to internalize the new
problem definition. Hereby a renewed 'goodness of fit' between institutions,
problem-solving styles of decision-making and the new policy paradigm can
be constructed. Under immobile corporatism there is no change, because of
a protracted 'decision-trap', but this does not imply that there is no learning
at the cognitive level. A condition of protracted corporatist immobilism has
produced two things: a heightened awareness of the mutual interdependen-
cies between societal interests and the government, and nostalgia over the
feat of success of past policies. In the eye of the larger public a protracted corporatist stalemate increases the costs of open defection, of refusing to agree
over 'public regarding' priorities. As we have argued above, these elements of
learning under stress, take place under increasing threats of government intervention.

Two forms of paradigmatic policy learning under corporatism can now be
hypothesized. First, as noted above, there is the form of paradigmatic learning which is imposed upon organized interests by state actors, if the latter are
able to recast the rules-of-the-game and threaten or undermine the privileged
status of the social partners in the relevant policy domains under consideration. A second form of paradigmatic policy learning can ensue when there is,
with the unfolding of corporatist immobilism, a shift in the balance of power
between the separate interests of organized capital and labour. Paraphrasing
Karl Deutsch, those who lose power must learn. Learning, in other words,
will most likely affect the weakened actor. The dominant actor may want to
walk away from corporatist immobilism, but the possibility to do so is not a
sufficient condition for it to happen. As Wolfgang Streeck rightly observes,
corporatist institutions are likely to regain their usefulness if the weakened
actor's learning curve leads in the preferred direction of the dominant actor
(Streeck, 1984).

We agree with Hall that policy learning, conceived of in terms of deliberate
attempts to adjust policy in response to past experience and new information, is driven by failures and attempts to improve performance, beginning
with adjustments in policy instruments and techniques to keep policy devel-

opment on the right track. The relationship between institutional and paradigmatic change in corporatist systems is far more contingent. One trajectory is that accumulated policy failures lead to a major outside intervention and a break-up of failing corporatist institutions together with paradigmatic reform. A second trajectory involves a significant shift in the balance of power, leading to proactive learning of the weakened party, in the direction of the normative priorities of the stronger force, reinvigorating the corporatist institutional framework. This form of paradigmatic change after a long phase of immobilism, may allow for quite a fundamental shift in cognitive and normative priorities, managed through long-established and respected methods of decision-making. We conjecture that such a shift, if managed with corporatist continuity, ensures a more adequate, equitable and effective implementation than the far more uncertain, painful, and politically risky strategy of a state-led institutional and paradigmatic overhaul.

In the following three chapters our three dimensions of policy learning in terms of instrumental adjustment, institutional reform, and paradigmatic change under corporatism, will be put to use in the study of adjustment and reform in the three core policy domains of industrial relations, social security, and labour market policy in the Dutch welfare state during the past two decades.

Note

1   Other domains, not analaysed in this book, include work organization and corporate governance (see Streeck 1992).

Chapter Five

Corporatism Regained:
External Adjustment, Wage Moderation,
and Trade Unions

WHEN, ON 24 NOVEMBER 1982, the leaders of the central union and employers' organizations, Mr. Wim Kok and Mr. Chris van Veen, announced that they had reached an agreement on 'central recommendations concerning aspects of employment policy', nobody could have foreseen that this would be the beginning of a new era in Dutch industrial relations. Later, the 'Accord of Wassenaar', named after the residential area near The Hague where Mr. van Veen lived and the deal was prepared, became a celebrated symbol of corporatism regained. At the time, it came as a complete surprise to the outside world. In preceding years, everybody had grown accustomed to failure. Since the formal return to free collective bargaining in 1970, the central organizations, usually prodded by the government, had tried to negotiate an agreement every year. Only once, in 1972, did they succeed. No less than seven times did the government impose a wage stop or some limit on wage increases. The 'Accord' took away the threat of another wage freeze and there has been no intervention since. With the distance of years, the 'Accord of Wassenaar' has risen in status. *Wassenaar* has become to Dutch industrial relations of the past fifteen years what *Saltsjöbaden* (1938) was for Swedish labour relations in the 1950s and 1960s: the place where the central organizations of unions and employers had begun a reorientation towards a coordinated and bipartite model of negotiated central guidelines for responsible wage bargaining.

There are further reasons for the Accord's claim to fame. First, *Wassenaar* marked the return to wage moderation as the dominant strategy for investment and job growth of the Dutch trade unions. The central organizations recommended to forego nominal wage increases and suspend the payment of cost-of-living adjustments, due in January and July 1983 and 1984, in order to create a financial basis for negotiations over employment stimulating measures, in particular via working hours reduction. Dutch unions, impressed by soaring unemployment, convinced themselves that improving the profitability of Dutch industry was a *sine qua non* for whatever strategy of recovery and job growth. In exchange, employers lifted their ban on negotiations over a working week under forty hours. In brief, the Accord was one of those manifestations of the 'change in policy and mentality', of normative and cognitive

81

change, in policy priorities and what is needed to get there, alluded to in Chapter One.

Second, the agreement marked the first step in the transition from a centralized but faltering system of collective bargaining to a decentralized yet highly coordinated system. The Accord was only a recommendation, but, as we will show in this chapter, one with great organizational and normative authority. It was not an old-style central agreement with legally binding implications for affiliated unions, member firms and employers associations. At the time, observers saw this as a weakness, a kind of bloodletting in order to rescue the system of central consultation and a concession in order to make it palpable for employers, because the economic recession of the 1980s had shifted power in their favour and political changes had left the unions without an ally (Reynaerts, 1985).

But the argument can be turned around, for soft agreements are easier to reach. They decrease the likelihood of a 'joint decision trap' by lowering the consensus requirement in this kind of multi-level bargaining. They relieve the negotiators from the requirement to ask all of their members for approval of everything they sign and make approving members less vulnerable to pressure of members who disagree. Disagreeing members can no longer hide, but must defend their deviant course on their own. There are indications that Mr. Kok might not have been able to convince the radical unions in his federation who had voted against similar proposals in previous years and might not have signed the Accord had it been a classical central agreement with precise and binding figures for maximum wage increases. Reading from the recent account of its chief negotiator, Mr. de Haas (1996), Philips might have done something similar to Mr. van Veen.

The Accord of Wassenaar may be called, with that typical 1990s expression, 'the mother of all accords'.[1] Not only have as many as 78 guidelines, joint opinions, reports of advice, recommendations, and agreements followed on issues varying from the use of alcohol at work, non-Christian public holidays, jobs for ethnic minorities, rights of part-timers, youth unemployment, training, absenteeism because of illness and wage moderation, but each has led to thousands of locally adjusted bargaining outcomes (Van den Toren, 1996). Not all these pieces of advice were heeded, some were even hardly known to lower level negotiators (van Heertum-Lemmen and Wilthagen, 1996). The 'shadow of central guidelines' falls most distinctly over the approximately thousand bargaining tables when the issues are quantitative and the effects can be easily seen and counted. As will be seen in this chapter, wage guidelines are a case in point.

In the following pages we want to explain why and how it was possible to create the conditions for a policy of voluntary wage moderation after a decade of policy stalemate. What was the policy learning process preceding the 1982 agreement? To this end, we summarize the troubled history of wage moderation and corporatism in the Netherlands. Next, we discuss the dynamics of voluntary wage moderation from 1982 to 1997, and try to understand how flexibility through corporatism works and is maintained. Before addressing these two questions, we introduce, briefly, the actors and the stages on which they meet.

THE TRADE UNIONS

The level of union organization is very moderate by international standards. About thirty percent of Dutch workers are member of a trade union. This is much lower than in all other small corporatist states except Switzerland, somewhat below the level in Germany and Britain, but ahead of France and Spain (Visser, 1991).

Moreover, Dutch unions are divided. Currently, there are three union federations of significance: the *Confederation of Dutch Trade Unions* (FNV), the *Christian-National Union Confederation* (CNV), and the *Union of White Collar and Senior Staff Associations* (VHP). Of the 1.9 million union members in 1996, the FNV organizes 1.2 million (63%), the CNV 350,000 (18%) and the VHP around 170,000 (9%). A fourth federation of mainly government employee associations has disintegrated; its central bureau and half of its 100,000 members will join the FNV; the others will remain unaffiliated. Independent unionism is significant in the health services, in railways, air transport, construction, and in the public service.

Unions of these different centres have no exclusive jurisdiction and must cooperate with each other in collective bargaining. Single table bargaining with employers is the rule. Under the 1927 Collective Agreement Act, employers who sign a contract with a union must apply its conditions to all comparable employees including those who are members of other unions. There are no obligations to negotiate on employers and no recognition rules for unions. Any union can enter the contest and try to secure a place at the bargaining table. Strikes for this purpose are in principle permitted (Schutte, 1995: 17). This implies that unions are always faced with the threat of exclusion, something which just happens often enough to pose a real threat. In the absence of a legal right of recognition for unions and given the threat of exclusion, coalition building is the only remedy.

Collective agreements have a legally binding status and usually contain a 'peace' or 'no-strike clause'. Since only those unions that sign are bound by a peace clause, employers are usually keen to involve all unions with significant membership. Unions prefer not to stand aside, because only signing unions gain the union representation rights established through collective bargaining and only they receive the annual employers' fee in compensation for the *erga omnes* application of agreements. This configuration has an built-in bias towards moderation of demands, since the most radical party on either side runs the largest risk of exclusion (Rojer 1996b). Exclusion has in recent years affected the FNV union at Philips (1996), Heineken (1995), and Dutch railways (1995), but is nearly always repaired before the next round of negotiations. Most agreements are negotiated on a yearly or two-yearly basis.

FNV and CNV have by and large the same internal structure. Each has between fifteen and twenty affiliates, mainly demarcated by sectors; if current merger plans are realized there will soon be but a few conglomerate unions left – possibly one for the private and one for the public sector, with a few smaller unions in between. Since the 1970s the largest union in each federation is the public servants' union which also organizes health, welfare, postal and communication workers. For the purpose of wage bargaining, the leading union is, in both federations, the *Industries' Union* (IB), formed in the early 1970s from mergers between the unions in the metal, textile and chemical industry. IB-FNV is present throughout manufacturing industry, except in printing and some parts of the agri-business

FNV and CNV purport to organize blue- and white-collar workers. Between them they are divided by tradition, religion and ideology. Party-political affiliations do not exist, but FNV is closest to the Social Democrats (PvdA) and the CNV to the Christian Democrats (CDA). The FNV was formed in the 1970s through a merger between the Socialist and Catholic sections in the Dutch labour movement. The CNV represents the Protestant tradition but has also attracted a number of unions organizing Catholic teachers and civil servants. The religious and ideological divide between the two centres has narrowed in recent years, and mutual co-operation has increased. Leaders and members of both federations share to an often surprising degree the same goals, but in the CNV there is more reluctance to join in strike action, not a much used instrument in Dutch industrial relations anyway. Job growth through wage moderation and working hours reduction, the prevention of large earnings differentials across firms and sectors, and the defence of an accessible and adequate social security system are among the main objectives shared by FNV and CNV (Klandermans and Visser, 1995). The VHP unions are less enthusiastic about these objectives and favour more individual, effort and status related rewards, but their view matters less.

Union density undulated around forty percent in the 1950s and 1960s but began to decline slowly in the late 1970s and plummeted to 25 percent in the 1980s. Later in the decade membership growth began to pick up and in the 1990s, amidst strong job growth, union density has climbed back to almost 30 percent in 1996 (see Figure 6). Union density in the private sector can be estimated in the range of 20-22 percent, in manufacturing it is 32 percent and in private services under 10 percent.

Two-thirds of Dutch workers do not join. This is occasionally mentioned in order to raise doubts with regard to the union pretense that they speak for all Dutch workers. Low membership levels certainly did not help them when their historical position of co-manager of social insurance came under attack (see Chapter Six), or when they wanted to claim a new role in the labour mar-

Figure 6: Union density in the Netherlands, 1950-1996

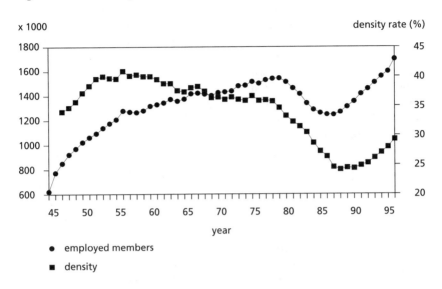

ket (Chapter Seven). On the other hand, in the classical domain of industrial relations and collective bargaining the legitimacy of their position is not in doubt. At no stage during the past fifteen years have Dutch employers tried to destabilize the unions or tried to create a union-free environment.

Moreover, opinion research does show a relatively high and stable approval rate of Dutch unions, their policies and leaders (Klandermans and Visser, 1995). Three out of four workers support the view that unions 'are necessary institutions for the protection of collective employee interests'. Moreover, in elections to the mandatory works councils, which take place every third or fourth year, unions attract two-thirds of the votes. These councils apply to all establishments with 35 or more workers, have a set of strong rights of approval and advice concerning management decisions, and are found in nearly all larger and in more than fifty percent of smaller establishments with less than a hundred employees (Visser, 1995).

Table 13 shows that Dutch unions, in spite of the rise in part-time employment discussed in Chapter One, mainly represent full-time workers with standard contracts and that they are underrepresented among women, young people and non-native workers. They have made gains among women (in 1975 the share of female members was just over ten percent), but they are nowhere near the Swedish or Danish unions, in which women now make up half of the total membership (Visser, 1991).

Table 13: Union membership in 1995/1996: composition and levels

	membership	share	density
FNV	1,197,000	64%	19
CNV	350,000	19%	5.5
MHP	163,000	9%	2.5
other	170,000	9%	2.5
total	1,880,000	100%	29.5
employed	1,520,000	81%	29.5
not employed	360,000	19%	–
sex	male	77%	34
	female	23%	20
age	15-24 years	8%	15
	25-44 years	55%	28
	45-64 years	37%	40
nationality	native	94%	29
	non-native	6%	21
working time	> 35 hours	81%	31
	20-35 hours	16%	23
	12-19 hours	3%	13
employment contract	standard	95%	31
	flexible	5%	11
duration of employment			
	long (>=5 years)	90%	31
	short (<5 years)	6%	13
	unknown	4%	–
sector	manufacturing and utilities	23%	43
	construction	12%	13
	trade, retail and hotels etc.	6%	42
	transport and communication	11%	15
	financial services	2%	5
	other private services	3%	37
	public administration	18%	39
	education	17%	21
	health	5%	32

	membership	share	density
firm size	1-9	5%	15
	10-99	23%	24
	>=100	67%	32
	unknown	5%	–

Source: Own calculations from CBS 1995 and 1996 labour force survey, FNV statistics, and Klandermans and Visser, 1995

The figures in Table 13 illustrate the dilemma of Dutch trade unions. Many unions, especially those in industry, represent older workers, mostly male breadwinners in full-time jobs with considerable tenure. Newcomers, men and women, start more often and work a longer part of their lives in temporary jobs than in the past, they work more frequently in part-time jobs, obtain less job security and are more difficult to organize (Klandermans and Visser, 1995). In their policies, Dutch unions have slowly begun to shift their weight to the second group, ahead of the slowly shifting composition of their membership. In 1986, both FNV and CNV, under pressure of membership decline, began to draw up projects that could make them more effective in a changing membership market. A more market – or target group – oriented approach became the basis for a more positive policy towards women, part-time and flexible workers. Typically, Dutch unions have gone through the learning curve of, first, trying to deny, then, to prohibit flexibility (Douma, 1997). When that did not work, they demanded quantitative restrictions. Still later, they have come around and adopted a policy of negotiated flexibility, in which they try to regulate with *bonafide* employers a phenomenon the rise of which they cannot stop. Success does not come easy and anecdotal evidence suggests that unions are hardly present among vulnerable groups and flexible workers in sweat shops, many of whom may be illegal and exploited by *malafide* employers (Braam, 1994).

EMPLOYERS ORGANIZATIONS

Dutch employers are well-organized – an estimated 60-70 percent of all employees in the private sector work in firms that join an employers' association, a level comparable to Germany, Belgium or the Scandinavian countries (Traxler, 1996; van waarden, 1985). Nearly all firms with a hundred or more employees, including all major multi-national and many foreign firms, have taken up membership.[2] In some sectors there is considerable rivalry between employers' associations organizing large and small firms, as well as opposition from specialized organizations. In construction, for instance, there are seven employers' associations partaking in collective bargaining for 180,000 employees, compared with three unions. In banking, on the other hand, there is one employers' association which organizes all but a handful of small foreign banks and negotiates with the five trade unions the sector agreement for 99 percent of the 100,000 staff. In metal engineering, the powerful *Federation Metal-Electro* (FME) negotiates on behalf of 1,250 firms with 187,000 employees in all, one third of whom are members of a union. Philips and Hoogovens (the only steel producer) are member but negotiate their own agreement. The 30,000 small firms in the sector – the dividing line is less than 30 employees and many are no more than repair shops – negotiate the sector agreement for 246,000 employees through a federation of twelve employers' associations.

Eighty-three percent of Dutch workers are covered by a collective agreement, not counting the government sector. The large majority of firms negotiates these agreements jointly with the help of an association. About 520 agreements apply to a single company; nearly 200 to a sector.[3] The first type covers 14 percent of private sector workers, the second nearly 69 percent (see Table 14). This division has hardly changed over the past twenty years; few

Table 14: Collective bargaining, structure and coverage in 1993

type of agreement			workers covered	coverage rate
covered by company agreements			650,000	14%
covered by industry agreements			3,300,000	69%
– directly			2,800,000	58%
– through extension			500,000	10%
total coverage private sector			3,950,000	82%
not covered			800,000	17%
coverage public sector			850,000	100%
coverage total economy			4,800,000	85%

	size	no.	%		share
company agreements	< 2,000	479	67%	200,000	3%
	> 2,000	43	6%	500,000	10%
industry agreements	< 10,000	133	18%	400,000	9%
	> 10,000	65	9%	3,700,000	78%
all agreements		720	100%	4,800,000	100%

Source: calculated from: Van den Toren 1996: tables 3.1 and 3.3

sectoral agreements have disintegrated, in some new services sector agreements have been established. Collective bargaining is fairly complete in manufacturing, but in business and personal services, with many small and new firms, its existence is often frail (Smit, Schilstra and Pauwe, 1995).

Traditionally, most multi-national firms, although prominent members of the employers' associations, have negotiated their own agreements. Their size and multi-plant character give these agreements the significance of sectoral agreements. Some, like the agreements at Philips, AKZO-Nobel, Unilever, have been trend-setting in the past. Today, the largest company agreement covers the 90,000 staff of the privatized PTT. Although decentralization has become a watchword in the Netherlands just as elsewhere in Europe, employers have been keen to keep pay bargaining, and distributional conflict, out of the firm. This explains why sectoral bargaining has continued, with a slight shift in recent years to allow more local variation through the use of framework agreements. Company agreements are negotiated under the control of headquarters, since management is keen on avoiding competition and union presence in their plants. There are hardly any employers who like to switch from unions to works councils as bargaining partner. They usually appreciate the professionalism and reliability of union negotiators, and fear that bargaining with the works council would jeopardize the consultation role of the latter (Teulings and Hartog, forthcoming). Formally works council are barred from wage bargaining and the councils cannot legally call a strike. Another contributory factor to the continuation of sectoral bargaining is that in the exposed sector many agreements define minimum terms and conditions only and permit some variation among firms. Under severe economic stress, unions allow hardship or opening clauses.

The high degree of stability of multi-employer bargaining, and extended coverage, is also supported by the 1937 Extension and Nullification of Collective Agreement Act. This law allows the Minister of Social Affairs and Employment to declare the collective agreement binding upon non-organized employers, if the agreement covers a 'substantial majority' of the industry's employees.[4] The official explanatory note to the 1937 Act indicates three purposes: firstly, to increase the coverage of collective bargaining to all employees; secondly, to protect the collective agreement against unfair competition, in particular from employers who try to dodge contractual obligations by discontinuing membership; and, thirdly, to encourage coordination in wage bargaining, thereby allowing the state to play a minimal role in wage determination (van Peijpe, 1985). In the 1980s, as part of its deregulation policy, the Centre-Right government had considered to strike the law from the statute book, but it soon realized the importance of this legal instrument in the process of controlled decentralization of wage bargaining which the Netherlands was undergoing. The final verdict was that the Act had to remain, and be implemented without change, 'in the light of its relevance for the existing social order, the preferences of employers' and employee organizations, and the its importance for maintaining labour peace'.[5] The neo-liberal attack on the idea of promoting collective bargaining would come much later, in the 1990s, and have some interesting consequences.

Currently, extension applies to 17 percent of all firms and 9 percent of the employees in the private sector.[6] Extension helps to explain the high level of collective organization of employers and extensive coverage rate of collective bargaining in the Netherlands (Traxler, 1996). In order to avoid the imposition of binding regulations, employers must reach a company agreement with the unions and conduct bargaining on their own, which for most firms is a costly option.[7] If they are to be covered by a sector agreement, they may as well pay a small fee and seek to influence its content. The trade unions are in a more ambiguous position. On the one hand, extension helps to prevent low-wage competition from non-union firms, on the other it creates free riders.

There are three major employers' and business associations, each of which participates in central consultation. Large and medium sized firms are members of the *Federation of Dutch Industry* (VNO) which has recently teamed up with the *Dutch Federation of Christian Employers* (NCW). Employers in the small firm sector, with less than fifty workers, join the *MKB-Nederland*, and agricultural businesses combine in *LTO Nederland*. Together, these peak associations form the *Council of Central Business Organizations* (RCO) for the purpose of joint action vis-à-vis the unions and the government. Attempts to establish a fourth peak association of employers in public and subsidized services have failed. VNO-NCW has currently about 130 affiliates, mostly industry federations. Since 1996 it is no longer directly involved in wage bargaining; the special NCW department which used to prepare and monitor negotiations has been transferred to the *General Employers' Association* (AWVN), one of the largest and oldest affiliates with direct members in the entire exposed sector, among which many of the country's largest multi-national firms (e.g., Shell, Unilever, Akzo-Nobel, Heineken). AWVN does not itself sign collective agreements, but assists firms in negotiations. With the FME it is the most important counterpart for the IB unions.

CONSULTATION

Physical and social distances in the Netherlands are small. Top officials and their advisors in trade unions and employers' associations meet frequently. They have easy access to Cabinet Ministers, key policy makers and top civil servants. Various foundations, councils, boards and committees allow for frequent, protracted and multiple contacts. For the purpose of wage policies the most important is the Foundation of Labour (STAR, *Stichting van de Arbeid*). STAR is a private foundation, founded in 1945, owned by the central union and employers' organizations, and intended as their meeting place.

Unions and employers have ten seats each on the governing board and the chair rotates between VNO-NCW and FNV. The wage coordinators of both organizations run the influential *Wage Committee* of the STAR. The principal accords and agreements of recent times have been negotiated within the STAR. Twice every year, in the Spring when next year's budget is prepared, and in the Fall when a new round of wage negotiations is about to begin, the Foundation meets with a delegation from the Cabinet (van Bottenburg, 1995).

The Social-Economic Council (*Sociaal Economische Raad*, SER) is a tri-partite organization. Since its recent reorganization, employers and unions each have eleven seats, the other eleven are occupied by crown members appointed by the government, usually professors of economics, the President of the Central Bank, the Director of the Central Planning Bureau and, recently, some ex-politicians. The SER was founded in 1950, as the top of a three-tiered – nation-wide, sectoral, and firm level – system of consultation.[8] In practice, the Industry Boards which employers and unions could organize if they wanted, flourished only in retail, food, drinks and agriculture. At firm level, the works councils gained significance only after legal changes in 1971 en 1979 (Visser, 1995). The SER's function was mainly to serve as advisory council to the government. In the first twenty years of its existence its role in setting the targets for wage policy and advising the government on the expansion and organization of the welfare state was very important. In the 1970s and 1980s the SER was less and less able to render unanimous advice and influence government policy.[9] Increasingly, the SER was being used, or made itself useful, as a means of delaying difficult decisions and other ad hoc Expert Committees became more important (Klamer, 1990). In recent years its role has been overshadowed by the Foundation. In 1995 Parliament has revoked the SER's prerogative to be consulted on social and economic policy before the government introduces new legislation. So far this has had few consequences.

FLEXIBLE ADJUSTMENT AND CORPORATISM.

In *Small States in World Markets*, Peter Katzenstein argues that smaller states often rely on corporatist strategies to smooth the process of industrial adjustment. This reflects not only domestic factors like consociational democracy or class compromise, but also their vulnerable position in the world economy. Because they are highly dependent on trade, smaller democracies cannot employ protectionist measures to insulate themselves from changes in the international economy. Instead, they must specialize in internal coordination, between unions, employers and state actors. Corporatism, according to Katzenstein (1985: 22-30), provides a device for harnessing social forces, facilitating flexible response and easing, but not avoiding, the burden of adjustment.

Democratic or social corporatism comes in two variants: Social Democratic corporatism, characterized by strong Social Democratic parties and trade unions, as in Scandinavia, and Liberal corporatism, characterized by weaker and divided labour movements and stronger business communities, as in Switzerland and the Netherlands. Both variants, however, share

> 'an ideology of partnership, expressed at the national level; a relatively centralized and concentrated system of interest groups; and voluntary and informal coordination of conflicting objectives through continuing bargaining between interest groups, state bureaucracy, and political parties (Katzenstein 1985: 32)

This is an adequate characterization of Dutch industrial relations in the 1940s and 1950s, and in recent times.

SUCCESS AND FAILURE OF A LOW WAGE STRATEGY

The Netherlands has been late in industrializing and a substantial portion of its industrial base and transport facilities were destroyed or taken away in the Second World War. In 1945 everybody important in the Dutch policy making elite agreed that unemployment could only be avoided if the country embarked upon a program of rapid industrialization (Dercksen, 1986; Fortuyn 1981; de Hen 1980). The task to find new outlets for exports and maintain a favourable balance of payments became even more daunting with the loss of the Dutch East Indies and the establishment of the Republic of Indonesia in 1949. It was therefore necessary to restrain wages and produce more cheaply than in neighbouring countries. In the first decade after the war there was a near complete consensus about this strategy; the Communist opposition was soon marginalized under the effects of the Cold War.

Annual wage guidelines were formally issued by the *Board of Government Mediators* (CvR), which acted under the responsibility of the Minister of Social Affairs.[10] In reality, guidelines were jointly determined by the *Foundation of Labour* (STAR) and the government, and implemented by the CvR in consultation with the Foundation. After the establishment of the *Social-Economic Council* (SER), it was given a role in the process: its macro-economic advice was providing the context for the annually adjusted statutory wage guidelines. Between 1945 an 1959 this system operated almost unopposed and without significant changes. According to John Windmuller (1969: 392) 'no other system of administered wage determination has done well for an equally long period of time'. In nearly all surrounding countries similar controls had broken down a few years after the war (Flanagan and Ulman, 1971).

The corporatist adjustment strategy, based on industrialization, with capital imports made available under the American aid of the Marshall Plan and exports of manufactured goods driven by low wages, had given the Netherlands a competitive edge over neighbouring economies. Full employment, then a concept mainly applying to male workers, was restored and maintained over two decades. In the European Economic Community, of which the Netherlands was one of the founder states, Dutch wage policies sometimes drew the criticism that it 'operated as a bounty on exports and as protection against foreign competition' (Windmuller, 1969: 392), and there were accusations of 'social dumping' (Pen, 1963: 218). Around 1960, wages were an estimated 20 to 25 per cent below those in Germany and Belgium. In border areas, workers crossed into these countries for jobs and in 1961 a much discussed paper, entitled 'The Netherlands – A Social Paradise?' (Hoefnagels, 1961), compared Dutch unions and social policies unfavourably with the achievements of its neighbours.

Nobody did foresee that the country was on the brink of a so-called 'wage explosion' as a result of wage restraint, too much and too long. Its success became its undoing. When in the early 1960s labour reserves dropped to under one percent, supplementary or so-called 'black' wages became widespread. In 1959, modest and complicated allowances for sectoral differentiation from the national pay norm had been introduced, but under the conditions of a tight labour market sectoral negotiations proved impossible to monitor. In 1963 the STAR was given the task to negotiate and oversee the operation of statutory wage guidelines, but central union and employers' federations were not up to the task. Wage drift was incorporared into central agreements and as a result wages 'exploded' with annual increases of 13 percent in 1963, 15 percent in 1964 and another 10 percent in 1965. By the mid 1960s the system was in ruins, an attempt by the government to hand control back to the CvR backfired. The trade unions did not want to return to the old system, which in their eyes had outlived its purpose of assuring full employment and had placed them in the impossible position of telling their members not to accept wage increases which had already been conceded by local employers. The central employers' associations were reluctant to give up statutory controls entirely, because they knew that their members could not resist wage pressure. Under the statutory regime, they had practically disarmed and discontinued their mutual resistance funds. By the end of the 1960s wages were on a par with West Germany and Belgium, and labour's share in net enterprise income had risen from under 70 to nearly 80 percent in 1970 and 83 percent in 1973.

THE TROUBLED MANAGEMENT OF A HIGH WAGE ECONOMY

By 1970 the Netherlands had become a high wage economy and one of the wealthier countries in the world. The problem was to find a new way of determining wages that was adequate for a high wage economy which was still based on a labour intensive industrial base. At variance with the 1940s, this had to be done in a society whose population was much less restrained by the memories of crisis, war and unemployment, and whose elites commanded much less authority over their followers.

Until well into the 1960s Dutch society was a 'segmented' or 'pillarized' society. The image of 'pillars' (*zuilen*) refers to the segmented organization of social, cultural and political activities and services – from nurseries to funeral parlours, and everything in between: schools, hospitals, insurance, sports clubs, cultural associations, women's leagues, unions, employers' associations, newspapers and broadcasting companies. Rigid separation of membership, supporters, clients or interest categories was combined with a high degree of elite control within each of these segments. Between these pillars, elites cooperated through interlocking directorates (Daalder 1966; Lijphart 1968). This system had emerged around the turn of the century as the result of the competition between Catholics, Protestants and Socialists and their fight against the spirit of nineteenth century Liberalism. In the 1960s the system began to disintegrate with astonishing speed. Among its phenomena and effects were a decline in religious identity and allegiance, looser ties between religion, party and interest organizations, demands for participation, and insecure leadership.

Trade unions, employers' organizations and government representatives proved unable to work out an agreement over a new voluntary wage policy. All agreed that the *Board of Government Mediators* had to go and free collective bargaining should in principle be restored. But the government's insistence that it should retain the power to reject agreements which it deemed 'excessive' was unacceptable to the unions. In protest against the new Wage Act which after two years of bickering reached the statute book in 1970, the two major union federations, later united in the FNV, organized protest strikes and withdrew temporarily from the SER and the STAR. This was only the prelude to the noisy lack of consensus which was to characterize the 1970s. Other events which marked the transition to a new era were the unofficial strike wave of 1970 in the Rotterdam port, which challenged a stultified union leadership and signaled the re-emergence of a radical Left; the successful opposition in 1972 to a plant closure in the AKZO corporation by means of a factory occupation, which drew widespread support from church leaders, local union leaders, students and newspapers; leadership clashes within the main union confederation, as well as well as a string of strikes in metal engineering and in printing over income redistribution in 1972 and 1973. A new generation of union leaders made its appearance in the 1970s.[11] Union rulebooks were generally revised to allow for more membership participation and the ban on Communist membership was lifted.

As can be seen in Table 15, the Netherlands did partake in the international trend of increased worker militancy in the 1970s, although levels remained very modest by comparison (Crouch and Pizzorno, 1978). Under the statuto-

Table 15: Incidence of strikes 1950-1995; the Netherlands compared with other countries

	workers involved 1960-67	workers involved 1968-73	workers involved 1974-79	workers involved 1980-89	workers involved 1990-95	working days lost 1960-95
Netherlands	3	6	2	4	6	20
Belgium	13	21	26	10	4	98
Germany (West)	2	5	5	4	14	28*
Germany					22	
France	148	155	81	25	5	104**
DK	9	17	40	27	23	117
SW	0.4	2	6	10	12	77
UK	41	74	57	44	10	268
US	17	24	15	4	3	196

Sources: 1960-89: M. Shalev (1992, p. 105, Table 3.1); 1990-95: calculated from ILO, *Yearbook of Labour Statistics 1996*, Geneva 1996, and OECD, *Labour Force Statistics*, Paris, various years
Relative involvement, workers involved in stoppages (strikes and lockouts) per thousand workers in employment
Volume, working days lost due to stoppages, per thousand workers in employment
All figures expressed as annual averages (geometrical means)
* 1990-93; 1960-93
** 1990-94; 1960-94

ry wage policy, strikes had been of questionable legality, and the strikes that occurred were mostly unofficial (Albeda and Dercksen, 1994). In 1960 the Supreme Court had ruled that strikes were, in principle, acts in breach of contract. In the 1970s the courts developed a more permissive view. After the statutory wage policy ended, the 1960 ruling was partially overturned by the 1972 decision of the Amsterdam Court of Appeal which ruled that strikes are legal unless some circumstance makes them illegal. While the right to strike is not regulated by law, judges have tended to accept the legality of strikes if used as a means of last resort when contracts have expired and efforts to renegotiate a new contract have demonstrably failed (Betten, 1985; Rood, 1991). In 1986 the Supreme Court ruled that the provisions of the European Social Charter are directly applicable to the Netherlands, thus establishing the legality of the right to strike. With a reference to the European Social

Charter, the judges had in 1983 already thrown out the ban on strikes for public employees, in existence since 1903.

Employers rearmed. In 1973 they reinstalled the mutual resistance funds and strengthened the leadership of their central organizations. In contrast to the 1960s, they were less ready to concede wage increases. Postwar wage restraint had encouraged the development of labour-intensive industries, but general wage rises and expensive social policies had changed the Netherlands into a high cost economy. Textiles, clothing, and soon shipbuilding were in trouble and could not be rescued despite ambitious public schemes which lasted until well into the 1980s. Relationships with the unions and with the government were strained, especially during the Left-of-Centre government led by Mr. Joop den Uyl (1974-77). This was the first-ever, and only government dominated by the Social Democrats. This government was given a rough ride since it was only half-heartedly tolerated by its divided Protestant and Catholic coalition partners.

From the start, Den Uyl was confronted with the sobering effects of the 1973 energy crisis, to which his government responded with mandatory wage, price and energy controls. Since he saw the support of his trade union allies rather than the cooperation of employers as the key to political survival, these controls were packaged with policies aiming at income redistribution and social protection, in particular through the system of net linking of social benefits to contractual wages. In 1974 the statutory minimum wage was made to function as the absolute social minimum, at a rate varying from seventy percent for single persons without family responsibilities to a hundred percent for breadwinners. The minimum wage itself was indexed to wage developments in order to ensure that everybody would participate in real income improvement.

Moreover, since the late 1960s, beginning with a tri-annual agreement at Philips in 1967, the unions had been able to secure the inclusion of automatic price escalators in annual collective agreements. This tightly inter-related system of automatic adjustments limited the autonomy of policy makers severely. By 1980, automatic price escalators determined 75 percent of the annual wage increases. With very small real wage gains, and with special allowances for low-paid workers, price escalators, often paid in flat rates, must compress wage differentials across skills and make it very difficult for unions and employers to negotiate an adequate response to labour market disparities.[12]

CORPORATISM WITHOUT CONSENSUS

The years between 1976 and 1982 are characterized by a policy stalemate (see: Wolinetz, 1987, 1989). All participants are convinced that something must change, but disagree over priorities, policies and instruments. Yet, they continue to seek partial agreements and compromises within the corporatist institutions in which they keep meeting. This rarely leads to agreement; in less than half of the cases in which the SER was asked advice, employers and unions agreed; most of its positions were watered down; delays extended over many years; and consequently the SER's influence on government policy was minimal. Increasingly, Mr. Kok, as leader of the FNV, 'had to accept without agreeing'.[13]

Employers and the government did not see eye to eye on anything at all. In 1976, nine CEO's of major multination firms had taken the unprecedented step of an open letter to Prime Minister Den Uyl with the warning that his policies destroyed the climate for private business. Reduction of public expenditure and control over the expansion of the welfare state now became their major preoccupation. Relations with the Centre-Right government (1977-81) under Mr. Andries van Agt were hardly any better. This government was weak, internally divided, in particular within the newly formed Christian Democratic party, and had hardly a majority in Parliament. Van Agt did not achieve anything which either the unions or the employers found of much importance.

Relations between the government and the unions were also strained. Mr. Wil Albeda, the Minister of Social Affairs from 1977-81 and an ardent supporter of corporatism and central wage policies, did everything to talk the social partners into a social contract. When he failed, he resorted to statutory interventions, like his predecessors. He saw wage moderation as the only way to prevent cuts in public sector employment and social benefits. The hands of the government were tied by the system of net linking between benefits and wages, and by the mechanism of wage determination in the public and subsidized sectors. Salary increases for civil servants were centrally set by the Minister of the Interior, after consultation with the unions. From 1962 onward this had been done on the basis of the development of contractual wages in the private sector. In the course of the 1970s workers in health and social services, public transport and other subsidized enterprises had also been elevated to the status of 'trend-followers' (Fase, 1980). Combined with the linking of a growing volume of social benefits to private sector wages, this meant that perhaps as much as sixty per cent of the rise in the annual budget was predetermined and no government could afford not to be interested in private sector wage bargaining.[14] However, employers had grown wary of intervention, which had many distorting effects, and unions were disappointed by the very few things the government had to offer.[15]

In the next chapter we analyze the 'growth to limits' in social expenditure. Here we note that the rise in social charges and taxes in the late 1970s was associated with a slow-down in the growth of after-tax wages and 'the employed did make some payment', but there was 'a limited responsiveness of the bargaining system to pressures emanating from an appreciating currency and an expensive welfare policy' (Flanagan, Soskice and Ulman, 1983: 131). The share of gross labour costs in net enterprise income rose according to the

Central Planning Bureau's figures to 90.5 percent in 1980. With rising long-term interest rates there was a severe squeeze on profits and investments.[16]

In 1977 employers started their counter-attack and wanted the elimination of the escalator clauses, but within weeks, impressed by a wave of strikes, they were forced back to the bargaining table and conceded the issue. The most tangible effect was that price compensation had now become untouchable – as a symbol rescued through struggle. However, worried by a continued decline in manufacturing jobs and a severe crisis in the ship-building industry, the leadership of the IB-FNV started in 1977 to reverse its radical stance on income redistribution and gradually adopted a policy of wage moderation and working-time reduction. In 1979 IB gained the support of the FNV and CNV federations, there was even a draft of a central agreement, prepared in the Wage Committee of the *Foundation of Labour*, but at the last minute the FNV had to withdraw because of implacable opposition from affiliates who claimed the banner of defence for low paid-workers and benefit recipients (Nobelen, 1983; van Voorden, 1980). What Peter Svensen (1989) wrote about egalitarian wage policies in Sweden, applies even stronger to the Netherlands, since unlike Sweden it did not have an active labour market policy (see Chapter Seven), and no mechanism for the redeployment of excess profits either. Attempts to introduce a kind of investment wage in order to tap 'excess profits', one of Den Uyl's proposed structural reforms, were defeated. Without these compensatory mechanisms, Svensen shows, an egalitarian wage policy with high increases for low-paid workers and low increases for high-paid workers tends to produce wage drift among the second group and structural unemployment in the first.[17] Ultimately, this weakens the independent bargaining power of unions in both groups. Unemployment and union weakness, finally, reduced the employers' need for central wage bargaining.

THE ROAD TO WASSENAAR

The oil crisis of 1979 hit the Netherlands much harder than the first oil price hike in 1973 (van Zanden and Griffiths 1989). The recession was exceptionally severe, even by European standards (see Chapter One). As in Peter Hall's social learning model of institutional change, discussed in Chapter Three, under pressure of the crisis the debate over a the need of a fundamental reorientation of policies is intensified and becomes more political and public. In its 1976 report on the Netherlands, the OECD wrote that in spite of the sharp increase in unemployment since the energy crisis of 1973 'public concern has been less than one would have expected only few years ago' and attributed this to the highly sophisticated system of social security and income guarantees.[18] Later on the mood changed entirely. In national election studies carried out in 1977, 1981 and 1982 more than half the respondents spontaneously named unemployment as the most important problem of the nation (Andeweg and Irwin, 1993: 192). After the second oil crisis, the population surveys of the Social-Cultural Planning Bureau (SCP), a government sponsored institute for social and policy research, picked up a noticeable shift in attitudes, revealing a growing wariness and pessimism about the future.[19] A stream of gloomy projections of above average labour force growth, jobless economic growth and ever rising unemployment, possibly to one million unemployed in the next decade, did not fail to make their impression.

Table 16: Some economic indicators 1964-94

	1964-73	1974-79	1980-83	1984-90	1991-96
GDP (in constant prices)	5.6	1.5	-0.3	2.9	2.5
labour productivity	5.5	2.5	1.5	1.5	1.0
employment growth	0.7	0.3	-1.3	1.8	1.5
consumer price inflation	5.8	7.4	5.5	1.4	2.6
nominal wage rate	12.2	10.2	4.0	3.0	2.6
real wage rate	6.4	2.8	-1.5	1.5	0
unemployment rate	1.5	5.1	10.1	8.2	6.2

Average annual changes and rates, calculated from CBS, *95 Jaren Statistiek in Tijdreeksen*, The Hague, 1995, en DNB, *Annual reports*, various years

In the wake of the failed central agreement of 1979 a remarkable shift in policy orientation surfaced. In its regular policy memorandum of March 1980 the Central Planning Bureau called for a reconsideration of the linking mechanism. In his annual reviews, the President of the Central Bank, Mr. Jelle Zijlstra, kept repeating that public finances had got out of control, with devastating effects on inflation, interest rates, and private investment (Messing, 1987: 551-5). The 'financing deficit', which measures the budget deficit plus the interest paid on long-term loans, had climbed from 4 to 8 percent during the first Van Agt government (1977-81) and then jumped to 10.2 percent in 1982. As a consequence, repayment on loans had become the largest item on the budget. In a similar vein, the Scientific Council for Government Policy issued an alarming report on the state of Dutch manufacturing in June 1980, with a biting critique on the 'waiting for corporatism' attitude.[20] Ignoring the usual corporatist machinery, the government responded with the installation of an *ad hoc* commission, chaired by Mr. Gerrit Wagner president-director of Royal Dutch Shell, and a membership of experts with indirect representation from business and labour. Not wasting time, the commission recommended, in straightforward language, that the country was in dire straits and private enterprise needed all the help it could get, that profitability needed a boost through lower wage and energy costs, that the operation of the labour market should be improved through decentralized wage bargaining allowing for larger wage differentials, that the introduction of an investment wage should be considered as a means to increase the commitment of workers, that the salary system for public sector workers should be disconnected from the private sector and public sector expenditure must be reduced, that social security should be reconsidered with an eye to providing greater discipline and more incentives to work, and that support to ailing industries should be phased out and be replaced by a general system of supplying credits to industry (van Dellen, 1984) With hindsight, this reads as a catalogue of the policy measures adopted over the next fifteen years. All recommendations have been taken to heart, except the investment wage, which was quietly removed from the agenda after 1982.

Politically, 1982 is a turning point. Following the elections of 1981, there was an attempt to patch up the Centre-Left coalition of the Christian and Social Democrats. The resulting government, again led by Mr. van Agt (CDA) and with PvdA-leader, Mr. den Uyl, as Minister of Social Affairs, was hardly functioning and fell after only nine months. To underline his ambitions, Mr. den Uyl had added 'employment' to the name of his Ministry, and drawn up a very ambitious 'employment plan', but failed to get the necessary public finances (see Chapter Seven). Early in 1982 he had a damaging fight with the unions over his attempt to introduce 'waiting days' in sickness insurance. The fall of this cabinet raised the level of drama and ended the political basis for a Social Democratic management of the crisis. New elections brought to power a true 'no nonsense' austerity coalition, led by Mr. Ruud Lubbers, and relegated the Social Democrats to the opposition for nearly the full length of the 1980s.

The new coalition of Christian Democrats (CDA) and Liberals (VVD) commits itself to a three track strategy of, firstly, a drastic reorganization of public finances in order to reduce the 'financing deficit', lower interests and inflation; secondly, economic recovery through improved business profitability, lower labour costs, industrial restructuring and less regulation; and, thirdly, work-sharing without extra costs to business in order to alleviate the unemployment problem. Unveiling its plans on 22 November 1982, two days before *Wassenaar*, the government declares that 'it is there to govern'[21] and has decided to suspend the payment of price compensation, due in 1983, and freeze the salaries of public servants, the minimum wage and social benefits. This puts the trade unions in a tight corner. Strikes are out of the question, unemployment is soaring, membership is in steep decline and morale is low. Moreover, a defence of the price escalators for the employed puts the unions in a morally awkward position. Hence, for them the conclusion of an agreement with employers, accepting the agenda of the employers but with the addition of the issue of working hours reduction, is the least of two evils (Catz, 1983). For employers, on the other hand, the Accord is a chance to forestall government intervention, because even the new government toyed with ideas to impose job-sharing and make-work solutions, like the governments of France and Belgium had done.

THE RESPONSE TO WASSENAAR

The response to Wassenaar was swift. On 12 December 1982 Parliament accepted a special 'umbrella law' which allowed the opening of existing agreements and the suspension of price compensation in order to facilitate negotiations over job redistribution and working hours reduction. Although negotiations over shorter hours proved cumbersome, in less than a year two-thirds of all collective agreements were renewed, mostly for two years, during which the payment of price compensation was suspended and a five percent reduction of the average annual working hours was to take place. By 1985, cost-of-living clauses had virtually disappeared; less than ten percent of all collective agreements included a fully paid escalator clause.[22] Average real wages fell by nine percent in real terms. The share of labour in the net enterprise income, still 89 percent in 1982, fell to 83.5 percent in 1985.

Wassenaar gave the new Centre-Right government a jump start. For the next two years it could leave wage determination to the social partners. Assured of restraint, the government had its hands free to get control over public sector finance. The unions' acceptance of real wage decline in the private sector made the government's decision to reduce public sector pay, minimum wages and social benefits seem 'less unfair' and 'easier to sell' (Wellink, 1987: 359). In the Spring of 1983, preparing the Budget for 1984, the government decided to play its card as the country's largest employer and step up restraint. The unveiling of its plan to reduce public servant salaries, minimum wages and benefits with 3,5 percent on January 1984 caused an uproar among the public sector unions. Later in the year they organized their largest-ever postwar strike, only to find out that they had become isolated. When an increasingly hostile public turned against them, the unions were quick to cite the avalanche of civil court orders requiring them to end the strike. In the consultations that followed the actual cut in pay became three percent and the bitter pill was sweetened by a reduction of the working week of government employees to 38 hours, taking effect in 1986.

In ordering the unions and their members back to work, the judges had cited disproportionate damage to third parties and insufficient consultation as reasons for their decisions, but ruled that civil servants have a right to strike. In other words, in the future wage restraint in the public sector would have to be negotiated. 1982 is indeed the start of the unlinking of private and public sector wages and the development of autonomous labour relations in the public sector. In 1985 Parliament approved new legislation ending the 'trend following' mechanism in the subsidized sector. In principle, employers and unions were free to negotiate wages, as in the private sector, but within limits set by the Cabinet. After an official union complaint and intervention from the ILO, the government conceded further bargaining freedom. In the government sector, a non-binding Expert Conciliation and Arbitration Commission, chaired by the ubiquitous Mr. Albeda, was installed for reference of labour disputes between the government and the civil service. In the next ten years labour relations in the government sector were normalized; while civil servants lost most of their special privileges with respect to pensions and dismissal protection, civil servants unions gained the right to strike and to collective bargaining. This process was negotiated from start to finish between the unions and the government and completed in 1993 with the introduction of eight sectoral bargaining jurisdictions (e.g., central government, local government, police, education, and so on).[23] The conclusion is that the private sector can no longer be taken hostage and that the government has gained more authority if it wants to cast a 'shadow of hierarchy' over private sector wage bargaining

JOBS FOR WAGES: AN UNREQUITED EXCHANGE

In Wassenaar employers dropped their veto, but not their objections against the reduction of the forty hours working week. In the words of Mr. Van Veen, employers realized 'that without additional policies, economic recovery will not be sufficient for a return to full employment in the foreseeable future'. But he added that the two camps had 'remained divided on just one issue: working hours reduction'. In his account,

> 'the unions, with support of the political establishment, had chosen a collective reduction of working hours, from 40, to 38, 36, and 34 hours, and ultimately 32 hours by the year 1990. Employers resisted this one-sided approach (...) and had to rise to the challenge in order to implement job redistribution through a variety of instruments and to stay within the constraints of a balanced policy of economic recovery'.[24]

The fact of the matter is that in the Netherlands the 32-hours working week has been realized. But, as we have seen in Chapter Two, this did not occur in the collective manner which the unions initially wanted and which was so much feared by Mr. van Veen and his rank and file. Five months after the Accord of Wassenaar, employers once again pleaded for an individual rather than collective reduction of working hours[25], but it is only after the first collective round of 1983-84, that they stepped up their campaign to promote part-time jobs and increased flexibility in working hours arrangements (Visser 1989).

With regard to part-time jobs, Dutch trade unions initially shared the sceptical view of other European unions (Casey, 1983; Conradi, 1982). In 1981, the FNV had published a position paper in which the inferiority of employment rights, wages, fringe benefits, and career prospects in part-time jobs and the lack of union membership among part-timers were highlighted.[26] The federation did not want to help create a secondary job market and demanded first an improvement in statutory protection for part-time workers. At this time, the FNV fully subscribed to the strategy of the *European Trade Union Confederation* (ETUC), adopted at its Milan Congress, to seek a reduction of the working week to 36 hours by 1984.[27] The only collective reduction of the working week realized by the Dutch unions, from 40 to 38 hours on average, was accomplished in the bargaining round of 1983-4. From the mid-1980s the movement towards shorter working hours stalled.

In 1983-84 the reduction of working hours took place in the context of massive labour shedding and helped to save *existing* jobs. The Central Planning Bureau estimated that 25 percent of the reduction of working hours in the private sector has been translated into extra jobs and that the remainder was recaptured by employers through increased labour productivity and work intensity. An enterprise survey of the Ministry of Social Affairs and Employment showed that in 78 percent of all enterprises, with 54 percent of all employees covered by collective agreements, there had been no replacements. IB-FNV observed that the piecemeal steps to a shorter working week occurred mainly through extra days off, that the condition of unchanged or longer operating hours had frequently been violated, and that employers more often than not had cut the least productive hours.[28] In the public sector, where owing to formal staff planning procedures, control by the trade unions was easier, hiring occurred at a rate of 65 percent of vacated hours. In 1984-85, when the economy moved out of the recession, the unions did gear up for another round, still without pay compensation, in an attempt to create *new* jobs. But employers declared any general move to less than 38 hours 'off limits' and upgraded their 'Joint Committee for the Preparation of Wage Policies', which serves as a coordination platform and counterpart of the coordinating activities of the FNV. Employers upheld their veto until 1993.

A recession-induced campaign for shorter working hours, like the 1983-84 campaign, has the characteristics of 'public regarding' behaviour of insiders in order to absorb or keep people in employment who would otherwise be unemployed (Visser, 1990; see also Lindbeck and Snowers, 1988). New jobs as replacement of vacated hours are the criterion by which such a campaign stands. Precisely for this reason, Mr. Wim Duisenberg, ex-Minister in the Den Uyl cabinet and in 1982 the new President of the Central Bank, had his reservations about Wassenaar. In his view the promise to honour working hours reduction with new jobs undermined the willingness of workers to continue wage restraint for the sake of improving the profitability and investment prospects of firms.[29] This is exactly what happened in the second half of the 1980s, when the unions found it increasingly difficult to convince their members to continue wage restraint.

Yet, despite Mr. Duisenberg, in the early 1980s a significant and growing number of Dutch workers was prepared to bring a sacrifice and accept working hours reduction whilst realizing that this would lead to a decline in their monthly income. Between 1979 and 1983 the percentage of Dutch workers in favour rose from 27.9 percent in 1979, to 35.5 in 1981 and 37.6 in 1983, but then dropped to 25.0 percent in 1985.[30] If they could be assured that others would do the same, as many as 71.5 percent of Dutch workers would accept shorter working hours with a small income loss (Smirzai, 1981). According to SCP figures, the percentage of workers who disagreed with shorter working hours if this implied a loss of income hovered around forty percent. The opponents were overwhelmingly lower-paid workers and breadwinners, and they were the card-carrying members in the unions, especially in industry.

The leaders of the Dutch unions had the courage to continue on the road of wage restraint and work sharing, in spite of continued job and membership losses. The central organizations repeated their will to continue wage moderation in two new but less significant agreements in 1984 and 1986. These agreements did not promise specific tradeoffs, like the Accord of Wassenaar, but confirmed the 'agreement to agree' of the social partners and their willingness to address the evils of the nation, above all youth unemployment (1984) and unemployment in general (1986). In practical terms, little was accomplished; the plan to create part-time jobs of 25 to 32 hours per week for school-leavers and apprentices, which had been developed in a previous agreement between unions and employers in metal engineering, was soon abandoned as it proved a formidable handicap in recruitment. In 1990 they added an agreement on 'extra jobs for ethnic minorities', but again the results on the ground proved disappointing.

The trade unions were unable to maintain their united front on working hours reduction. In 1986 the VHP unions abandoned the FNV-led coalition for shorter hours and within the FNV the public servants union gave priority to the recovery of the relative wage losses they had suffered earlier in the decade. By 1987 the campaign for shorter working hours was dead. A year later the will to continue wage restraint seemed exhausted. The international economic upswing between 1988 and 1991 encouraged unions to raise their aspirations and renewed membership growth helped to restore confidence. With the Dutch 'jobs machine' under full steam, wage pressures in the exposed sector reappeared. As was shown in Chapter Two, in this period nearly all job redistribution took the form of extra part-time jobs. The unions in industry, with mainly full-time workers, felt cheated. For them the relevant issue was the reduction of working hours and jobs for full-time and shift workers, but between 1987 and 1993 annual working hours of full-time workers decreased with only 0.3 percent cumulatively. For the annual wage round of 1989 the IB-FNV claimed a 4 percent wage increase which shocked

Figure 7: Annual changes in contractual wages, wage costs, and inflation

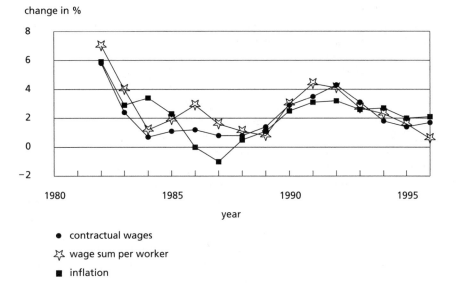

change in %

- ● contractual wages
- ☆ wage sum per worker
- ■ inflation

the policy-making elite into predicting the end of moderation and the return of the problems of the 1970s.[31]

From Figure 7 we can derive the picture that wages and unit labour costs, under the influence of an appreciating guilder following the turmoil of German unification and the EMS crises of 1992 and 1993, did increase. The unions do realize a modest increase in the real wages of their members. But the party is over almost before it has begun. 1990 is the year that politicians discover that 'the country is sick' and in 1991 a major overhaul of social security upsets all agendas and puts the unions once again on the defensive (see Chapter Six). In 1992 the economy moves into recession and a number of major firms, like electronics producer Philips, aircraft manufacturer Fokker, or Daf-trucs, are in deep trouble. 100,000 jobs in manufacturing, ten per cent of the total, are cut between 1992 and 1994. Unions return to wage moderation as their dominant strategy, but according to the government this has taken them too long. In order to shorten the 'brake time' in external adjustment, the instrument of a wage freeze, as defined in the Wage Act, is revived.

A NEW SHADOW OF HIERARCHY

In the Autumn of 1992, Mr. Bert de Vries, the Christian Democratic Minister of Social Affairs and Employment in the third Lubbers government (1989-94), a coalition with the Social Democrats led by Mr. Wim Kok, who himself holds the post of Finance Minister, threatens to impose a wage freeze. It remains doubtful whether there was a sound legal basis for such action. The Wage Act of 1970, revised in 1988, does empower the Minister to order a temporary wage stop or impose a maximum, but only on the very restrictive condition of a major economic crisis.[32] This condition did not exist in 1992 (see Chapter One), nor did it in 1993, when the threat was repeated.

The social partners were nonetheless impressed. In November 1992 the central organizations of unions and employers recommended a 'breathing space' of two months, during which expiring collective agreements are to be prolonged, and the negotiations over new agreements suspended in order to absorb the new facts of the international recession. In this period employers begin a campaign for zero wage increases ('zero is necessary, zero is enough') and unions halve their wage demands. Early in 1993 many unions negotiate multi-annual agreements in which nominal wage increases did not keep pace with price inflation (see Table 17).

Table 17: Nominal wage flexibility in the 1990s

years when agreements applied	annual basis*	level basis**	CPI
1988		0.8	0.5
1989		2.0	1.1
1990		3.5	2.5
1991		3.5	3.1
1992	4.3	4.4	3.2
1993	3.1	2.9	2.6
before 'breathing space'	5.1	4.6	
after 'breathing space'	2.6	2.2	
1994	1.5	0.8	2.7
before 'New Course'		1.1	
after 'New Course'		0.5	
1995	1.3	1.4	2.0
1996	1.6	1.8	2.1

Source: SZW and DNB, *annual reports*; data recalculated by Dr. Wiemer Salverda
*   change between years, taking into account date when provisions in agreements take effect
** change between agreements on annual basis, regardless of date when provisions take effect

During the year 1993 relations between unions and employers, and of both with the government, are tense. The government's decision to lower disability allowances and reduce eligibility upsets the bargaining agenda and for the unions it becomes the major issue to repair the damage through collective reinsurance. Encouraged by the government, employers put up resistance and want to concentrate instead on measures to lower the increasing tax and social contribution wedge between gross and net earnings. In most sectors they nevertheless strike a compromise: reinsurance does take place, be it optional and varying across firms, and with increased payment by employees (Rojer, 1996a).

Unhappy with these developments, the government begins, once again, to threaten with intervention. In August 1993 Minister de vries did begin preparing a wage freeze for 1994, but his policy intention met with a negative advise from the Social Economic Council and major legal experts.[33] At the same time, under the influence of policy advisors in the Central Planning Bureau, the Ministry of Economic Affairs and the OECD, the possibility of withdrawing the 1937 Extension of Collective Agreements Act is brought into the debate.[34] The critics point out that by declaring the 1993 collective agreements binding the government sanctions with one hand what it has wanted to prevent with the other. Other points of criticism are that the practice of extension helps to maintain cartels, prevents the foundation or expansion of small firms and low-wage jobs for vulnerable groups in the labour market. They believe that without extension and, by implication, without sectoral agreements, more low-wage competition and more low-productivity jobs would be generated. The government toyed with the idea to discontinue extension of collective agreements and in 1994 the outgoing Minister of Social Affairs and Employment lists the repeal of the 1937 Extension of Collective Agreements Act as one of the four measures that might help to increase the flexibility and job growth in the Dutch labour market.[35] This attack draws the unions and employers together. In 1993 they publish a joint defence of the 1937 Act, but at the same time they offer a more flexible use by reviewing the rules on dispensation.[36]

The government is also stepping up its pressure to obtain wage restraint in order to stop the destruction of jobs. The unions complain that the massive job losses occur despite of increased profits and reproach that employers did not honour their pledge to do everything possible to combat unemployment. At the same time, they try to entice the employers into a new agreement with the promise that they 'can lead their members' and deliver wage restraint if, on their part, employers concede a new round of working hours reduction. In this constellation a new accord seems improbable, and yet, this is what happens. In December 1993 the central organizations sign a new accord, this time called '*A New Course. Agenda for collective bargaining in 1994*'. Employers get further decentralization and flexibility, the unions a promise that the central employers organizations will give up their blanket resistance against working hours reduction and that local union representatives or works councils will be involved in negotiations over local solutions. Both parties stress the need to increase the employment/population ratio and they recommend part-time work as a possible solution to the combined pressure of work and child care. With job creation as a first priority, the will to continue restraint is confirmed and many unions now conclude multi-annual agreements under the rate of inflation in 1994 and 1995.

From Table 17 we learn that the impact of the new accord is again large. In 1994 there is a complete standstill on wages. In 1995 employers concentrate on a reduction of early retirement entitlements which together with imminent measures of deregulation provoke the largest postwar strike in construction (Van der Meer, 1996). Employers have to tone down but the issue is now on the agenda and has become part of attempts to change the system of pension savings. Unions push the issue of working-time reduction on the agenda in 1996, but the results are mixed. Central employers do give up central coordination on the issue and suspend their mutual resistance insurance fund, but in half of all cases, among them metal engineering and Philips, employers refuse to make a deal and offer a wage increase in stead. In 1997 the movement for shorter hours has again halted; about half of all full-time employees will move to an average working week of 36 hours in the next year or so. For the coming years, reflecting the buoyancy of the Dutch economy and job market, the unions prepare a small wage increase and concentrate on qualitative issues, in particular training, parental leave, and employability.

The new issue in recent years has become the reduction of the distance to the formal labour market and the creation of jobs for 'vulnerable groups'. Specific measures, lowering the tax and social contributions wedge for low-paid workers, have been taken and will be discussed in Chapter Six. The job creation plans for people which need help to find jobs are discussed in Chapter Seven. Here we would like to draw attention to the new use of the 1937 Extension and Nullification of Collective Agreement Act. The government has made its application dependent on the 'substantive outcomes' of wage bargaining, in particular measures which are believed to be beneficial for the job prospects of unskilled workers, for instance through the creation of lower entry wage scales and new scales for target groups, for instance, long-term unemployed workers. Only if negotiators show their goodwill and promote these 'public regarding' objectives will they, without further ado, obtain the public protection against non-organized firms and low-wage competitors. In the interest of collective organization and the prevention of an uncontrolled low wage sector, Dutch employers' associations and trade unions have responded to the challenge. Hence, the new 'shadow of hierarchy' has been a success. The proportion of collective agreements with entry wage scales at or near the minimum has risen from six percent in 1993 to 68 percent in 1995 (Venema et al., 1996). Table 18 shows how these scales relate to the minimum wage.

Table 18: Lowest wage scales of regular jobs, entry and target group scales as a percentage of the minimum wage, by industry, end 1996

sector	regular lowest scale	entry scale	target group scale
manufacturing industries	116.2	105.1	101.2
construction	133.0	100.0	110.1
trade, restaurants and hotels	111.7	103.3	103.2
transport and communication	107.5	118.3	100.0
commercial services	108.7	101.0	100.1
social, public and other services	105.0	100.0	100.0

Source: SZW, Labour Inspectorate
Calculated for adult wage earner of 23 years, weighted by number of employees covered by collective agreements

As a consequence, the average level of the lowest contractual wage levels has decreased from 111.8 percent in 1994 to 108.3 percent in 1996; the most recent estimate is that eight percent of all employees are paid according to these lowest-level scales. Freeman et al. (1996) show that the upward effect of mandatory extension on wages is almost zero. They argue that the blissful lack of preoccupation with relative wages in Dutch collective bargaining depends upon the absence of an open non-union, low wage sector. Without this instrument, wage moderation would be more difficult to achieve.

CONCLUSIONS

The Accord of Wassenaar marked the return to a policy of voluntary wage restraint on the part of the unions, a policy which they did continue, with some hesitation, during the next fifteen years. Table 19 summarizes the effects, by comparing 1973-82 with 1983-96: under similar quantitative conditions of external trade, the relations between employment growth, labour costs and relative income shares of labour and capital were reversed. As we explained in Chapter Two, labour got richer only because it got more jobs.

The *renewal* of the corporatist strategy of flexible adjustment in 1982 was the result of a strong signal from the market – in particular unemployment and the erosion of union bargaining power. The 'puzzling' of previous years had led to new insights but needed the 'powering' of a new political and economic situation. The policy of wage restraint did not begin with a consensus, but produced a consensus. It took some courage of union leaders to start an unrequited exchange of wage restraint for jobs. Nobody could assure suc-

Table 19: World trade, employment, and labour costs, 1973-96

	1973-82	1983-96
relevant world trade (annual % changes)	4.7	5.3
employment		
hours	− 1.6	0.9
persons	− 0.8	1.4
production	1.9	3.0
real labour costs	3.8	0.8
employment growth (annual changes x 1000)		
labour years	− 33	50
persons	− 31	55
labour share in value added (%)	1.2	− 0.8

Source: CPB, L. Bovenberg, 1997/2, Table 2

cess, and there was no apparent success in the first years after *Wassenaar*, at least not for the trade unions and their members. Only later did job and membership growth pick up. Profits and investments came first, and it took trust and belief in the goodwill of employers to continue. Hence, wage moderation in the 1980s cannot be explained by its outcomes, like it might be in the 1990s. In press interviews of early 1997, Mr. Johan Steekelenburg, the departing FNV chairman, pointedly remarked, that the justification of the policies of his organization were indeed the new jobs and the new members.

Comparing the major accords of 1982 and 1993, there are obvious similarities and differences. Both are typical examples of external adjustment, a lowering of the real exchange rate for goods and services sold on foreign markets. With the Dutch guilder invariably, since 1983, pegged to the German Mark, the adjustment had to come from changes in wages and productivity. The wage leadership on both occasions was in the hands of large unions and employers associations in the exposed sector. The weight of the public sector was neutralized after 1982, by a government which optimally exploited the tactical position created by the Wassenaar Accord and the kind of extra power a newly elected government usually has.

Both accords were negotiated under a 'shadow of the market' and a 'shadow of hierarchy'. In 1982 employers seized the chance to regain bipartite autonomy, and saw the deal with the unions as the lesser evil; in 1993 they had learned to value the unions as more trustful partners than the government. Only two years before, in 1991, the central employers' federations had withdrawn from a tripartite 'Common Policy Orientation Pact' signed in 1989, in which all participants had promised to give highest priority to the struggle against unemployment. In March 1991, employers wrote a so-called 'stand still' letter and announced that they would not participate in the customary Spring session between the STAR and the cabinet. The object of their anger was the government, the third cabinet led by Mr. Lubbers (1989-94), but with the participation of the Social Democrats and an activist Christian Democrat at the helm of the Ministry of Social Affairs and Employment. Employers began to express doubts about the intentions of the government and feared that a tripartite Pact, however vague, might be used as a ploy 'to bring the state back in'.

In the past fifteen years, the trade unions and employers have disagreed many times about policies, but their cooperation, the success showing in job growth and, finally, the political attack on corporatism have drawn them closer. In the 1990s social partners confess that they need each other and that the country needs them. This is the most conspicuous message of the 1992 advice of the *Social Economic Council* on how to prepare the country for the membership of the Economic and Monetary Union. The advice, which went under the significant title 'Convergence and Concertation Economy', was written in the record time of less than half a year and was again a typical 'agreement to agree'. While the SER, the most typical 'piece de resistance' of Dutch corporatism, conceded that in the past it had been plagued by indecision, it argued, in a Katzenstenian vein, that European integration required a revitalization of corporatist adjustment strategies in response to international economic pressures and European policy competition.[37]

There also are differences between the two accords, both in content and form. In 1982 the emphasis was on the restoration of profits as a condition for job creation, and on the redistribution of jobs as a means to stem the rise in unemployment. In 1993 job creation and job redistribution remained the prime objectives for the trade unions, but the containment of labour costs was combined with a cautious support for expanding domestic demand, made possible by low inflation, a large trade surplus, a strong currency, and improved public finances. The years after the accord, in particular 1996, marked the transition to a new type of exchange, between wage moderation and fiscal compensation, setting in motion a virtuous circle of more jobs, less per capita taxes, hence more spending power while paying flat wages to those already in employment (see Figure 7). Although export-led growth remained important, as it had been in the 1980s, the explanation of the job creation record in the mid-1990s is based on domestic-led growth, concentrated in services tied to the local economy. It is this structural change towards an American-type service economy, accelerated by wage moderation, fiscal compensation and job-redistribution, which has allowed the Netherlands to be relatively unaffected by the recession in Germany and other European economies.

The 1993 accord is a further step in the process of organized or controlled decentralization of Dutch industrial relations. *Wassenaar* led the return to bi-

partite wage bargaining; *A New Course*, coming after the trust-building experience of eleven years, promised a further step towards decentralization,
with the increased involvement of local bargainers. Officially, the central employers' organizations do no longer give binding advice to member organizations. On an Informal basis, coordination between representatives of major
multinational firms, central and major employers' associations is frequent
and intense. Corporatism is more than ever entrenched at the meso- and micro-levels of sectors and firms (Van den Toren, 1996; Visser, 1995).

A protracted, 'voluntary' policy of wage moderation is not just a matter of
leadership, courage and intentions, but needs a solid organizational and legal
basis. We recall that nearly all bargaining with employers takes place at a single table and that threats of exclusion generate pressure towards compromise
within the union camp. In addition, we must consider that most collective
agreements in the exposed sector are negotiated by one union, the Industries'
Union of the FNV.[38] All negotiations are led or coordinated by appointed
full-time officials, who are themselves supervized by union headquarters; officials rotate across regions, sectors and firms; deviance is sanctioned; voting
and ratification procedures are usually across-the-membership. Coordination is further supported by a central strike fund which in multi-sectoral and
conglomerate unions like the IB is an essential instrument for the prevention
of large wage differentials across sectors and firms. As a federation, the FNV
has also retained a central strike fund from which unions, if engaged in a strike
approved of by the federation, are reimbursed.

Low wage differentials across sectors and firm – as distinct from differentials reflecting different skills and levels of education – are not only important
for the organizational viability of multi-sectoral industrial unions, but also vital for the continuation of a policy of voluntary restraint. Membership support for a policy of sacrifice, without immediate benefits for oneself, depends
on a sense of fairness. As it turns out in the Dutch case, union members can
be convinced of the wisdom of a policy of protracted restraint even before it
shows results, but support is embedded in close 'networks of civic engagement' through which the norm that everybody should play his or her part is
spread and upheld. Fairness is a behaviourally observed norm, if others are
not acting according to the norm, its force as a rule is weakened.

Does this mean that a wage moderation policy can or should be continued
endlessly? Probably not, or not by itself. Wage moderation needs legitimation
through political exchange—it is a means towards some end which trade
unions and their members find more important: e.g., full employment, job redistribution, decent public services, a high level of social security, better
labour market chances for vulnerable groups, job protection, training and
leave rights. Moreover, wage moderation for the sake of low-cost competition in export markets has no end. If one's competitors in high-cost
economies do the same, stronger medication is needed. The temporary advantage of lower costs is a means to increase labour force participation, espe-

cially in services, and helps to lower dependency, social charges, taxes and wage costs. It can help to break the vicious circle of 'welfare without work' and create the conditions for welfare reform in which the main protective tenets of the welfare state are retained. This has been the major rationale for wage moderation policies in the Netherlands and remains relevant in a context where broad unemployment still affects one in five in the labour force. The Central Planning Bureau estimates that half of the job growth of the past fifteen years can be attributed to wage moderation. This clearly demonstrates the importance of this particular policy instrument. But it is no panacea for all ills – the struggle against persistent long-term unemployment and the improvement of labour market chances of unskilled workers need other policies.

Notes

1   This expression was actually used by Mr. Alexander Rinnooy Kan, chairman and chief negotiator for the employers from 1991 to 1996, in reference to the Wassenaar Accord, in his speech at the 25th Anniversary of the *Dutch Industrial Relations Association*; see Rinnooy Kan (1993).

2   In the small-firm sector the density rate, measured in terms of employment in organized firms, is lower; in retail, for instance, density is probably only 25 percent and in construction only 5,500 of the 13,000 firms are organized (van der Meer 1996).

3   There are currently 900 to 1,000 collective agreements in force, but in Table 14 we have disregarded the 200 or so which contain only a single (non-wage) clause (see Van den Toren, 1996).

4   What a 'substantial majority' is has not been defined and may vary across industries. Extension can only happen after a request by the parties to the agreement and advice from the Wage Committee of the *Foundation of Labour*. In practice, this advice is only asked when firms, excluded unions or employers' associations have filed an objection (Schutte, 1995: 62).

5   Rapport 'Deregulering inkomensvorming en arbeidsmarkt', 25 May 1984, Tweede Kamer, zitting 1983-84, 17031, no. 4.

6   In sectors where neither employers nor unions are sufficiently organized, for instance in retailing or in hotels and restaurants, a bipartite Product and Industry Board may step in and issue a so-called ruling with minimum conditions.

7   Most multi-national companies have, however, preferred company bargaining and have obtained the freedom to do so from the relevant associations. Some smaller companies have gone to the pains of setting up a 'yellow union' with which to negotiate a contract. Since the Netherlands has ratified ILO convention no. 98 on freedom of bargaining, something it did only in December 1993, this should have become more difficult.

8   As defined in the 1950 Industrial Organization Act.

9   One of the most important advisory functions of the SER was to give an annual advice on macro-economic prospects and policies. Significantly, between 1972 and 1982 there never was a unanimous advice.

10   The legal basis was the Extraordinary Decree on Labour Relations of 1945 which remained in force, with regard to wage setting, until 1968 with a significant change in 1963. Other chapters of the Decree, with respect to dismissal controls for instance, are still relevant, although with many changes since its original version (see Windmuller, 1969; Van der Heijden, 1995).

11   Windmuller (1969: 223) observes that 'Dutch union leaders have the same tendency to deal with their members in a spirit of benevolent authoritarianism or high-handed paternalism which they want employers to abandon in dealing with their employees'. According to Pen (1973: 223), this 'went un-noticed for a long time, [but] now draws attention from critics in and outside the union movement'.

12   De Wolff and Driehuis (1980) observe that in the second half of the 1970s, when officially regis-tered unemployment stood at 200,000, employers in manufacturing kept complaining about finding skilled workers. Yearly, some 50,000 jobs remained vacant.

13   A typical expression of his, according to Mr. Johan Steekelenburg, one of his successors as presi-dent of the FNV (NRC Handelsblad, of 9 March 1994), quite characteristic for the man and the con-sensus requirement in corporatism.

14   In 1976, the grand old man of Dutch economics, professor Jan Tinbergen, advocated a return to a statutory wage policy along the 1950s model, but this was seen as entirely unrealistic. However, the underlying analysis of Professor Hans van den Doel, one of his co-authors, that a system with many publicly guaranteed social rights is vulnerable to free riders who leave their 'unpaid bill' to society, be-came a major theme in the discourse on wage determination and the welfare state during these years.

15   Deeply disappointed, Mr. Albeda later wrote, prematurely as it turned out, that the failure to achieve wage moderation before the unemployment catastrophe of the early 1980s was 'proof of the bankruptcy of the Dutch consultation system' (Albeda, 1987: 311).

16   According to OECD figures (Historical Statistics 1980-1988, Paris, 1990), the real interest rate in-creased from 1.2 percent in 1974-79 to 5.3 percent in 1980-86.

17   In the second half of the 1970s, wage drift, defined as the difference between contractual and ac-tual hourly wages of full-time workers, averaged 15 percent on an annual basis, in some manufacturing industries 20 to 25 percent. In the recession of 1981-3, wage drift completely disappeared or was neg-ative (H. van Reyn, 'De ontwikkeling van de verdiende lonen en de regelingslonen in de jaren 1972-1982', in CBS, Sociaal-Economische Maandstatistiek, 1983, no. 8). The single most important factor explaining annual changes in drift were the government-imposed wage stops or ceilings.

18   OECD, Economic Survey of the Netherlands 1976, Paris, 1977: 11.

19   See SCP, Sociaal en Cultureel Rapport, 1980, 1982 en 1984, Rijswijk.

20   WRR, Plaats en toekomst van de industrie, The Hague, 1980, rapporten aan de regering no. 18.

21   Prime Minister Lubbers, cited in *NRC Handelsblad*, 22 November 1982

22   FNV, *Annual Report 1985*, Amsterdam 1986: 9.

23   Mr. Hans Pont, who as top civil servant advised the Minister of the Interior in the process, had been the chief behind-the-scene organizer of the public servants strike of 1983 and was Mr. Kok's successor as Chairman of the FNV (1985-88).

24   Cited from Mr. van Veen's contribution in A. Knoester, *Lessen uit het verleden. 125 jaar Vereniging voor de Staatshuishoudkunde*, Leyden and Antwerp: Stenfert Kroese, 1987: 300.

25   RCO, *De arbeidsduur nader bekeken*, The Hague, April 1983

26   FNV, *Een deel van het geheel. FNV-visie op deeltijdarbeid*, Amsterdam, July 1981.

27   We must assume that the objections to part-time work by the German unions, not least because it was believed to weaken the struggle for a collective reduction of the working week (Casey, 1983: 415; Conradi, 1982: 42-8), played a role as well, since the leaders of the Dutch and German union federations, DGB and FNV, meet annually. According to Mr. Johan Steekelenburg, from 1985 Vice-Chairman and from 1988 Chairman of the FNV, in later years his German colleagues repeatedly expressed their unhappiness with the acceptance of part-time employment by the Dutch unions (interview with public radio, 17 April 1997).

28   IB-FNV, *Arbeidsmarkt op drift*, Amsterdam, 1986.

29   De Nederlandsche Bank (DNB), *Jaarverslag 1982*, Amsterdam, 1983: 27.

30   The difference in the size of the unemployment problem and in trade union policies is a plausible explanation why in these years the popularity of uncompensated working hours reduction was much lower among German workers. U. Engfer et al. (1983) report that 13.7 percent of the German workers supported a reduction of working hours 'ohne Lohnausgleich' in 1981. The Dutch figures are from the Social-Cultural Planning Bureau, *Sociaal en Cultureel Rapport 1982*, The Hague, SDU: 219 (Table 11.4) and *Sociaal en Cultureel Rapport 1984*, The Hague, SDU: 285, Table 11.8.

31   Frank van Empel, "Meer loon dan werk. De vakbeweging gaat tot de aanval over", *Elsevier*, 7-10-1989.

32   *Wage Act*, 1988, art. 10 and 11. Before 1995, the Minister needed to ask the SER for advice before taking his final decision. A wage order, in the sense of the 1988 Act, takes immediate effect and applies to all wages, irrespective of whether they are the result of collective or individual bargaining. Arrangements which contradict the order are null and void. A wage order has a maximum duration of one-and-a-half year (Schutte, 1995).

33   Minister of Social Affairs and Employment, letter to the Social Economic Council and to Parliament, of 25 August 1993; SER, 'Tijdelijke bevriezing lonen 1994', advice 1993/13; P.F. van der Heijden, 'Loonwet 1994: Collectieve onderhandelingsvrijheid ingevroren', *Nederlands Juristenblad*, 1993, 1133-35.

34   G. Zalm, 'Betekenis en toekomst van de Algemene Verbindend Verklaring', lecture to the *Dutch Industrial Relations Association*, Utrecht, 19 December 1991. Finance Minister in the Kok government (1994-), Mr. Gerrit Zalm (VVD) was at the time director of the Central Planning Bureau.

35   SZW, *Sociale Nota 1994*, The Hague: SDU, 1994; the other three measures were the repeal of the 1919 Labour Act and the introduction of a new Working Time Act, realized in 1996, greater freedom for temporary job agencies (also realized), and withdrawal of preventive dismissal controls (withdrawn by the current Minister, see Chapter 7).

36   Foundation of Labour, 'Enkele aanbevelingen in relatie tot het avv-beleid van cao-partijen', May 1994.

37   SER, *Convergentie en overlegeconomie*, The Hague, advice 92/15, 20 November 1992.

38   As from 1998, following the merger with three other private sector unions, this union will negotiate about 500 of the 900 or so collective agreements.

Chapter Six

Corporatism Unrestrained:
Reversing the Spiral of Welfare without Work

IN THE SUMMER OF 1991, the Dutch government, a coalition of Christian and Social Democrats, announced a major welfare reform package, reducing the level of protection and entitlements under the disablement and sickness compensation programs. Although there was a widespread conviction that the programs had been misused and that changes were necessary, the reforms proved to be very controversial, and politically risky. On 17 September 1991, on the invitation of the entire union movement, nearly one million people marched the streets of The Hague in what was probably the largest such demonstration in Dutch history. The Social Democrats, in particular, were deeply divided over the measures and relations with its natural union ally, the *Confederation of Dutch Trade Unions* (FNV) were at an all-time low. The PvdA's chairwoman had to resign and the party lost one-third of its members. Mr. Wim Kok, party leader and Finance Minister in the third Lubbers government (1989-94), nearly had to step down. Only by calling a special party conference and putting his position on the line, did he rescue his position and his party's support for the reforms. There were other casualties – later the party's Junior Minister, responsible for the implementation of the package, lost both the confidence of her party and her job. In the general elections of May 1994 the Social Democrats lost one-quarter of its electoral support, which, all in all, was better than expected.

Why did they do it? The target of the reform was the disability insurance program. This workers' insurance, later extended to include all citizens whose disability prevented them from earning a living, had been introduced in 1967 and was at the time seen as the crown on the Dutch welfare state. It was the only such insurance in the world, except New Zealand, with equal treatment of *risque professional* and *risque social*. At the time of its introduction, the responsible Minister estimated an inflow of no more than 200,000. In 1980 the number reached 660,000 and by the end of the decade it was no longer unthinkable that soon there would be one million disabled, out of a labour force of six million. Skilfully dramatising the situation, the Prime Minister, Mr. Ruud Lubbers, went public and declared: 'the Netherlands is sick'.[1] No longer was the problem defined as a financial one; in the 1990s the problem of disability became to be seen as a problem of governability.

Figure 8: Sickness and disability absenteeism in selected European countries, in 1990

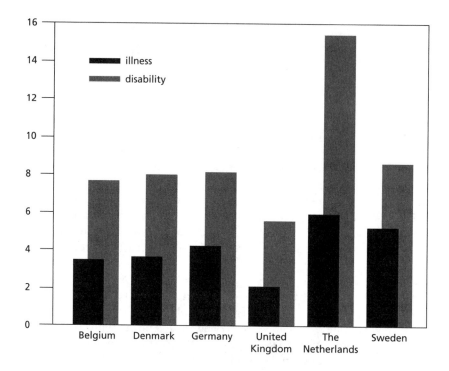

Source: *Sociale nota 1995*, p. 82.

The social policy reform undertaken by the Lubbers and Kok governments in the 1990s no longer involved the mere tinkering with entitlements, benefit levels and eligibility criteria. It introduced a new provision logic of private providers and managed competition in the execution of compulsory social insurance. In addition, the reform unleashed an attack on the principle of self-governance in social security administration and implementation – a hitherto sacred principle in the history of Dutch social security. Even in 1945, the planners of the post-war welfare state, inspired by Beveridge and the conviction that a New Deal was necessary, had been unable to overrule the coalition of interest groups and Christian political parties in favour of self-rule. Nor had the two prior Right-of-Centre governments of Mr. Lubbers (1982-86; 1986-89), both bent on welfare cost containment, mustered the courage to change the rules-of-the-game. A grandiosely announced 'system change' in social security, finally implemented in 1987, tightened up unemployment insurance and introduced minor changes in the disability program. The institutional makeup of bipartite social security sovereignty remained in tact while the state relapsed in its usual 'remote control' mode.

It was only under influence of dramatic new figures and a paradigmatic cognitive change in defining the ills of the welfare state as a crisis of inactivity, that the spiraling number of disability claimants could be dramatized into a crisis of ungovernability. In this crisis the state had to act and restore its authority over the interest groups. But how could the disability problem get out of control so badly in the first place? Why did the social partners, the unions in particular, act so self-serving in the domain of domestic compensation, while behaving in a 'public regarding' manner in the area of external adjustment? In the previous chapter the unions were the heroes, most of the time, here they are the villains of the piece, not the only ones, but nevertheless. Why is it that their responsibility for the commonwealth could not be counted on in the case of social security? Was there an exchange involved between their 'public regarding' behaviour in wage bargaining and their 'rent-seeking' complicity in exploiting the disability programs as a means to smoothen the process of modernization of the Dutch economy in the 1980s? These are the questions we wish to answer in this chapter.

A DEVIANT PATH AND A MAJOR CRISIS

In the postwar era of economic prosperity, many elected governments in Western Europe and North America launched an effort of wholesale social policy reform to counter what Beveridge had called the 'five great evils of Want, Disease, Idleness, Ignorance and Squalor'. After a decade of depression and war, universal schemes for disability, sickness, and old age were introduced. Most importantly, the welfare state assumed the political responsibility for the plague of unemployment. The austere 1950s witnessed a modest expansion of social security, but coverage was extended and levels of entitlements became more generous under the benign conditions of sustained economic growth and full employment in later years. The energy crisis and monetary instability of the early 1970s, however, brought the 'Golden Age of Capitalism' to a halt. The reappearance of mass unemployment provoked a dramatic increase in expenditure. By 1980 the welfare state had 'grown to its limits' in many Western European countries (Flora, 1987).

In the European history of postwar welfare state growth the Dutch trajectory stands out. Until 1955 the Dutch welfare state, measured in terms of social security coverage, lagged far behind countries like France, Germany and the United Kingdom (see Figure 10). After 1955, in a period of less than two decades, the Netherlands transformed from a welfare laggard into one the most generous and extensive welfare states in the world (Flora and Alber, 1986; Cox, 1993; Hemerijck and Van der Veen, 1995). In 1977 the *Financial Times*, with slight hyperbole, noted that the Dutch had succeeded in estab-

Figure 9: Social security coverage in Western Europe, 1940-1970

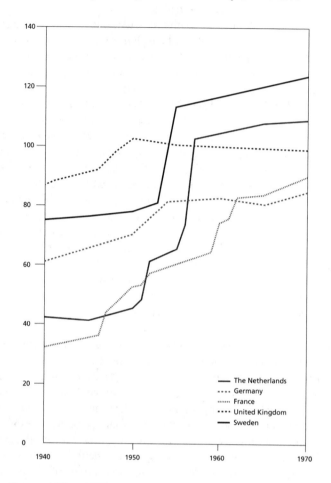

Source: Flora and Alber, 1981.

lishing 'one of the world's most prosperous and enlightened welfare states, with minimum wages higher than in any other industrial society, high labour productivity, remarkably few strikes, and a widely developed social security network'.[2] In 1979, in terms of productivity per men per hour the Netherlands ranked second only to the United States, ahead of West Germany, and by several distances ahead of the United Kingdom and Sweden (Madison 1982: 130, Table V-2). In 1980 the incidence rate of taxes and social security contributions had risen to 52.2 percent of the national income in net terms, up from 38.5 percent twelve years earlier. This was the fastest increase in any West European country and brought the Netherlands nearly on a par with

Sweden.[3] This is the country about which *The Economist* wrote, in January 1982, that 'if somewhere must be found to ride out the recession, Holland must be the nicest, comfiest place to choose'.[4] At that time, unemployment was rising at a rate of 10,000 per month, and more than one million Dutch people of working age were supported by the welfare state.

DEVELOPMENT WITH FAILING CONTROLS

There are essentially two reasons behind the postwar welfare state trajectory of late development and rapid expansion. One is closely related to the specific institutional legacy of social policy before the war; the other to the postwar strategy of external adjustment and wage restraint, discussed in Chapter Five.

The administrative heritage of a social security system, based on bipartite self-governance and shared responsibilities between private interest groups and public authorities, at first retarded welfare state growth, but later made it impossible to apply the brakes. In this fragmented system, overview was lacking, supervision wanting, and authority dispersed. Consequently, nobody could be held responsible and nobody did take responsibility. This conclusion was reached gradually, but it was not until in the 1990s that the political consequence of accumulated negative policy outcomes was translated into a path-breaking effort of institutional reform.

The postwar wage restraint policy was successful in creating a low cost export base for Dutch manufacturing products. At first, wage costs and social provisions were held back in support of the policy. Later, its success provided the basis for expansion of social policy legislation. This was the promise for which the unions and their members had willingly exercized restraint. Beginning with unemployment insurance and old age pensions in the 1950s, social security coverage was extended, new programs were introduced and benefit levels raised. However, when as a consequence of wage hikes and expansive social policy programs the Netherlands made its forward leap and became a high-wage economy, it was only a matter of time before the economy was saddled with a series of structural crises of its still mainly labour intensive manufacturing industries. In the second half of the 1960s coal mining was shut down, the textile, clothing, footwear and leather manufacturing all but disappeared, and shipbuilding began its long-term decline. Tens of thousands of workers lost their jobs. As will be discussed in the next chapter, there never was a labour market policy which might have addressed problems of regional industrial decline or competence training of workers who had been made redundant. These workers were helped with negotiated social plans in which the unions tried to cushion the pain of redundancy with extra severance payments above otherwise modest unemployment insurance and social security payments. Slowly but surely this contributed to a rising volume of social security claimants.

Initially, the postwar evolution of Dutch social security was slowed down as a consequence of the continuous political disagreement over the responsibility of the organization and administration of social policy between the different religious and political groups – Liberals, Protestants, Catholics, and Socialists – which made up Dutch society. The difference with the swift implementation of a strategy of external adjustment is striking. The consensus across the party spectrum and between the two major economic interest groups created the precondition for a tripartite strategy of wage restraint in which the guidance of a strong and resolute state was accepted. In the field of domestic compensation, by contrast, the prewar divisions over the responsibility and organization of social policy revived and prevented the state to take a similar engaging and directive role.

The position of the Catholic People's Party (KVP) and its ambiguous doctrine of subsidiarity has been crucial. Together with its Social Democratic ally, the Catholic People's Party (KVP) was the party in government. With industry in ruins and the country in need of reconstruction, the role of the state in holding down wages and prices was easily justified.[5] But the party could never be mollified by its coalition partner and accept a similar leading role for the state with respect to industrial organization, education, or – the field that concerns us here – social policy. In these domains, the Catholic doctrine of subsidiarity most of the time went in unison with Protestant apprehension about the state taking over responsibilities which God has given to individuals. Together with the liberal 'laissez faire', the home-made Calvinist doctrine of 'sovereignty in one's own circle' of family, firm or church, had been a mighty ideological weapon against state intrusion in social policy.

This position had a natural ally in the employers camp. Irrespective of religious affiliation, employers believed that they were better able to control the costs of social insurance and prevent illegitimate use if not an expansionist state bureaucracy but industry itself was responsible for implementation. For this purpose they soon formed Industry Insurance Associations (IIAs, *bedrijfsverenigingen*), after the German pattern. The main Socialist unions, in agreement with the Socialist Party, preferred social insurance to be run by the state, both on ideological and practical grounds: it would contribute to the emancipation of the workers, free them from dependence upon and control of employers, and benefits would probably be more generous. But although they were the mainstream in the Dutch union movement, between 1918 and 1960 the Socialist unions were always outnumbered by the Catholic and Protestant unions combined. In 1921 they conceded the issue in what was probably the first central agreement between unions and employers, the Posthumus-Kupers memorandum, named after the two leaders of the largest peak association of employers and the Socialist union federation. In this understanding the unions accepted that not the state but industry should run the workers' insurance on the conditions that the IIA's would be placed under bipartite governing boards with an equal number of seats for the unions.

This agreement cleared the way for further social policy legislation (Mannoury, 1967).

Industrial self-governance by the social partners in social security has its origins in the Industrial Injuries Act of 1901, the first major social security act. This act was directly inspired by Bismarck's social security legislation and was intended as the first of the three classical insurances for workers. However, the dispute over who would administer these laws and control implementation delayed the introduction of a Workers Sickness Insurance and Workers Disability Act, the latter of which in Germany also included a pension for workers who could no longer work because of old age.

The Industrial Injuries Act (1901) introduced a compulsory insurance. However, with regard to the administration of the new insurance inspiration was found in Austria (Mannoury, 1967). Hence, unlike its German specimen the insurance was not administered by semi-public associations of employers, but by a National (later Social) Insurance Bank, which was a service organization under supervision of the central state. Premium payment, however, was differentiated by industry and depended on the risk of injuries in a particular industry. A coalition between the Protestant party and some employer groups to copy the German model lock, stock and barrel failed. Only when the Minister promised that employers were allowed to opt out, individually or in combination, from the compulsory insurance, did the Act pass Parliament. One of the consequences of the struggle against the new law was the foundation of the first employers' association in the Netherlands.

A Disability Act was introduced only in 1919, but implementation was truncated to a very lean old age provision (as in German, called 'rente') for workers above the age of seventy years. The Socialists and the Association for State Pensions had wanted a universal, state guaranteed old age pension, after British and Danish models, but they lost. The actual level of the new old age pension for workers, disguised as disability allowance, was very low, not earnings related. The administration was entrusted to regional Councils of Labour (*Raden van Arbeid*), whose ailing existence was given a new impulse by the Protestant Minister presiding over social policy in the years before the First World War. Unions and employers held seats on the governing boards of these Councils, but the president was appointed by the government.

The third and most important piece of legislation, the Sickness Act, was enacted in 1913, but the contention over who should be responsible for its administration, held up its actual implementation for seventeen years (Rigter et al., 1995: 50). The original Bill was little else than the Dutch rendering of the German *Krankenversicherungsgesetz* of 1883, but stiff opposition by the medical profession caused the enacted version to merely contain insurance against the loss of earnings caused by illness and not the equally important insurance for treatment of illness. This part was adjourned *sine die*, that is, until the Nazi-Germans imposed the health cost insurance funds in 1942 (Mannoury 1985: 197). The remaining part was an improvement for those with longer illnesses, but made things worse for others. The 1909 revision of the Civil Code already obliged employers to continue full payment of wages 'for some short period'. The new Act provided for payment during a half a year, at a rate of seventy percent, to start after three so-called waiting days. Under the new insurance, workers had to pay premiums withheld on weekly wages.

Following the 1921 memorandum, employers and unions wanted to administer the new insurance through the industrial insurance associations which had already become involved in the administration of the Industrial Injuries Act for firms who had opted out of the compulsory scheme. However, the regional Councils of Labour had not enough work with running the disability insurance, and also wanted to run the new law, after the model of the Austrian *Bezirkskrankenkassen*. In 1930, after years of stalemate, the law was finally implemented; both organizations, the bipartite IIA's and the regional Councils of Labour were entrusted with the task of implementation. This dualism – sometimes with an open war of competition between them – was to last until 1952 (Mannoury, 1967).

The prewar legacy conscripted the postwar expansion of the welfare state into a very muddled administrative structure. Attempts to change the fundamentals of social security organization consistently failed, until 1993! Not even the interruption of five years of war and occupation did accomplish that. Appointed by the government in exile in London, a state commission chaired by Mr. A.A. Van Rhijn, inspired by the Beveridge report of 1942, advised the first postwar government to introduce a universal welfare system, organized on a tripartite basis, run by the social partners but under the supervision of the state, quite similar to the evolving policy of external adjustment (Rigter et al., 1995). In 1946, however, the social partners, represented in the *Foundation of Labour* (STAR), advised against the proposed central supervision, in line with the 1921 compromise. In 1948, a second state-commission, also headed by Mr. Van Rhijn, proposed the establishment of a Central Administrative Office charged with the supervision of the IIA's. The proposed bill did not make it through Parliament, where the Protestant opposition enlisted the support of the Catholic People's Party for an amendment which left the bipartite IIA's free to administer social insurance as they saw fit or, if they wanted, to work together in a shared insurance administration office (GAK). The fateful Stapelkamp-amendment defined the *status quo* for the next decades and drastically curtailed the leverage of the state in the otherwise expanding realm of social security. In 1952 the amended Organization of Social Security Bill (OSV) was enacted; the idea of a Central Administrative Office had been dropped and supervision was entrusted to the new Social Insurance Council (SVR), based on tripartite representation with a minority vote for the government. The new act made an end to the prewar dualism and entrusted the Industry Insurance Associations with a monopoly in the administrative and implementation of workers' insurance. A number of 19, later 23 IIA's, each representing a particular branch of industry, was responsible for collecting premiums and paying out benefits. This provided the social partners with a high degree of institutional power within the Dutch welfare state. In the 1970s the associations, which used to operate on the basis of private law, were granted public status under the new Civil Code, book 2. This brought the IIA's in the mire of public regulation on financial solvency and accountability, but the relationship with the state remained characterized by a form of 'remote control'.

The fragmented nature of social security administration in the Netherlands became mirrored in a complicated pattern of social policy provisions. Haphazardly, this evolved into a three-tiered system of universal or people's insurance, workers' insurance programs, and social provisions. The first tier of universal insurance is based on the principle of social solidarity, financed through general taxation, and is geared towards providing non-working citizens with a minimum income. Beginning with the emergency decree on old age pension in 1947, this was a postwar novelty in the Netherlands. In 1956 the decree was changed into a General Old Age Pensions Act which guaranteed everybody over the age of 65 a flat rate public pension, which was made inflation-proof in the next year. In 1959 the General Widows and Orphans Act was established, followed in 1963 by the General Family Allowance Act. Abolishment of the Health Cost Funds, imposed under German occupation, was already unthinkable after 1945; the funds were given a new legal basis in 1965 and extended to include exceptional medical risks and long-term hospitalization in 1968. All universal insurance programs are implemented and administered by government agencies, in particular the general tax office (revenue) and the Councils of Labour (payment), except in the case of the Health Cost Funds which remained in the hands of private associations with links to the different religious and ideological groups.

Workers insurance, the second tier of the Dutch social security system, is based on the principle of economic equivalency and provides for earnings-related benefits to wage earners in the case of illness, accidents or unemployment. Benefits are financed by compulsory contributions levied on employers' payrolls and employee earnings. Eligibility depends on the employment history of claimants and benefits represent a percentage of previous earnings. This second tier is managed, as we have already seen, by autonomous bipartite Industry Insurance Associations. Sickness insurance dates from 1930. Prewar unemployment insurance had been on a voluntary basis, administered by special funds attached to the trade unions with government subsidies on premiums, following the so-called Danish system. During the occupation the unions had to stop their activities and the funds were discontinued. In 1945 they were not re-established; in line with the Atlantic Charter of 1941 and the Beveridge report of 1942 insurance against unemployment was now to be a government responsibility. The trade unions did not resist the take-over by the state – their experience with administrating the debt-ridden and overburdened funds during the 1930 recession had not left them with fond memories –, even though they regretted the loss of a useful selective benefit for membership retention. The 1949 Unemployment Insurance Act guaranteed income maintenance, at eighty percent of last earned wages during 26 weeks; claimants had to be involuntary unemployed, to engage in an active search for new employment, and be willing to accept all commensurate job offers, which, in turn, was contingent on the level of education, work history, age, previous income, and residence. In 1964, at a time of extreme labour scarcity, a supplementary Unemployment Relief Act guaranteed a further two years of continued benefits, not means-tested and at 75 percent of the last earned wage.

In 1967 the Labour Disability Act replaced the Industrial Injuries Act of 1901. Like unemployment this insurance came under the control of the IIA's. Disability insurance benefits were also set at eighty percent of last-earned wages. Under the scheme, workers who had received sickness pay for one year, could apply for benefits. The new act removed the distinction, crucial in prewar legislation, between disability as a consequence of injuries during work, and disabilities which might have their cause elsewhere but likewise incapacitate people from earning an income. Besides the equal treatment of *risque professionel* and *risque social*, the Minister responsible for the new law insisted on a general, solidaristic rather than industry-related or variable system of premium payment (Veldkamp, 1968). The new act inaugurated the novelty in the Dutch social security that claimants were entitled to benefits irrespective of whether the illness or disability had actually occurred or developed while on the job. In 1976, a General Disability Act extended coverage to the self-employed, civil servants, and persons who had developed disabilities from birth. Although a social provision, it was decided that the social partners should administer and implement the new provision as they did with regard to the related disability insurance. With this act the Dutch welfare state reached its apogee.

Social provisions, the third tier, provides the public safety-net for citizens who do not or no longer have other entitlements, income or means of subsistence. For instance, after the expiration of the unemployment insurance benefit, someone still unemployed is transferred from the earnings-related private to the public tier of the welfare state. In 1965, the National Assistance Act replaced the Poor Laws of 1854 and 1912; this is the 'final stanza' of the Dutch welfare state. Assistance is financed by general revenue and administered by municipal social service agencies. Benefits are set at the so-called social minimum, since 1974 pegged at seventy percent of the statutory minimum wage for a single adult. Although coverage is theoretically unlimited, public assistance is means-tested and recipients must register at local Public Employment Offices and be available for work. Payment of the benefits is administered by the municipal social service administration. Originally, public assistance was placed under the responsibility of the Ministry for Culture, Recreation and Social Work, later to the Ministry of Health and Social Work (between 1955 and 1972 Health had been the responsibility of the Ministry of Social Affairs), but in 1987 public assistance was united with the other two tiers under the supervision of the Ministry of Social Affairs and Employment.

Throughout the postwar period there were attempts to streamline the splintered institutional structure of social security. All these attempts consistently failed because of the joint veto-powers of organized business and labour, represented in the governing boards of the Industry Insurance Associations, the Foundation of Labour and the Social and Economic Council, the Christian Democratic forces in and outside parliament, and the ambivalence of the Social Democrats between corporatism and statism (van Doorn, 1981). In its content, the system was a typical example of the 'compensatory' continental model, based on the principle of industrial insurance against occupational risks, financed by payroll social security contributions, the central role of the (male) breadwinner, geared to the defence of the traditional family, the quasi-private administration of social security and the strong focus on income replacement rather than on active labour market policies (Esping-Andersen 1990). What is specific for the Netherlands within the group of continental welfare states, is the degree to which the breadwinner principle was applied in employment, incomes and social policy. In no other country with a comparable modern economy had paid work of married women been discouraged to such an extent. One of the Christian-Democratic politicians, Mr. Wil Albeda, who held the post of Minister of Social Affairs between 1977 and 1981, summarized the ideological bias and its consequences with clarity:

'The emphasis placed on the breadwinner principle in our system of social insurance was based upon the widely held belief that a married women should stay home and care for the house and the children. Child payments and public housing proceeded from this same view. The low degree of participation of women and the high birth rate in the Netherlands belonged together' (Albeda, 1990: 87).

Interestingly, it was the deep crisis of the particular policy content of the continental model, its built-in tendency to keep many people inactive and to compensate for the loss of income, which created, many years later, the conditions for reform in the institutional makeup of Dutch social security. But first the welfare state would 'grow to its limits' while the controls of restraint would increasingly falter.

FROM EXPANSION TO CRISIS

There were various developments which contributed to the rapid expansion of social security expenditure in the 1970s. To begin with, there was the extended coverage of the programs both in terms of the risks and the people to which these programs applied. The number of people depending on income transfers of all the programs taken together doubled between 1970 and 1985, from 1,6 million to 3,2 million, not counting the annual average of about 300,000 workers on sickness leave. The two disability programs produced the largest absolute rise: from just under 200,000 to around 700,000; unemployment benefits increased ten-fold, from 68,000 to 682,000; the number of people depending on public assistance more than doubled from 63,000 to 180,000. Recipients of old age pensions rose from 1,2 to 1,6 million.[6] Excluding students, the number of people in working age without paid work and without social benefits, mainly housewives, remained more or less constant at 2,2 million. In the same period paid employment stagnated at around 4,8 million jobs. Consequently, the dependency ratio deteriorated fast. Excluding old age pensions, the number of employed persons per benefit recipient decreased from 14.8:1 in 1970 to 5:1 in 1980 and 2.9:1 in 1985. If indeed the unpaid income of housewives were to be added up to this dependency rate, there is only 1.2 person with a paid job for everyone depending in one way or another on the earnings which that job brings.[7] It goes without saying that such shifts raise formidable questions of cost-sharing and financial solidarity.

The second factor was the overall rise in benefit levels which was associated with the net linking of all benefits to wage developments (Vording, 1993). In 1969 the Netherlands had introduced a statutory minimum wage. Its level was set relatively high since it was supposed to cover the costs of living of a one breadwinner family with two children.[8] The minimum wage was then made to serve as an anchor for all transfer incomes. The lowest level of any social benefit was set at seventy percent of the minimum wage for a single person moving up to hundred percent in the case of a family. In 1974 the controversial decision was taken to link the minimum wage and, indirectly, the related social security benefits, to the contractual wage developments in the private sector. Twice every year, levels were adjusted so that low-paid workers and social benefit recipients would not just catch up with inflation but also be assured of their share in the overall increase in wealth of the nation. At this time virtually all private sector contracts contained automatic price escalators, which made them inflation-proof. The result of this system was that, when new contracts were negotiated between unions and employers in the private sector, government costs went up automatically. The same applied to the salaries of an increasing number of civil servants and the various semi-public employees of the welfare state. This necessitated the generation of extra revenue through taxation and premiums, which resulted in higher wage costs and lower disposable incomes, especially at the lower end of the wage hierarchy. Special allowances for low-paid workers cushioned these affects, but added to the costs of employers and the likelihood of unemployment. Together, the growing volume of benefits and their linkage to inflation and pay rises in the private sector, led to higher costs that were insufficiently met by either social charges or taxes.

Table 20: Volume of social security claimants: unemployment, sickness, disability and public assistance (x 1000)

	unemployment	sickness	disability	public assistance
1972	108	229	229	83
1973	110	241	253	9
1974	130	258	280	102
1975	196	265	311	117
1976	213	271	359	120
1977	207	275	490	111
1978	207	287	543	104
1979	218	292	572	107
1980	236	292	611	112
1981	359	275	637	123
1982	507	259	651	13
1983	616	247	666	15
1984	659	249	685	167
1985	649	244	703	180
1986	625	262	718	179
1987	612	276	725	179
1988	599	287	739	178
1989	580	315	758	178
1990	538	345	790	176
1991	525	345	801	175
1992	539	340	805	174
1993	602	343	805	170
1994	678	290	789	166
1995	698	304	753	164
1996	707	301	733	155
1997	707	300	722	144

Source: Ministry of Social Affairs and Employment (1998)

In 1953 social insurance premiums had amounted to only five percent of national income in net terms; in the next decade they rose to eleven percent and by 1970 they had reached fifteen percent. On a steady climb in the 1970s, they peaked at 24 percent in 1983 and than flattened out to 20 percent in the later 1980s. As this did not meet costs, the government's share in social security more than doubled during the 1970s and was partly financed through its non-tax income from the natural gas resources and by increased public borrowing.[9] The rise in the government's share essentially reflected two developments. First, a growing number of claimants under the programs no longer qualified for insured status. As a consequence of rising unemployment among school-leavers and adolescents and of longer spells of unemployment affecting a growing number of workers, the proportion of insured workers among the stock of unemployed decreased steadily to only sixteen percent in 1986. The number of people depending on welfare allowances only rose in proportion.[10] Second, in the second half of the 1970s governments tried to slow down the rise in social charges in order to contain the rise in labour costs and encourage wage moderation. More than once this was done by subsidizing employers' contributions to social security, with the unintended consequence of lowering employers' resistance to wage demands of the unions.

By comparison, tax revenues remained rather stable, with a slow increase during the 1970s from 26 to 30 percent of the net national income. Even with the income from gas, this was considerably less than government expenditure. The problem of the 'financing deficit', calculated as the difference between government revenue and expenditure, minus the amount paid on long-term loans, was born. Until 1979 it never exceeded 4.4 percent, but then began to rise dramatically to 10.7 percent in 1983. It would become the major preoccupation of economists and governments in the 1980s (Andeweg and Irwin, 1993: 209-10). The windfall benefit of huge gas resources in the Northern part of the country turned out a blessing in disguise. It produced the so-called 'Dutch disease': 'a sickness whose syndrome is the use of temporary income, in the Dutch case obtained from the unexpected gas revenues, in order to finance current expenditures. The symptoms are increased government expenditures and a hard currency' (Metze 1990: 25). The consequence was that the gas-induced high value of the guilder put Dutch export at a disadvantage. The extra resources were not used for long-term ventures to modernize industry, but employed to shore up ailing sectors (shipbuilding) and finance social security.

It is paradoxical that when the expansion of the welfare state was anchored on a tripartite incomes policy, the political and cultural pre-conditions for a successful implementation of the policy were already gone. As such it qualifies as an example of transposition, the use of a once successful decision-making rule in another domain and for other purposes, a technique which was discussed in Chapter Four. In this case it was a recipe for policy failure.

The successful policy of wage restraint in the first decades after the war did suggest to policy makers, in particular to governments, that if they paid the right price wage moderation could be purchased. This was in particular the leading idea of the two Christian Democratic Ministers of Social Affairs, Mr. Jaap Boersma (1971-3, 1974-77) and Mr. Wil Albeda (1977-81), who led the department in the 1970s, both with a career in the Protestant union movement (CNV) and both on the left of their party (ARP), and later of the CDA. The right price, so it seemed, was a higher level of social protection for those without work and the granting of special provisions for the low-paid.

Table 21: Elections to the Second Chamber, 1972-1994

	1972	1977	1981	1982	1986	1989	1994
CDA*	31,3	31,9	30,8	29,3	34,6	35,3	22,2
PvdA	27,3	33,8	28,2	30,4	33,3	31,9	24,0
VVD*	14,4	17,9	17,3	23,1	17,4	14,6	20,0
D66	4,2	5,4	11,0	4,3	6,1	7,9	15,5
GL*	10,8	4,3	6,2	5,6	3,1	4,1	3,5
RPF/GPV/SGP	4,0	3,1	4,0	4,2	3,1	4,1	4,8
CD*	-	-	0,1	0,8	0,4	0,9	2,5
SP	-	-	-	-	-	0,4	1,3
Elderly Party	-	-	-	-	-	-	4,5

Source: *Compendium voor Politiek en Samenleving in Nederland.*

* Party and predecessors

Abbreviations:

PvdA	Social Democratic Party
CDA	Christian Democratic Appeal
VVD	People's Party for Freedom and Democracy (Liberals)
D'66	Democrats '66
SGP	Political Reformed Party (Calvinist)
GL	Green-Left Party
GPV	Reformed Political Union (Calvinist)
RPF	Reformed Political Federation (Calvinist)
CP	Centre Party/Centre Democrats (Ultra-Right)
SP	Socialist Party

Table 22: Cabinet composition 1971-1994

	prime minister	minister of social affairs	ministries
1973-7	Den Uyl (PVDA)	Boersma (ARP)	KVP(4) ARP(2) PVDA(7) D'66(1) PPR(2)
1977-81	Van Agt (CDA) I	Albeda (CDA)	CDA(10) VVD(6)
1981-2	Van Agt (CDA) II	Den Uyl (PVDA)	CDA(6) PVDA(6) D'66(3)
1982	Van Agt (CDA) III	De Graaf (CDA)	CDA(9) D'66(5)
1982-6	Lubbers (CDA) I	De Koning (CDA)	CDA(8) VVD(6)
1986-9	Lubbers (CDA) II	De Koning (CDA)	CDA(9) VVD(5)
1989-94	Lubbers (CDA) III	De Vries (CDA)	CDA(7) PVDA(7)
1994	Kok (PVDA)	Melkert (PVDA)	PVDA(5) VVD(5) D'66(4)

Source: *Compendium voor Politiek en Samenleving in Nederland*, pp. A-0500-121

In 1973, after extended negotiations, the Netherlands got its most Leftist government of the postwar period. Dominated by the Social Democratic Party, led by Mr. Joop den Uyl, in unison with two minor Left of Centre parties, it was based on a coalition with two of the Christian parties. Of these, the Catholic People's Party (KVP) had lost half its electorate in a decade and was searching for a new identity, and the other party, the Protestant ARP, had just embarked on a radicalizing course. Hit by the crisis of 1973-74, which, all in all, lowered national income by two percent, the government drew up a series of temporary measures, including wage and energy cost restraint. True to the government's political credo of 'redistribution of wealth, knowledge, and power' and its belief that 'the strongest shoulders should carry the heaviest burdens', the crisis measures were embedded within policies favouring the low-paid. This was consistent with the preference of the Industries' Union (IB) and the FNV. Mr. den Uyl and Social Affairs Minister Boersma believed that the linking mechanism, guaranteeing a 'parallel development of earnings and benefits', combined with progressive fiscal policies, would help to contain social security spending costs because it would induce the unions to apply the brakes on wage rises (Toirkens, 1988; Hemerijck 1995). As it turned out, it did not. The unions, especially the IB, wanted more, but Den Uyl was unable to deliver on his promise of structural reforms. Of these, only the new Works Councils Act reached the statute book in 1979, under another government. It made the council a body elected by and from the employees with stronger legal powers of consultation, not unlike the German *Betriebsrat* (Rogers and Streeck 1994; Visser 1995). The bills on 'openness of non-wage incomes' and 'collective employee profit-sharing schemes' never made it; taken over by subsequent governments, the proposals were continuously watered down and later dropped. A fourth reform proposal, meant to stop speculation with agricultural and building land, caused the government's fall. New elections produced a very large gain for Mr. Den Uyl, but at the expense of smaller parties on the Left, and the Social Democrats proved to be unable to negotiate the Christian Democrats into a new coalition.

Originally, Mr. den Uyl and his cabinet had acted upon the belief that the crisis was temporary, and that expansionist fiscal policies were a means to spend the country out of the crisis. His second budget, for 1975, written one year after the energy shock of 1973-74, explained that:

'the Netherlands, with its strong external position (!), not only because of its gas resources, is among the few countries in the industrial world which can and should (!) allow itself an expansive, compensating budget. The situation on the domestic front, with its ever higher and persistent level of unemployment, is another reason'.[11]

In 1976, however, Mr. Wim Duisenberg, who held the post of Finance Minister, put on the brakes and formulated his so-called 1% norm or rule that total public expenditure should not rise with more than 1 percent of the net national income per year. This was a considerable revision of the projected 2.4 to 3 percent at the time (Van Zanden and Griffiths, 1989). The new Centre-Right administration, led by Mr. van Agt, was a weak coalition, internally divided, in particular in the case of the Minister of Finance and later European Commissioner, Mr. Frans Andriessen, and the Minister of Social Affairs, Mr. Wil Albeda.

The Van Agt administration followed the policy legacy of Den Uyl, in particular with respect to wage policies and the linking of social benefits. It was unable to bring public finances under control (Toirkens, 1988) and was locked in internal fights (Hemerijck, 1993). Initially, Mr. Duisenberg's norm was adopted and in 1978 the government announced a further reduction in spending and a series of small curtailments in the index for calculating civil servants salaries and social benefits, to be implemented in small steps until 1981. But because of internal obstruction from spending departments, little support in Parliament and no support from the unions, little was accomplished (Toirkens, 1988). The 'financing deficit' which had decreased to just over four percent in 1977 doubled during Mr. van Agt's tenure.

In this period wage developments were the key issue of economic and social policy making, since wage rises determined sixty percent of the rise in the annual budget. For the Finance Minister this was sufficient reason for application of the 1970 Wage Act and impose a wage freeze. According to Mr. Albeda this would be ineffective, as unions would immediately make up for losses. Moreover, it would worsen the 'social climate' for much needed consultation with the unions. Various compensating measures, varying from employment programs, redistributive income measures, the imposition of restraint on non-wage incomes, small increases in welfare contributions, and tax reductions, were offered in order to attract the unions into a political exchange and accept voluntary restraint. The internal cabinet clash between Finance and Social Affairs escalated in the second half of 1979. When the so-called 'almost accord' of 1979 between the central organizations, so carefully arranged by Mr. Albeda, floundered, the Finance Minister clamoured for an extended wage freeze for a period of two years. As this demand was considered outlandish, even by his Liberal coalition partner, he rapidly lost support in parliament. Early in the next year, Mr. Andriessen resigned from the cabinet. The commitment to concertation had triumphed over the objective of fiscal restraint, but not for long.

The second oil crisis of 1979 hit the Netherlands much harder than the first and left the country's economy and public finances in a much greater disarray. Mr. Albeda had no option but to apply the Wage Act and impose a wage freeze. Final talks with the unions produced no results; they made it clear that no further deals could be expected before the next elections, from which they expected a political change (Nobelen, 1983). The general elections of 1981 did result in a patched-up coalition between the Christian and Social Democrats, but the new government lasted only nine months, from September 1981 to May 1982. Deeply divided and with little outside support, the new administration immediately fell back into policy immobilism.

It might have seemed to the governments of the 1970s that the linking of benefits to wages was a necessary condition for wage restraint and would provide a built-in brake on rising claims of and rivalry between different groups. However, when tripartite bargaining over wage restraint faltered, the linking system spurred social security expenditures. Moreover, it made the government the prisoner of the outcome of negotiations and tactical games between unions and employers (Hemerijck, 1995). Exacerbated by two major external (energy) shocks, this resulted in a very fast rise of the volume and costs of the welfare state. The Dutch welfare state had lost the incomes policy guiding principle upon which it was erected without being able to fall back on alternative steering mechanisms, in part because of its weak institutional position in the policy domain of social security. This sums up the welfare state crisis in the Netherlands. The government was responsible for setting the maximum levels of provision, but had neither control over the upward drift of these levels nor influence upon the criteria of application of the norms of provision. The system had few built-in mechanisms for self-restraint, invited participants to a 'liberal use' of the possibilities of the various systems, and was therefore rife for a classical 'tragedy of the commons' (Hardin, 1968).

THE SMALL STEP APPROACH TO WELFARE STATE RETRENCHMENT

The fall of the short-lived Centre-Left cabinet, after a decade of corporatist immobilism, opened the way for the formation of a true 'no-nonsense' austerity coalition. The Lubbers administration which came to office in November of 1982, committed itself to a drastic reorganization of state finances and curtailment of social security benefits. One of the first measures of this government was the severance of the automatic linking mechanism between private sector wages, public sector wages and transfer payments, to be followed by a three percent cut in 1984. The revised Linking Act of 1980, on linking the minimum wage and, indirectly, social benefits to average changes in contractual wages, was never applied between 1982 and 1990; each year Parliament allowed its dispensation, usually with some compensatory measures for the lowest incomes or so-called 'real minima'. [12]

Assured of wage restraint in the private sector and without the linking mechanism, the intra-cabinet tussles now came to revolve around the size of the singular departmental cutbacks. In these games the new Minister of Social Affairs, Mr. Jan de Koning, as he himself declared, came to speak 'the language of the Ministers of Economic Affairs and Finance.[13] This gained him the stature of being the second most powerful politician in the government

Figure 10: Development of the statutory minimum wage as percentage of the average wage

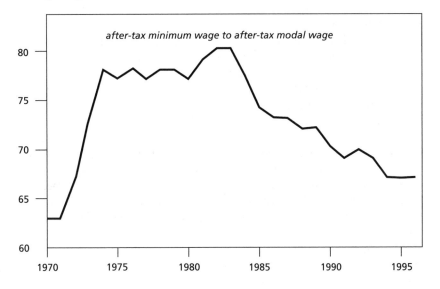

after-tax minimum wage to after-tax modal wage

Source: CPB, L. Bovenberg (1997), figure 11.

and in the Christian Democratic party, after Mr. Lubbers. His realism held the government on a solid course of austerity and welfare retrenchments in which the salami-principle of small slices was relentlessly applied. Large and brusque steps were to be avoided, since they were likely to provoke conflicts which might halt or, worse, reverse the policy of retrenchment. The risk of a major social conflict would have been too large; with small steps 'the pattern is rather that this year's anger is replaced by next year's anger'.[14] At the same time the door to the unions was always kept open, but they always went out empty-handed

The next step, after lowering and freezing the rise in benefits, was to change the system and reduce the claims on the social security system. This was announced as a 'system reorganization'. Already in 1982, Mr. Louw de Graaf, the Junior Minister responsible for social security had written a policy memorandum, titled 'Reorganization of the System of Social Security', in which he argued the case of a fundamental reform.[15] The plans that were finally presented and adopted by Parliament were far more modest. The Minister, De Koning, again chose a cautious line, in correspondence with his philosophy of doing one thing at the time. The 1987 'system reorganization' did not change the institutional structures and responsibilities in social security implementation. The only organizational change was the placement of public assistance under the jurisdiction of the Ministry of Social Affairs and Employment, a reform that had been advocated since 1945, bringing all income maintenance programs under one roof. With respect to the involvement of the social partners and the bipartite autonomy in the administration of social insurance no adjustments were made.

The major changes concerned a reduction in eligibility, benefits levels and duration of unemployment insurance. When the original laws on unemployment insurance and extended relief had been introduced nobody had anticipated a persistent high level of long-term unemployment. The aim was to make the much expanded system less costly. Paying heed to European legislation, the male (breadwinner) bias in the old laws was removed. Under the new law[16], unemployment insurance and unemployment relief were integrated and the costs of financing extended benefits shifted from the government to employers and employees. Benefits were lowered from eighty to seventy percent of last earned wages. Tighter eligibility rules required that beneficiaries must have worked at least 26 weeks during the 12 months prior to unemployment. Benefits could last from six months to five years, depending on one's job history and age.[17] With respect to disability, the other culprit in the social security spending crisis, the reforms were modest by comparison. Maximum benefit levels were also reduced to seventy percent, but the effect of this measure was often undone by setting more favourable conditions in collective agreements, at least during the first years of disability. A sharper distinction was introduced between physical disability and unemployability, and the latter category was placed under stricter rules and lower benefits. Moreover, the so-called 'labour market consideration' in the disability scheme (see below) was repealed.

With the adoption of these austerity measures in parliament, the second Lubbers government (1986-89) promised 'peace on the social security front'; after the 'system reorganization' of 1987 there would be 'neither improvements nor setbacks'. The results of the reform effort, however, were mixed (Van der Veen, 1995). The cuts were substantial and did generate savings. From 1985 on social expenditures stabilized. But this was as much the effect of the economic recovery and the growth in jobs; in the early 1990s costs would again increase. Registered unemployment fell, but long-term unemployment remained high. The narrowing of eligibility for unemployment insurance put the pressure on the disability program. Even the Minister's administrative order of 1987 that older workers could, under conditions, be dismissed, did not take away that pressure.

THE CRISIS OF INACTIVITY

By 1990 there was broad, public awareness that the Dutch welfare state, like many other continental welfare state, was trapped in a pathological vicious cycle of, what Esping-Andersen has recently coined, 'welfare without work'

(Esping-Andersen, 1996). In response to the shocks of the 1970s, the 'compensatory', transfer based, welfare states of France, Germany, Belgium, Italy, Spain and the Netherlands, had embarked on strategies of modernization and labour shedding in response to industrial restructuring. While the Scandinavian welfare states pursued a strategy of integrating as many people as possible into the labour force by subsidizing entry and preventing exit, the continental model tended, by contrast, to subsidize the exit of older men and discourage the entry of women. The principle of the industrial insurance of occupational risk, the primordial role of the breadwinner, the quasi-private administration of social security and the focus on income replacement rather than an active labour market policy have in conjunction magnified the continental crisis of inactivity.

In the second half of the 1980s, the Dutch economy began to suffer from a negative spiral, a devastating interactive logic between the labour market, labour-saving investments, and the system of social security. Firms in high-wage economies can only survive if they are able to increase labour productivity. This is most commonly achieved through labour-saving investments and by laying off less productive workers. Under the principle of traditional breadwinner family dependence, increased inactivity drives up taxes and payroll social security contributions. This, in turn, puts pressure on wage costs, which provides new ground for reassessing the remaining workforce in terms of their level of productivity, most likely leading to another round of dismissals. A vicious cycle of high wage costs, low net earnings, exit of less productive workers, rising social security contributions, elicits further layoffs and intensifies the spiral of welfare without work. Jobs disappear in sectors where productivity increases stagnate and prices of goods and services cannot be easily raised. Moreover, if service sector salaries are linked to exposed sector wage developments, and productivity in services lags ('Baumol's disease'), this leads to a loss of jobs in the labour intensive service sector. In other words, the crisis of inactivity helps to create a new class of non-employed, low-skilled, permanently inactive, welfare-dependent citizens, who are unable to gain access to the formal labour market.

Advanced welfare states confronted with spiraling inactivity and declining activity are, in due course, no longer able to preserve generous welfare standards. The peculiar combination of the growing volume of inactive citizens who receive welfare benefits and the declining number of citizens with paid jobs undermines the financial and social foundation of the welfare state. A high tax burden for social services and large social security contributions pushes the gross wage costs upwards. This is reflected in the so-called 'tax and social contributions wedge', which indicates the difference between the labour costs of employers and the disposable income of workers. The marginal wedge, in addition, indicates how much of a salary rise or, in the case of newly hired workers, how much of their additional income, will be spent on taxes and social security contributions, thus failing to lead to a net wage increase for workers. High average and marginal wedges are neither good for the economy nor good for job growth.

Different continental welfare states, employed different social policy provision to subsidize exit and discourage entry (Kohli et al., 1993; Naschold and de vroom, 1994). The Netherlands seems to have pushed the continental strategy of labour supply reduction to the extreme. While in Germany and France early retirement provided for the main exit route from the labour market, and in Belgium extended unemployment had similar functions, in the Netherlands generous and lenient sickness and disability insurance served this purpose. How much disability pensions became the 'escape route' for elderly workers is revealed by a comparison with Germany and Belgium. Per 10,000 wage earners between 55 and 64 years, there were in 1987 434 with a disability pension in Belgium, 262 in West Germany, and 980 in the Netherlands (Prins, 1991: 10). There are no reasons to believe that the health of workers, safety conditions in workplaces, or medical care in the Netherlands are so much worse as to warrant these large differences. Among the Dutch insured population between the age of 55 and 64, there were in 1986 more people drawing disability benefits than there were people with a paid job (Aarts and De Jong, 1992). Although the volume of disability benefits did not grow as fast as in the 1970s, this was no sign that inflow into the program had decreased. More people had reached retirement age and left the system, but there was an increasing number of people under 35 years of age entering the program and the average age of people in the program decreased.

Aarts and De Jong (1996) consider four factors which explain the exceptional growth of the disability program in the Netherlands. First, as we have already noted, the scheme does not make a distinction between different causes of disability. Second, the so-called 'labour market consideration' provision stipulated that in assessing the degree of disability, the diminished labour market opportunities for partially disabled persons should be taken into account. As a rule-of-thumb, disability was redefined in terms of the worker's incapacity to find a job similar to the one held before. During the 1970s this rule-of-thumb came to be interpreted in terms of a relation between productivity and wages. If productivity had fallen relative to the worker's last earnings, he or she should be considered incapacitated. Medical doctors, on the payroll of the Industry Insurance Associations, generally applied the 'labour market consideration' with leniency. The 'labour market consideration' was repealed in the 1987 reform. Third, the disability and sickness schemes are closely related. In general, workers receive sickness benefits during the first year of illness, after which they can apply for a benefit under the disability program. The financing of the two programs differs; sickness pay is primarily financed by employers while disability benefits are financed from workers' contributions. We recall that contributions were set at uniform, nation-wide rates, unrelated to the sector-specific risk factors in different industrial branches. In most collective agreements sickness benefits are guaranteed at a level of 100 per cent of last earnings and most extend supplements to disability benefits for a year or longer.

These three factors, i.e., the broad definition of disability, the incorporation of labour market chances into the calculation of disability, the close relation with sickness pay and extended benefits, together with the institutional element of bipartite autonomy in Dutch social security administration, allowed for the liberal deployment of these schemes to shed labour and divert unemployed workers to sickness and disability channels rather than overt unemployment. This peculiar collusion of interests and institutions between the government, employers, workers and trade unions produced an enormous problem of moral hazard.

The improper use of social security disability pensions for industrial restructuring, first introduced in the wake of the 1973 oil crisis, matched with the strategic and material interests of the trade unions and employers, and with the government's own desire to keep the official unemployment figures down. Disability pensions were more attractive to redundant workers than unemployment benefits, even more so after 1987. Benefits would probably continue until retirement age, be topped up in collective bargaining, and claimants didn't need to be available for work. Using the sickness and disability route instead of layoffs, employers bought off worker resistance and kept good relations with the unions, while the costs were born collectively. Confronted with rising labour costs, including social security contributions, the disability scheme allowed employers to externalize part of the cost of restructuring and to hire younger and cheaper productive workers. The use of the sickness and disability route was a way to circumvent cumbersome and time consuming dismissal procedures and a way to avoid industrial conflict.

The Dutch law on dismissals is tough and includes, since the 1945 Extraordinary Decree on Labour Relations, preventive controls. Dutch employers need a special permit from the regional director of the Public Employment Office for nearly all types of dismissal. For elderly workers, above 45 years, employers have to observe a prolonged period of notice, up to a maximum of 13 weeks. In case of collective dismissals the period of notice may even be longer. If an employer makes 20 or more workers redundant within three months, he is obliged to notify not only the regional director of the Public Employment Office, but also the works council and the trade union. The regional director then puts the request aside for one month to give everybody involved the time to negotiate a 'social plan'. Although the consent for dismissal is granted in 85 per cent of the number of requests, delays can be very long. Paying for sickness leave for one year and then letting the disability scheme take over, may be cheaper than either keeping less productive workers on the payroll or seeking his or her dismissal.

In the mid-1970s early retirement schemes also became an important exit route for elderly less productive workers in the Netherlands. Early retirement schemes are administered by individual firms or industry funds in ways that are quite similar to sickness benefits. Entitlements and contributions are negotiated between the trade unions and companies or sectoral employer associations, usually as part of the wage package. Government involvement has been limited, except in its capacity as employer. Recently, discussions have flared up over cost containment – the schemes are very popular – and the introduction of flexible retirement pension schemes with extra individual insurance.

From a Schumpeterian perspective, there is an element of virtue in the use of social policy in economic adjustment. While high gross wage costs, including social security contributions, compel firms to rationalize and modernize production, high replacement ratios and generous social insurance policies permit industrial restructuring and modernization to proceed without industrial conflict. Throughout the 1980s, this use of social policy as a productive constraint went ahead with few questions asked. Come the 1990s, with a stronger economy, considerable job growth and a decline in overt unemployment, but no significant drop in the volume of inactivity and long-term unemployment, a policy reassessment became unavoidable. For a large number of people, Dutch social security may have served as an 'inactivity trap', leading to a tremendous waste of human resources. Rising costs continue to be a cause of concern, but in the face of an emergent inactivity crisis public attention shifts to a concern with the apparent lack of controls. The escape from the labour market through one program or another appears unstoppable. With this awareness, the crisis of the Dutch welfare state is no longer first and foremost defined in financial terms; it has become a crisis of governability.

THE BUURMEIJER PARLIAMENTARY INQUIRY

When the Social Democrats (PvdA) regained office as partners in Mr. Lubbers third cabinet in 1989, social security reform took on a different tack. Economic recovery allowed for partial restoration of the linking mechanism. For the PvdA this had been an important political precondition for the acceptance of government responsibility. Linking was applied in 1990, in 1991 and in the first half of 1992.

Around 1990, a new policy consensus was emerging that the level of labour force participation had to increase. In particular the Scientific Council for Government Policy (WRR) was very focal in advocating this view and in 1990 the Council published a major study in which it argued that attention should shift from the seemingly improved unemployment rates to the still very low participation rates. The low level of labour force participation was identified as the Achilles' heel of the Dutch welfare state. The WRR advocated a new approach based on the creation of 'simple' and 'cheap' jobs for workers with little experience and low skills. Only a strategy which would induce more people into employment was believed capable of reversing the negative cycle of high taxes and social security contributions leading to high gross wage costs and causing round after round of reorganizations and lay-offs in order to defend one's corner in an increasingly competitive international market.

The policy recommendations of the WRR inspired top-level civil servants at the Ministry of Social Affairs and Employment to design a new contingent system of linking, which was enacted in 1992. The new Conditional Linking Act made full indexation of social benefits to average wage developments conditional on two counts.[18] First, there must be no 'excessive' wage growth, i.e. wage rises which exceed the anticipated increases in inflation and productivity, with a consequent rise in unemployment. Second, there must be no increase in the number of social security beneficiaries with a consequent increase of the rate of taxes and social security contributions. For practical purposes, the two conditions have been combined in one formula, the so-called I/A or Inactive/Active ratio, measuring the number of benefit recipients as a ratio of the employed population. If the I/A-ratio exceeds a predetermined reference level, the unions know that the government will suspend the linking mechanism which raises benefits in correspondence with an average of contractual wage rises. At the introduction of the linkage system, the reference level of the maximum I/A-ratio was set at 86, later adjusted to 82.8 per hundred employed persons. In 1993, 1994 and 1995 the government froze the legal minimum wage and social benefits, because the I/A ratio had risen from 81.4 in 1992 to 85.8 in 1994. In 1996 linking was restored, reflecting the decrease of the I/A-ratio under 82.6. Higher levels of participation thus became the core policy concern of the Lubbers-Kok cabinet. This meant that the standard social policy routine of tolerating or subsidizing exit from the labour market was revoked. For the Dutch situation this also implied that eventually the bipartite souvereignty in social security administration and implementation would come apart.

In the Summer of 1991, after long agony, the government took its momentous decision to reorganize the sickness and disability programs. This came after an attack on the role of trade unions and employers in the administration of social security by the crown members in the Social Economic Council (SER) and elections for provincial councils which showed dramatic losses for the PvdA. The Minister of Social Affairs and Employment, Mr. B. de Vries went as far as to call the abolishment of the program 'a real option'. The SER had produced a divided advice on how to reform the disability program, because the FNV affiliates had refused to mandate the federation to negotiate a compromise. Consequently, the government could go its own way and ignore the Council's advice not to lower the level and length of protection against illness and disability. In response, the unions organized the largest postwar protest demonstration in The Hague. This episode marked the beginning of the end of the passive welfare state. It had various and far-reaching

Table 23: Ratio inactivity/activity and social security outlays

	i/a-ratio	i/a-ratio (excl. old age pensions)	social security outlays (in percentage GDP)
1972	48.0	17.7	12.9
1973	49.7	18.7	13.6
1974	52.2	20.5	14.6
1975	56.0	23.3	16.5
1976	58.6	25.2	16.4
1977	61.8	27.7	16.8
1978	63.6	28.9	17.4
1979	65.0	30.0	18.0
1980	66.2	30.7	18.6
1981	70.8	34.3	19.6
1982	76.8	38.7	20.7
1983	81.3	42.2	21.1
1984	83.4	44.0	20.2
1985	83.2	43.5	19.6
1986	82.8	42.9	19.7
1987	82.6	42.6	19.1
1988	82.1	41.9	18.5
1989	82.5	42.0	17.7
1990	82.1	41.9	18.7
1991	81.6	41.4	18.7
1992	81.3	41.1	18.8
1993	83.2	42.4	18.9
1994	82.9	42.0	17.9
1995	82.3	41.4	17.3
1996	80.3	40.4	16.7
1997	78.5	39.4	16.1

Source: Ministry of Social Affairs and Employment (1998).

political consequences. The PvdA, led by former union leader Mr. Wim Kok, went through a very deep crisis, lost a third of its members during the tenure of the third Lubbers administration, and a quarter of its electorate in the general elections of 1994. Relationships with the FNV and the unions were at an all-time low.

Notwithstanding major political and societal discontent, the cabinet's reform effort with respect to the sickness and disability schemes entered into force in two steps, in 1992 and 1993. The Act on the Reduction of the Number of Disablement Benefit Claimants came into force in March 1992 and introduced various financial incentives to discourage employers from using the sickness leave and disability schemes.[19] Employers who hire a partially disabled employee for a minimum of one year can qualify for a 'bonus' up to half the gross annual wage. Employers can be penalized with an equally large 'malus' if they discharge disabled workers in excess of the sector-specific average.[20] The second part of the reform package introduced new eligibility criteria and related benefit levels, and was approved by parliament early in 1993.[21] This produced a major tightening of the program. Under the new scheme, residual earning power rather than productivity relative to last-earned wages, determine the level of benefits. Many workers who in the past would have been granted full benefits are now only eligible for partial benefits. The reform mostly affects younger workers, while the rights of older workers, over fifty years old, have been largely untouched. The period during which new claimants will receive a full benefit has been substantially shortened, and income losses are particularly large for workers with higher earnings. Benefits for people in the disability program under the age of fifty have been reduced, in a limited number of years, from seventy percent of last earned wages to seventy percent of the legal minimum wage, with the possibility of an age-related allowance. Finally, medical re-examinations of beneficiaries already in the scheme are undertaken on the basis of more objective medical criteria, and the legal requirement for the partially disabled employees to accept alternative employment is tightened.[22] A new definition of 'disability' serves to oblige beneficiaries to accept all 'normal' rather than 'appropriate' jobs.

Under the new Sickness Act introduced in January 1994, the first two weeks (for enterprises with fewer than 16 employees) or six weeks (for all other enterprises) of sickness benefits are charged to the individual employer rather than to a general fund.[23] By way of making individual employers bear part of the cost of sickness leave, the measure, inspired by policy examples in Germany and Belgium, was designed to stimulate employers and employees to reduce absence caused by illness and accidents as much as possible. Employers were compensated by an average reduction of sickness benefit contributions by four per cent of gross wages. This has apparently helped to generate a drop in the absentee rate due to sickness, from 6.7 percent in 1993 to 5.5 percent in 1994.[24]

Trade unions have tried with some success to 'repair' the curtailments by demanding supplementary benefits to be included in the collective agreements. Unions observe that their 'bargaining space' has once again narrowed and deplore that they are forced to repair more and more elements of the welfare state that once were taken for granted (Rojer 1996a). As a result, the costs of sickness and disability have effectively become elements in collective bargaining, further reinforcing incentives to reduce sickness and disability absenteeism at the level of companies and industrial sectors. In 1994, for the first year in the history of Dutch disability legislation the population enrolled in the scheme actually fell.

By having re-defined the crisis of the Dutch welfare state as a crisis of governability, public attention has increasingly been directed towards the behaviour of interest groups and the institutional arrangement in which they operate. The publication of a report by the Public Audit Office in March 1992 became the prelude to institutional reform. The report diagnosed that the supervision of the tripartite Social Security Council over the implementation of Dutch social security had consistently failed in 1988 and 1989. Moreover, the Public Audit Office was extremely critical of the role of the Minister of Social Affairs and Employment and his Junior Minister charged with the responsibility for social security. By highlighting the ambiguous distribution of powers and responsibilities within the Dutch welfare system, against the background of the disability crisis, the report had far-reaching political echoes. The Lower House of Parliament decided, on the instigation of the Social Democrats but opposed by the Christian Democrats, to apply its heaviest weapon and begin an All-Party Parliamentary Inquiry into the functioning of the organization of the Dutch system of social insurance, with special attention to the implementation of the disability scheme between 1980 and 1992. Many former and current officials, civil servants, politicians, policy makers, administrators, union and employer representatives were, in televised hearings, interrogated by the committee, chaired by Mr. Flip Buurmeijer (PvdA). When the committee published its findings in 1993, it publicly confirmed what was by now common knowledge, namely that the social partners had made 'very liberal use', if not misuse, of the disability scheme.

The portrayal of the roles of the Industry Insurance Associations and the tripartite Social Insurance Council was devastating. The commission found that yes, the IIAs had handled applications for benefits timely and correctly, but there was no trace of a moral commitment towards helping people to recover and return to the labour market. The explicit objective of disability legislation to encourage revalidation and labour market reintegration had almost entirely been discarded. The Industry Insurance Associations had no existential interest in getting people off welfare, since their organizational survival and growth correlated with the number of inactive citizens. Moreover, there was a blatant lack of transparency in medical assessments. The Buurmeijer committee highlighted how successive governments had condoned these practices. Cabinets choose to wait for advice from the social partners rather than take the initiative of their own accord.

Already in 1967 the Social Economic Council had been consulted for advice on the future organization of social security. After seventeen years (!) the SER finally issued its recommendations, reaffirming the status quo by claiming that the involvement of the social partners in the execution and supervision of social security was indispensable for the proper functioning of the Dutch welfare state. A lack of political resolve had allowed the social partners to effectively govern Dutch social insurance all by themselves. Since the government gave priority to achieve substantive goals in other policy domains, like continued wage restraint, the Ministry kept itself at a safe distance from the contentious issue of social policy reform. However, the Buurmeijer committee rightly pointed out that the Industry Insurance Associations had since 1976 formally come under the jurisdiction of public law. This meant that the Minister of Social Affairs had *de jure* instruments of supervision. However, the Ministry choose to 'steer from a distance' and respect what was historically appreciated as the 'primacy of industrial self-organization'. The Buurmeijer committee also reproached the passive and indecisive position of parliament in this policy domain.

The overall conclusion of the Buurmeijer committee, with respect to institutional structures, roles and responsibilities in the Dutch system of social security, was that:

> (...) for too long necessary changes have failed to materialize in social insurance (...) The commission is of the opinion that this is the result of de position of successive cabinets, parliament and the social partners and the manner in which these parties have held each other in a paralyzing grip. The process of consultation and decision-making between the parties has been inadequate (...).[25]

The committee's conclusions gained broad public and political support, which at long last gave a strong impetus drastic changes in the institutional makeup of the Dutch system of social security. The Buurmeijer committee advised the government that the implementation of social security legislation should be monitored by a government agency that could operate fully independently of the social partners and their bipartite Industrial Insurance Associations. It suggested to dispense with the wholly ineffective tripartite Social Insurance Council. In short, the Buurmeijer committee articulated a clear-cut desire for corporatist disengagement – a separation of responsibilities for implementation and supervision. The larger part of the broached path-breaking legislative and institutional changes were enacted by the incoming 'purple' coalition, which came to power in 1994.

THE PARADOX OF PURPLE

The elections of 1994 produced a shift in the Dutch political landscape of historical proportions (Koole, 1995). The new government, led by Mr. Wim Kok (PvdA) is based on a so-called 'purple' coalition, combining the red of the Social Democrats and the blue of the (conservative) Liberals (VVD), with the Democrats (D66) in between.

In the elections of 1994 the reigning coalition of CDA and PvdA lost a dramatic 32 seats, coming down from 103 to 71 seats out of a total of 150. No single Dutch coalition had ever lost so much electoral support in one election. The Social-Democrats (PvdA) lost a quarter of their voters and went from 31.9 to 24 percent of the vote, a loss of 12 seats in parliament. Without the popularity of Mr. Kok things might have been worse. The election results were even more a slap in the face of the Christian Democrats who lost a third of their electoral support; they went from 35.3 to 22.2 percent of the vote, losing 20 seats. The two liberal parties were the winners of the election; D66 leaped from 7.9 to 15.5 percent and the VVD from 14.6 to 20 percent of the vote. Despite this metamorphosis of the Dutch political landscape, there was no readily available new coalition. Because the CDA lost so much electoral support, the other loser, the Social Democrats became the largest party. A restored PvdA-CDA coalition was only possible with the help of D66, but that party did not want to join the two losers of the elections. For the same reason a CDA-VVD-D66 coalition was impossible. On the invitation of Mr. Hans van Mierlo, D66 leader, the historical opponents of the left and the right in Dutch politics, PvdA and VVD, reluctantly, decided to join forces with D66 to establish a government without the Christian Democrats. A near-century of confessional rule ended.

The 1994 elections were the elections of popular discontent. The Lubbers-Kok coalition had paid a high price for its bold politics of welfare retrenchment; it was effectively voted out of power. In agreement with the analysis of Pierson, discussed in Chapter Three, the elections revealed how extremely risky welfare retrenchment is, since it imposes, in the words of Pierson, 'tangible losses on concentrated groups of voters in return for diffuse and uncertain gains' (Pierson, 1996: 145). However, in spite of this important political lesson, the new 'purple' coalition did not in the least slow down the ongoing reform effort. To the contrary, the new Minister of Social Affairs and Employment, Mr. Ad Melkert (PvdA), and his Junior Minister State Secretary for social security, Mr. Robin Linschoten (VVD), effectively stepped up social policy reform. However, on the insistence of the PvdA, on one condition: the level and duration of social benefits would not be tampered with. Taking heed to the advice of the Buurmeijer committee, the 'purple' coalition essentially pursued two reform approaches. First, financial incentives and limited competition have been introduced into the system as a way to improve efficiency and curtail problems of moral hazard. Second, the government has begun with a reorganization of the roles and responsibilities of various policy actors in the execution and administration of the Dutch welfare state.

The reform of sickness insurance was implemented in two steps in 1994 and 1996 with remarkable little ado. Since 1994, employers rather than sectoral funds pay the first weeks of sick leave. From March 1996, employers are legally obliged to continue sick pay coverage to a maximum of twelve months in the event of sickness of an employee.[26] The benefits cover seventy percent of the last-earned wage, but most collective and individual agreements put employers under obligation to supplement benefits to hundred percent. Employers are free to choose private insurance against the risk of sickness of their workers. They must, however, contract an occupational health service. In effect, this implies the full privatization of sickness benefits insurance.

The cabinet has decided to introduce financial incentives for employers as a stimulus to combat absenteeism due to disability. In order to bring more market forces into the social security system and limit moral hazards, the system is open to private insurers, with some differentiation of premium payments between sectors or firms with high or low disability track records. The introduction of the premium differentiation in the Disability Insurance Act is expected to come into effect on 1 January 1998.[27] This is supposed to ensure that contributions match actuarial risks and allows firms to opt out of public insurance and choose freely among competing private insurers to cover their legally mandated disability liabilities over a five-year period. This means that a form of 'managed competition' inside the walls of the Dutch welfare state will be established.

Social policy reform of introducing financial incentives into the system of social insurance, supposedly encourages firms to take preventive measures, such as improved health and safety conditions, against the risks of sickness and disability absence. Furthermore, the introduction of managed competition is expected to guarantee more effective implementation, by introducing incentives for private insurers and public administrators to revalidate the sick and disabled. Most likely, stronger incentives in sickness and disability schemes will put more pressure on unemployment insurance. Stricter eligibility criteria for unemployment insurance go hand-in-hand with a shift to public assistance for many redundant workers. By the same token, the greater financial burdens associated with sickness and disability could easily result in a greater reluctance of employers to take on employees whom they think might develop work-related handicaps. Already there are signs that health conditions are an issue in selection and that people with health problems are discriminated against. A new law, however, has made it unlawful for employers to ask health related questions during job interviews and undertake non-work related medical tests. Still, the number of difficult-to-place job seekers will most likely increase.

In 1995, the government introduced a number of changes in the Unemployment Insurance Act. In order to qualify for a pay-related unemployment benefit, an applicant must have worked at least 26 weeks in the period of 39 weeks (compared with 12 months before) prior to his or her dismissal and at least four years (used to be three years) in the five-year period preceding the dismissal. People who meet only the first requirement will have a right to an unemployment benefit equivalent to seventy percent of the minimum wage for a maximum of six months. The 'activating' content of the unemployment insurance has been strengthened. Eligibility for unemployment insurance benefits has been made conditional upon the willingness of unemployed persons to accept job offers and participate in training programs.

In the public tiers of the Dutch social security system the government has continued to individualize social policy provisions, in accordance with changes in the labour market, family structure and life styles. The General Widows and Orphans Benefit Act has been replaced by the Survivors Dependents Act in 1996. Under this new Act future surviving dependents will only receive benefits if they are not able to provide an income for themselves: people with children under 18 years old, people unfit for work and the elderly. Benefits will be means-tested with the introduction of the new Act. A new Social Assistance Act came into effect on 1 January 1996. The new Law introduces an individualized system of benefits standards of three basic norms. Single persons receive fifty percent of the minimum net wage, single parents seventy, and (married) couples hundred percent. Single persons and single parents are eligible for an additional payments by municipal social services if the norm is inadequate to provide for minimum subsistence. The new legislation also included an 'activation obligation', which stipulates that anyone who receives income support, except for single parents with children under five years of age and unemployed persons aged 57.5 and older, in principle must be available for work. In addition, the new Social Assistance Act gives local authorities more responsibility in implementing and enforcing income support. The revised act also specifies that municipalities and regional Public Employment Offices must cooperate more closely in order to facilitate their return to the active labour market of claimants.

It is still too early to evaluate the effects of the recent reforms. Whether social policy reform under the purple coalition has directly contributed to the observed drop in social security expenditure and the decline in the number of recipients remains controversial. Yet, a number of positive developments stand out. Social security spending has come down and the total number of people dependent on welfare has decreased from a peak of 925,000 in 1994 to 841,000 in 1995, reflecting a fall in inflow and a stronger outflow. Sickness absence has declined. Unemployment continues to decrease and even long-term unemployment is beginning to come down. Against the background of strong job growth, the I/A ratio has dropped from 82,3 in 1995 to 78,8 in 1997. This has allowed a fortunate purple coalition to restore the net linking of the minimum wage and social benefits to real wage increases.

It is very difficult, of course, to suspend a ninety-years old policy legacy of bipartite social security administration. Even without Christian Democrats, the ardent defenders of subsidiarity and bipartite sovereignty in social policy implementation, in power, corporatist disengagement proved a hazardous political enterprise. The Buurmeijer committee had advised to make a break with the legacy of bipartite social security administration and replace the tripartite Social Insurance Council by a new board, run independently of the social partners and the institutions they control. Over the long term, the committee envisaged to replace the Industry Insurance Associations with regional administrative bodies which should closely work together with Public Employment Offices in order to integrate policies of income replacement with active labour market policies, an idea which was also advocated by the OECD. This novel institutional set-up would establish a 'one-counter approach', combining the granting of benefits with schooling, training and job-searching activities.

The purple coalition largely endorsed the recommendations of the Buurmeijer committee over institutional reform. In 1994, the cabinet decided to amend the Social Insurance Organization Act of 1953 and make way for independent supervision. In 1995, the Social Insurance Council was replaced by two new bodies. The Council's supervisory responsibilities were placed in the hands of a new Supervisory Board, the *College van Toezicht Sociale Verzekeringen* (CTSV), with three independent government-appointed members and no ties to employers or trade union interests. The CTSV is assigned to control and supervise the ninety billion Dutch guilders spent each year on social security. The establishment of the CTSV must be understood as an attempt to restore the 'primacy of politics' and curtail the 'primacy of industrial self-organization' in the area of social security. The Social Insurance Council's coordinating tasks have been placed into the hands of a temporary institute with representatives of labour and management under an independent chairman. This institute, to which Buurmeijer was appointed chairman, played an important role in the preparation of a new institutional framework of Dutch social security, in which the IIA's would play a more submissive role. In 1997 a revised new Organization of Social Security Act (nOSV) was introduced to prepare for the introduction of market incentives in the implementation of social security legislation and in March 1997 the temporary institute was replaced by a more permanent coordinating tripartite body, named the National Social Insurance Institute (*Landelijk Insitituut Social Verzekeringen*, LISV). The board of the LISV contains independent members, employers' representatives and trade union representatives, and is headed by a government appointed chairman. The LISV sets the yearly premiums for the different social security schemes. Some thirty sector councils, made up of employers' and trade union representatives, will assist and advise the LISV with respect to social security governance in the different branches of industry. Supervision is assigned to the CTSV. The LISV will subcontract the actual administration of social security implementation to private, publicly recognized, agencies. Currently four such agencies have obtained a license. The government is preparing a full-scale revision of the Social Security Organization Act, which is expected to go into effect in the year 2000.

The appointment of three political administrators in the CTSV caused a stir in the politics of Dutch social security reform. In order as to restore the 'primacy of politics', Mr. Linschoten nominated three party politicians, without ties or understanding of the complexities of Dutch social policy, to supervise the former employees of the Social Insurance Council. Hated by their staff and ridiculed by the policy makers in field, because of their blatant lack of expertise, the CTSV supervisors headed straight for disaster. Within a year, the board was forced to hand in its dismissal. A parliamentary inquiry looking into the controversy criticized the 'staggering simplistic' procedures which Mr. Linschoten had used in selecting the CTSV-board and made his political position untenable. From its inception, employment and social security was considered the 'litmus test' of the purple adventure. In its policy memorandum of 1994, the Kok administration committed itself to creating 350.000 jobs during its tenure. As early as 1997, a year ahead of time, this target was reached. For 1996 and 1997, the government was able to restore 'net linking' of the minimum wage and social benefits. The trade-off of volume against income seemed to be bearing fruit. Notwithstanding these successes, the CTSV-controversy has revealed that institutional reform remains a politically risky and uncertain exercise.

CONCLUSION

Welfare reform is difficult, but possible, as the Dutch experience shows. It involves cumbersome, uncertain and politically risky processes of renegotiation over guaranteed social rights. As elsewhere, welfare state reform over the past two decades has revolved around two dimensions. First, there is a distributive element of freezes and cuts of benefits and the introduction of tighter – more provisional and selective – eligibility criteria, together with the use of financial incentives. Second, such distributive changes, are often accompanied by changes in the rules-of-the-game of social policy making, administration and implementation.

Welfare reform in the Netherlands went the whole cycle from distributive tinkering to institutional reform, with both incremental and more disjointed changes. There was no 'master plan' and at many times politicians suggested – and hoped – that the finish had been reached, before discovering that new problems demanded another round of painful changes. Learning, in this case, was very much a puzzling process in which all major political parties participated and, ultimately, claimed their primacy over the organized interest groups.

In the policy domain of external adjustment, analyzed in Chapter Five, we portrayed Dutch trade union movement as the principal learning actor, in coming to grips with the new realities of the political economy in the 1980s. In this chapter, state actors play the leading part. This should come as no surprise, as it is the political community who defines the manner and extent to which social rights protect the aged, the sick, the destitute and the unemployed by providing them with politically defined sources of income so as to enable these non-working citizens to make ends meet without necessarily relying on their poor labour market chances (Marshall, 1963; Esping-Andersen, 1990). Because social rights are designed to materially substantiate the life chances of citizens, they compel the political community to modify the distributive consequences of market processes. As a consequence, any standard of social rights is inherently subject to both upward and downward adjustment, depending as much on political commitments as on the contingencies of economic performance.

The process of social learning over social policy commitments in the face of intensifying economic constraints can be described in a number of stages, moving from incoherent cuts and redefining eligibility criteria towards more fundamental changes in the incentive structure of provisions and reforms of the larger institutional design of the welfare state. In the 1990s, with the important political support of the party which could claim the closest ideological ties with the welfare state and with the unions, the crisis of social security was redefined into a crisis of governability, hence legitimizing a new *Ordnungspolitik*, a major reform of the institutional makeup and incentive structure of social security. At the time when the purple coalition was formed, it was well understood that there was a clear need to restore the shadow of hierarchy over the bipartite corporatist organization of Dutch social security. This was probably all the more necessary because market signals are inherently weak in the area of protected social rights.

Notes

1   4 September 1990, opening address for the 1990-91 academic year at the University of Nijmegen

2   *Financial Times*, 1 November 1977.

3   OECD, *Historical Statistics 1960-1988*, Paris, 1990.

4   *The Economist*, 30 January 1982.

5   When in the mid-1950s the economy had surpassed its prewar level, industry was back on its feet and unemployment had fallen to less than three percent, the KVP's leadership began to make noises, on grounds of its subsidiary doctrine, that price and wage policy should once again be left to the free deliberations of employers and unions, a view which soon gained support from the large companies (see Windmuller 1969).

6   SZW, *Financiële Nota Sociale Zekerheid 1987*, The Hague, annually published with the budget; and OECD, *Economic Survey of the Netherlands 1996*, Paris 1996, p. 41, Table 3.

7   Own calculations on the basis of the SZW and OECD figures mentioned above.

8   Initially, the statutory wage had been fixed at or near the level of the lowest scales (for unskilled and inexperienced workers) in collective agreements, in order to prevent the need for a wage rise in structurally weak sectors.

9   The value of gas output quadrupled as a consequence of the 1973 price hike in oil prices and went up from 1.2 percent of GDP in 1970 to 5 percent in 1977 and 7 percent in 1980. By that time, 60 percent was converted into government income; and the gas resources represented 15 percent of total government revenue (OECD, *Economic Survey of the Netherlands 1986*, Paris 1986).

10   SZW, *Financiële Nota Sociale Zekerheid 1987*.

11   Ministry of Finance, *Budget 1975*, The Hague: Staatsuitgeverij 1974, 3; the exclamation marks are ours.

12   *Wet aanpassingsmechanismen* (WAM, 1980). As a result of the suspension of the linking mechanism and the three percent cut in 1984, the gap between average earnings of an employed worker and a worker on benefits has increased by some 12 percent between 1983 and 1989.

13   Interview with *de Volkskrant*, of 9 December 1983.

14   J. de Koning, 'De duizend handen van de markt', interview with *de Volkskrant*, reproduced in P. Broertjes, *Getto's in Nederland*, Amsterdam: van Gennep, 1989, 101-108, cited p. 104. In the same interview Mr. de Koning speculates whether a ten percent, rather than three percent cut in civil servants pay and social benefits – as preferred by his colleague and party rival at Finance, Mr. Onno Ruding – would have been better. In his assessment, written with hindsight, the risks would have been too large.

15   Already in 1967, the Social Economic Council (SER) had been asked to advise over a new organisation structure of Dutch social security. Because SER-advice was found wanting, in 1976 the so-called Lamers-committee, with only civil servants, was established. In 1979 this committee recommended the foundation of an independent supervisory board together with a regionalization of social security implementation—the old alternative, already in debate before the First World War. The social partners subsequently opposed the recommendation of the Lamers committee, since it contravened the principle of 'functional decentralisation'.

16   *Nieuwe werkloosheidswet*, NWW 1987. If benefits under the insurance system are exhausted and unemployment continues, a means-tested benefit, not related to previous earnings, applies. However, an interim benefit, depending on age and work experience, cushions older workers with longer work records from too sharp a fall in income. During the interim-period of up to two years the benefit will be lowered in equal half-yearly steps until (in the case of a single person) the minimum of 70 percent of the statutory minimum wage is reached. Eligibility for extended benefits is only granted to workers with at least three years of employment in the previous five years. Once the earnings-related benefit has expired, workers may be entitled to a welfare-based, not means-tested, unemployment benefit, again contingent on three years of employment in the previous five years, for a maximum of 12 months. Finally, active measures for schooling, with tougher sanctions, are introduced. Recipients must register at the Regional Employment Office and be available for work. Benefits can be reduced or suspended if recipients do not actively seek employment.

17   In 1985 workers under the age of 22 had already been excluded from unemployment relief and could no longer claim benefits for longer than half a year. On the other hand, from 1984 unemployed workers of $57\,^1/_2$ and older were no longer obliged to register for job search, while they were granted a special arrangement until the legal retirement age of 65.

18   *Wet Koppeling met Afwijkingsmogelijkheid* (WKA, 1992).

19   *Wet Terugdringing Arbeidsongeschiktheidsvolume* (TAV, 1992)

20   A recent court order has forced the government to withdraw this element. The judges reasoned that given the lack of distinction between *risque professionel* and *risque social* in Dutch law, the employer has too little control over the cause of disability and therefore cannot be held responsible for a higher than normal rate of disability. With the introduction of the Penalty Abolition and Reintegration Policy Promotion Act (*Afschaffing Malus en Bevordering Reïntegratie*, AMBER) in 1996, the 1992 'malus'-penalty in the disability scheme was abolished and the bonus-element reinforced.

21   *Wet Terugdringing Beroep op Arbeidsongeschiktheidsregelingen* (TBA, 1993).

22   In 1993, the first round of re-examination concerned 43,300 beneficiaries of less than 35 years of age. Little over fifty percent maintained their benefit; eighteen percent had their benefit reduced; nearly thirty percent lost their benefit; only two percent had their benefit increased.

23   *Wetsvoorstel Terugdringing Ziekteverzuim* (TZ, 1992).

24   From 6.2 to 4.9 percent without leave due to pregnancy. In 1994, benefit termination due to recovery, being found fit to work, increased by about 40 percent. The number benefits awarded receded by 15 percent, for private sector employees the number went down by even 25 percent. Days lost due to sickness spells dropped by 15 percent.

25   'Parlementaire enquête Uitvoeringsorganen sociale verzekeringen', Rapport enquêtecommissie (samenvatting), 1993, p. 75.

26   *Wet Uitbreiding Loondoorbetalingsverplichting bij Ziekte* (WULBZ, 1996). The basic policy conditions are still laid down by law.

27   *Premiedifferentiatie en Marktwerking bij de Arbeidsongeschiktheidsregelingen* (PEMBA, 1998).

Chapter Seven

Truncated Corporatism:
The Crooked Path towards an Active Labour
Market Policy

A RECOGNITION FAILURE

THE STATUS OF LABOUR MARKET POLICIES differs greatly between highly advanced welfare states. The Scandinavian welfare state is well-known for its strong emphasis on active labour market policy. In the word of Esping-Andersen, in the Scandinavian model, 'the right to work has equal status to the right of income protection' (1990: 28). By contrast, the continental welfare states have placed 'welfare before work'. While historically lacking an active labour market policy legacy, we have argued in the last two chapters, that the traditional passive character of Dutch social and economic policy is slowly giving way to activating measures. The regained confidence in corporatist adjustment strategies together with hard won social security reform, has led to a new definition of the problems of the Dutch welfare state. From the mid-1980s onwards, politicians, policy-makers, the social partners, and the larger public alike, came to realize that the low level of labour market participation was really the Achilles' heel of the Dutch welfare state. The current purple coalition is determined to create 'jobs, jobs, and more jobs'. Notably, the Social Democratic Minister of Social Affairs and Employment, Mr. Ad Melkert, champions the boosting of the 'activating' content of social policy combined with all kinds of job creation programs for youths and the long-term unemployed. Is the time finally ripe for an active labour market policy commitment in the Netherlands?

In his biting critique of the Dutch employment performance in the 1980s, Göran Therborn's main point had been that the Netherlands lacked an institutional commitment to a full employment and active labour market policy. He gave three examples to illustrate his thesis. First, the Manpower or Public Employment Service (PES, in Dutch *Arbeidsvoorzieniging*) was part of a bureaucracy, the Ministry of Social Affairs, whose main preoccupation was with social security and welfare provision. Other public employment services, embedded in the world of business and labour, and with a status of their own, were lacking. Second, the PES had no independent source of revenue to spend money on employment creation, competence training, or any active labour market policy. Available funds tended to depend upon and be subordinated to the costs of social security. If the latter rose, as they did, the former had to decline. Therborn's third and most captivating observation regarded the passive role of the state, demonstrated by a lack of commitment, authority and resources in the labour market policy domain.

By borrowing a concept which Gunnar Myrdal used in his *Asian Dilemma* with regard to Indian (under-)development, Therborn summed it all up with the qualification of a 'soft state', a state in which public authorities remain passive and ineffective with respect to the organization of society. In combination with the tendency of the Dutch welfare state to concentrate on measures compensating the loss of income caused by unemployment or want, this had turned the Netherlands into a 'soft welfare state' which, paradoxically and unintentionally, had given rise to the harsh reality of an underclass of long-term unemployed and unemployable workers who have become entirely dependent on the continued generosity of their fellow citizens. A 'strong welfare state', Therborn explains, is a state which is not just generous, but also capable of intervening in the economy and labour market in order to maintain and enhance employment.

Therborn's incisive critique did not draw much attention of the Dutch policy elite until in December 1988 when, in a public lecture, he added that a 'soft welfare state', with its neglect of the problem of persistent unemployment, tends to produce 'ghetto's' of people with dismal life chances and that the first signs of ghetto-ization were already visible in the larger Dutch cities, not least in connection with the racial concentration of long-term unemployment.[1] Around the same time, a research team led by another major sociologist, Kees Schuyt, published an important empirical study in which it was shown that in some cities true 'cultures of unemployment' had developed.[2]

Amidst various excuses that things were not much better in other countries, that Sweden had its own problems, that nobody could have foreseen the unemployment catastrophe, and that the employment gap had been larger in the Netherlands because of the extra influx of women into the labour market, assorted politicians did admit that 'Therborn is right in saying that the Netherlands never had an active labour market policy' (Mr. Marcel van Dam, PvdA, Minister of Housing in two cabinets and confidant of Labour leader Den Uyl), that 'we remained passive when it went wrong' (Mr. Wil Albeda, CDA, Minister of Social Affairs between 1977 and 1981), and 'have waited unnecessary long with the development of a labour market policy' (Mr. Koos Andriessen, chairman of the Christian employers and Minister of Economic Affairs from 1989 to 1994).[3] The Prime Minister, Mr. Lubbers, announcing his decision to seek a new term of office, admitted that 'we, I myself, have underestimated the nature and persistency of the unemployment problem'.[4] Most surprising, perhaps, was the 'mea culpa' of Mr F. Kruse, the Director-General in the Ministry of Social Affairs and the highest civil servant with responsibility for the Public Employment Service, who in a direct reply to Therborn agreed with most of the critique and confessed that 'with hindsight, we can say to have probably made the wrong choices' and conducted an 'inconsistent labour market policy, with patchwork measures based on ad hoc recipes and changing beliefs of various economic prophets', with wage moderation and lowering of the public debt as the only constants.[5]

It is not clear whether these events mark the turning point in the thinking about unemployment, inactivity and labour market policy. The fact of the matter is that between 1987 and 1991 a major change in thinking did take place, which led to new approaches, in terms of instruments, objectives and institutions. A reform of the public employment service was already under-way, after years of preparation and infighting, and in 1991 the new employment service was to function at arm's length from the Ministry, with direct involvement of unions and employers under a tripartite governing board, and with regional articulation. In 1987 the Scientific Council of Government Policy had already published a report on 'Active Labour Market Policy' in which it had recommended various aspects of the Swedish model, but the report that attracted real public attention, and helped to politicize the issue, was published three years later, also by the Council, under the title 'A Working Perspective'.[6] In this report the simple point was made that policy makers should not only or even in the first place look at unemployment, but at the net participation or the employment/population ratio. If they did, they would discover that over the past decades the rate had declined despite the increasing number of women who had entered the labour market, and that the Netherlands did worse than many other countries, in particular in comparison with the Anglo-Saxon and Scandinavian nations. In other words, policy makers had few reasons to be complacent, even if the official unemployment was decreasing. The low employment/population rate would erode the basis of the extensive and generous welfare state which the Netherlands still was, among other things by the perverse mechanism of 'welfare without work' which was later so well described by another Scandinavian academic, Gösta Esping-Andersen, in *Welfare States in Transition* (1996).

This new analysis of the inactivity bias in the Dutch welfare state had a perfect timing. With the disability crisis on their hands, policy makers needed all the academic and moral support they could get for making extremely unpleasant decisions. The new analysis provided one. In essence its story went like this: if we do not intervene now, reverse the dependence on welfare and get people back to work, there will be no welfare state to speak of in the near future. At the same time, it became apparent, especially among the battered Social Democrats in the government, that only if 'jobs, jobs, and more jobs' were created, the political fall-out of a strategy of stern welfare retrenchment could be minimized. This, finally, would become the credo of the 1990s, in particular of the new purple coalition, led by Mr. Wim Kok (1994-). The problem of missing instruments and failing institutions for an activating labour market policy would now gain a high place on the political agenda.

At first sight, the characterization of the Netherlands as a 'soft state' may seem odd or even out of place. Had the Dutch state not conducted – longer than any other industrialized market economy – a centrally guided wage policy? In Chapter Five we have seen that the particular societal conditions that made state guidance in wage determination policies possible were no longer available in the 1960s, that it took more than fifteen years before a new consensus emerged and that only when the state got control over its own finances it was again able to cast an effective 'shadow of hierarchy' over the bargaining table. A strong state need not be a large state. A restricted state, which carries out all the functions needed to secure basic public order, may well rate as a strong state precisely because it tries not to do 'too much' (Crouch, 1986: 181). From this angle, a soft state is a state which behaves passively in an environment of strong internal and external influences, and, therefore, has no capacity for *Ordnungspolitik*, a policy of institutional design, for instance, to commit itself and organize functional interests to an active labour market policy.

Yet, Therborn was right; in the domain of labour market policy the Dutch state was 'soft', that is, passive, behind-the-times and unable to organize or mobilize societal forces for a new approach to labour market policy (see also Braun, 1988). This in fact has a long tradition in the Netherlands; as we will show below. There had not been much of a labour market policy before 1940 (de Rooy, 1979), but that was hardly exceptional compared to other democratic capitalist countries before the war, except Sweden (Weir, 1992; King, 1995). Moreover, the successful policy of external adjustment, which produced two decades of nearly uninterrupted growth of income, productivity and employment after the war, and very low levels of unemployment indeed, did suggest that a specific labour market policy was not really needed. Occasionally, this assumption had been criticized. The OECD voiced its criticism in a report in which it praised the wage policy but criticized the absence of a coherent labour market policy in 1967.[7] But these voices were hardly heard, even though the shortage of labour and cost push inflation in the 1960s suggested that all was not well. It is curious that the subsidized emigration to Canada, New Zealand, Australia and South Africa of 100,000 Dutch people, only a few years before there was a shortage of labour and major companies went to North Africa and Turkey to import cheap labour, has never been a matter of evaluation of Dutch labour market policy at the time. By the end of the 1960s the idea was that the problem of unemployment had been solved, or if not, that it could be solved quite easily with sufficient political will and the right mix of fiscal, budgetary and wage policies affecting labour demand. There seemed little need for specific and costly policies of improving the matching of supply and demand, redeployment of redundant workers, or competence training, beyond some general policies of education, information and advice.

The recurrent theme in interviews with policy makers of the 1970s and 1980s is that the 1973 recession and its consequences took them by surprise (Heertje en van der Kolk, 1982). It was simply thought impossible that the ghost of the 1930s would return and we would experience a new period of mass unemployment. At first, the crisis was believed temporary, bad but temporary. The best thing would be to create extra jobs in the public sector and this, indeed, has been the first response. The fact that this was a different crisis, and that unemployment was there to stay, took a long time to be recognized. Mr. Wim Kok, chairman of the major trade union federation from 1973 to 1985, is on record that it took him and his fellow unionists up to 1980 to realize how destitute the unemployment problem actually was. Mr. Albeda, Social Affairs minister at the time, explains that in the 1970s nobody knew what an effective employment policy should look like. To stimulate the demand for labour through expansion of the public sector, the traditional response of the 1970s, seemed the best thing to do.[8]

RECEDING TARGETS

In a study of public labour market policies in the Netherlands between 1970 and 1982, Maarse (1984) has documented the gradual retreat of Dutch employment policies. Three broad conclusions are possible. With the rise in unemployment the targets slowly recede. In the 1960s an unemployment rate of 1 to 1.5 percent had been considered unavoidable 'friction' unemployment and the problem seemed to be that unemployment was often lower. In 1972, when unemployment is on the rise, the government accepts 2.5 percent as a tolerable level of unemployment; in its first budget, for 1974, the Den Uyl government considers 3 percent unavoidable, but soon the tone becomes more pessimistic and in 1976 the target is 150,000, 4-5 percent, to be attained in 1980 through many special measures; this figure is repeated in 'Compass 1981', the austerity program announced by the Van Agt government in 1978. The employment plan for 1982, written under the responsibility of Den Uyl during his brief fling as a Minister of Social Affairs and Employment, does not mention any target, but aims at creating 175,000 to 200,000 full-time, and an equal number of part-time jobs between 1982 and 1985. In reality, unemployment had surpassed the 500,000 mark by the end of 1980 and in the next three years 300,000 full-time jobs disappeared. In 1984 prime minister Lubbers announced that he would resign if unemployment exceeded the one million mark!

The second conclusion is that in the early 1970s active policies are mainly focused on the demand side, and particularly on job creation with public support in labour intensive sectors such as public infrastructure and construction and on job preservation through subsidies to ailing firms or sectors. Between 1972 and 1977 alone there were eleven such programs, many with special at-

Figure 11: Unemployment rates, 1945-1996

percentage of labour force

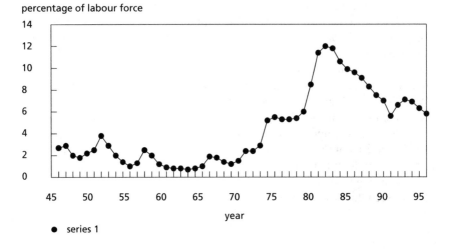

year

● series 1

Standardized rates.
Source: OECD.

tention to particular regions, adding up to a total cost of 11 billion guilder, of which 6.6 billion was in the budget of Social Affairs (Maarse, 1984: 99). Most of this is financed on a temporary basis. In the next two cabinets, in fact until the demise of Den Uyl's employment plan for 1982 and the fall of the second Van Agt cabinet because of the lack of political and financial support for that plan, this policy is continued, although after 1976 the financial resources for these demand stimulating policies no longer increase in real terms. After 1982, when the austerity coalition of Lubbers takes office, these policies of job creation in the public sector and aid to firms in financial difficulties are reduced and by 1985 they are abandoned.[9] Wage subsidies and additional employment programs make way for (re)training and education; new programs for handicapped workers are introduced, together with local initiatives for the young unemployed.

A third conclusion is that policies become ever more selective, targeting specific groups and dealing with the social and economic consequences rather than with the causes of unemployment. This conclusion squares with the passive bias in Dutch social policies discussed in the previous chapter. In its 1996 survey the OECD notes that financial incentives for active job search in the Netherlands have been particularly weak and that only in the 1990s the balance has shifted. In 1983, 95 percent of all the money spent on labour market policy is spent on measures to compensate income losses caused by unemployment, compared to 80 percent in Austria, 50 percent in Norway and only 20 percent in Sweden (Allaart 1988). This may have been the worst year, but even in 1990 still only 15 percent was spent on active policies of schooling and (re)training, wage subsidies, public works, and so on.

A DORMANT STATE MONOPOLY

The historical origins of Dutch labour market policy go back to the establishment of the first local public placement office in Schiedam in 1902. In 1914, a special State Committee on Unemployment, inaugurated in 1909, advised the government to give financial support to the growing number of local placement offices. Both the large unemployment explosions, one in 1917-18 and the other after 1929, led to a wave of local and private initiatives, to which a government more interested in upholding the value of the guilder and austerity, applied a strategy of control through lean subsidies (de Rooy, 1979). Unemployment insurance is mainly a private affair, organized by the unions, but is from 1917 on subsidized, usually at a rate of 100 percent subsidy on subscriptions, following the Danish model. This system disappears during war-time and does not return (see Chapter Six).

In 1917, fear of class conflict plays in the hands of reformers who succeed in stepping up government regulation through the establishment of a central department for unemployment insurance and labour exchange. With the integration of public placement activities and unemployment insurance, local labour exchanges loose part of their prior political importance. The right to unemployment relief is made contingent on obligatory registration at local placement offices. Increased public intervention reaches its pre-war apex with the introduction of the 1930 Labour Exchange Act. This Act established a public monopoly on labour exchange and placement activities. Private exchange and placement offices are banned and public employment offices set up. This government monopoly has remained intact until the new Public Employment Service Act of 1991, although from 1965 there was a slight opening up with the permission, under strict regulation, of licensed private labour exchange and temporary work agencies. Until 1940 labour market policy – if that term is applicable at all – is mainly a local affair, with increasing national regulation. During the occupation, the Employment Service is centralized and streamlined for the purpose of the German war effort and *Arbeitseinsatz* in Germany. This centralization is not reversed in 1945 (Van Bekkum, 1996).

The Extraordinary Decree on Industrial Relations of 1945, which was intended as a temporary measure but shaped postwar industrial relations and employment law for a very long time, determined that workers and employers had to ask permission to terminate any employment contract (Windmuller, 1969). Today, the Netherlands is among the few countries with has kept preventive dismissal control on the statute book, even though procedures have been shortened and the possibility of temporary contracts widened. Termination of a contract requires prior authorization from the director of the Regional Employment Office; dismissals without such authorization are void, but are likely to be granted for reasons of workers incapacity, redundancy or other 'substantial' causes. Special protection applies to special groups, for instance pregnant women, absentee workers due to illness, and members of work councils. Prior to the 1994 election it had been the government's intention to cancel preventive control on the grounds that existing procedures were cumbersome, costly, over-protective and inhibiting flexibility. It was also on the list of suspects of the OECD Job's Study and of the OECD's specific recommendations to the Dutch government.[10] In response to strong opposition by the unions, the Kok government (1994-) has dropped these plans and settled for a number of reforms which reduce the length of procedures and introduce more flexibility. In recent years, employers and workers have made greater use of voluntary termination of contracts, arranged before the lower district courts, usually with severance payment of one month salary for every year worked. In the case of collective dismissals, under Dutch and European law, the role of work councils, trade unions and the regional employment offices is spelled out in great detail, and involves notification, consideration of less harmful alternatives and, if unavoidable, the negotiation of a social plan (Visser, 1995).

In 1945 the tasks of the Regional Employment Offices were extended to advise on schooling and emigration, and, from 1948, the placement of partially handicapped workers in sheltered workplaces. With these new tasks the regional offices were transformed from a labour exchange to an administrative employment service. In later years, the social partners regained some of the influence they had lost in the 1940s. But, unlike their privileged status in social security administration, their role remained perfunctory. The service was run in a highly centralized and bureaucratic fashion from The Hague. All its activities were an appendix to the policy of external adjustment and continued wage moderation (Kruse 1987: 28). Between the early 1950s and 1991 the administrative structure, with provincial and regional offices under a central Directorate General in the Ministry of Social Affairs, hardly changed.

The central service is best described as a dormant state monopoly. In 1964 and 1967, the OECD criticized the Netherlands for its immanently 'passive' labour market policy stance. Under conditions of full employment, halfway through the 1960s, the service seemed redundant. Of course it could not be abolished or handed back to the market; as a member of the International Labour Organisation (ILO), the Netherlands is obliged to maintain a public employment service.[11] Until around 1970 the political interest in the operation of this service remains very limited. The service itself concentrates on its administrative tasks (registration of unemployed workers for social security purposes, and handling dismissal requests). In the margin, it develops informational activities for occupational choice, but most of its contacts are with people who need help because of a handicap, recurrent or persistent unemployment.

Until the first signs of the return of unemployment, the Public Employment Service operates on the sidelines of the Dutch political economy. In their 1964 memorandum the OECD Ministers stress the need for a more active approach to labour market allocation and better coordination between related policy domains of education, industrial relations, and social security. Priority should be given to improving the information function and to lowering regional and friction unemployment, and to preventive measures. This implies more emphasis on information, competence training, education and raising the quality of human capital. As a consequence, the Public Employment Service should not merely concentrate on marginal sectors and categories of workers with a weak position in the labour market.[12] This was a general study, not particularly addressed to the Netherlands and could thus be ignored. But soon after, the organization started a series of country studies and in 1967 the OECD published a detailed study of the Dutch labour market and manpower policies.[13] The Paris club is positive with respect to the regional articulation of the Dutch Public Employment Service, the consensual system of industrial relations, and the complementary employment programs offering additional and sheltered jobs to handicapped workers (Van der Veen, Hemerijck, and Burger, 1995). However, the report is very critical with respect to the lack of coordination between labour market policy and other social and economic policy domains. Moreover, it finds inspiration and vision with respect to the importance of training and education in preventing unemployment wanting. The OECD is critical of the organization of the PES and its failure to set the agenda for an active labour market policy.

Since the conclusions of the OECD were not overly negative, Dutch policy makers hardly took notice. However, the three cooperating Trade Union Confederations used the report to raise the issue in the Social Economic Council (SER) and characterized existing policies as 'patchwork'. The following year, the SER takes up the issue and publishes a rapport which underscores the negative image which both employers and unions have of the Public Employment Service. The Service seems to be involved only in the administrative handling and placement of the unemployed. The dual function of the local labour office, as registration office for the unemployed and as labour exchange for workers who want to change jobs or employers who look for staff, does not go well together. In practice, this means that workers who do have jobs avoid the office, and so do employers. Less than fifteen percent of all job changes are in fact handled through the service, although at this time the Extraordinary Decree of 1945 still stands and requires prior permission for termination of contracts from the Director of the Regional Employment Service. The SER suggests that this requirement should be dropped. It also suggests that the employment offices should no longer be involved in social security administration and that the registration requirement for unemployed workers should be replaced with the requirement that benefit claimants actively seek work. Finally, the employment offices should also become more outward oriented and seek cooperation with firms, other public agencies, unions and regional centres for vocational training and education.

The advice is written against the background of the tight labour market of the late 1960s. The existing PES seems completely redundant in dealing with job search for workers with jobs. Cost push inflation and lower growth rates do however suggest that the Dutch labour market needs improvement. The political response is tepid but typical. The involvement of the social partners is welcomed and officially recognized by the establishment of a special SER commission, ex. article 43 of the 1950 Industrial Organization Act, which gives the new commission the prerogative to give direct advice to the government and other relevant policy actors. This new *Labour Market Council*, with 39 members from the employers' organizations, unions and crown members, is inaugurated in 1969. Initially, the expectation is that the council will help to overcome the fragmentation of policies and rivalry between the various Ministries, and make the employment service more effective in the field. For this purpose regional councils are established. This initiative never was to bear fruit. The resurgence of unemployment and the experience of immobile corporatism in the 1970s, undermined this early effort at tripartization (Van Bekkum, 1997). We must wait for the early 1980s before another initiative towards the building of a tripartite, corporatist framework for labour market policy does take root. In response to unemployment and the first large-scale initiative to create jobs in the public sector, the central office of the PES frustrates any attempt at tripartization. Instead, it sees a chance to create a more prominent role for itself, fighting it out with Economic Affairs and Education. It fails predictably and leaves behind a battered service (van Voorden, 1975; Kruse, 1987).[14]

In the meantime, the local labour offices try to improve their services (Rigter et al, 1995: 394). Initially the idea seems to have been to restructure both the internal and external positioning of the local office, with more coordination with social security agencies, and a separation of the various functions and groups served by these offices, showing in the physical outlay. This attempt at renovation is smothered by the unemployment crisis of the 1970s and the resistance of the social partners to finance joint activities. The 'new style labour office' initiative starts in 1973 with four experiments. These experiments were hardly successful, but served to prove how difficult it really is to integrate labour market policy and social security administration. They showed that compartmentalization reigned at all levels of government. There are doubts all around but the operation is nonetheless continued, with some delay. From 1979 to 1985 all labour offices are refurbished according to the 'new style' model. In reality, the operation is tuned down to not much more than an internal reorganization and facelift. The other elements of the 1969 SER advice are not heeded: the PES remains responsible for dismissal regulation and unemployment registration. The objective of creating a more market oriented, outward orientation of the service, is by and large unsuccessful.

The service hardly takes initiatives and is still everybody's laughing stock.

The 'new style' operation was launched against the background of preparing the service for new tasks in a tight and increasingly complex labour market. When the operation was finally on its way, unemployment had risen to five percent. From the mid-1970s the problems of rising long-term unemployment for older and unskilled workers, a shortage of jobs and traineeships for school-leavers and a shortage of skilled workers to fill job vacancies existed side by side, and on all three counts the PES continued to receive bad notes. Local employment offices are overwhelmed by the new influx of unemployed whom they can hardly help. The administrative task of registration of the unemployed appears to beguile all other activities of the office, who fall victim of a negative cycle of poor performance. The perception that the labour offices are receptacles with card-boxes of unattractive vacancies and unemployable people is reinforced and leads to further stigmatization of its clients and frustration of its staff.

In the late 1970s, in the face of rapidly increasing unemployment, it becomes clear that the PES is not up to its task. The service is particularly unpopular with employers. If they have vacancies they really want to fill, the labour offices are the last place to turn to. The local offices are seen as reservoirs of hopeless cases; increasingly employers make use of temporary job agencies. In response to regional unemployment, concentrated in the Northern provinces, the older industrial areas at the Eastern and Southern borders, and increasingly in the major cities, local authorities, faced with the disintegrating social consequences of rising unemployment, also raise their voices. The local services continue their attempt to improve their image and become more client-oriented. In 1979 the Public Employment Service receives permission to set up its own temporary job agency, called 'Start'. This venture is very successful, and 'Start' has become one of the big players in this vastly expanded business. It is run independently from the PES, although its offices are often located in or near the same building. But the problem is not just a matter of internal organization and physical appearance. In a report on active labour market policy, published in 1987, the Scientific Council for Government Policy (WRR) highlights the extent to which employment offices have, under conditions of rising unemployment, been confronted with strain and work overload and poor quality of staff. The WRR estimates that only sixty percent of the registered unemployed in the polluted files of the PES can be considered effective labour supply. Furthermore, the absence of a sectoral orientation and the great emphasis on finding regular work with open ended employment contracts rather than temporary and flexible work leads to inadequate handling of clients.[15] In agreement with the SER advice from 1969, the WRR explicitly criticizes the fact that the local employment offices are only focused on unemployed workers and appear to have nothing to offer to employed workers who want to change jobs.

TOWARDS A TRIPARTITE SOLUTION

Around 1980 the idea is revived to involve the social partners in more direct ways with the operation of the Public Employment Service. One background factor is that unions and employers increasingly negotiate over employment and training in their regular collective bargaining, and have come to realize the need of an effective employment service. The idea is picked up by the Social Affairs minister, Mr. Albeda, who agrees with the social partners that the Public Employment Service has lost its link with the reality of labour markets. The Minister realizes that the 'new style' operation is not enough and that the legal framework in which the PES operates has become a dead weight. Both the Labour Exchange Act of 1930 and the Extraordinary Decree of Industrial Relations of 1945, still operative, have become dated. Above all, Mr. Albeda fears to have a disaster on his hands with soaring unemployment and ineffective public employment services. His preferred change of direction concerns a new legal basis and a new institutional structure which involves the social partners, but all within public law and under the roof of the Ministry of Social Affairs (Van der Veen, Hemerijck, and Burger, 1995: 397). To this end he asks the Social Economic Council for advice over a new structure for the Public Employment Service.

Infighting by the Ministry of the Interior, the lobby of the Dutch Association of Municipalities (VNG) and larger cities such as Amsterdam, Rotterdam, The Hague or Utrecht begins immediately. They all want a decentralized service, not a tripartite service. There is pressure to consider the whole issue in the context of the 'major reforms of the organization of the central government' which are commenced by the Lubbers government: scaling down the public sector, privatization, decentralization, deregulation, restructuring and re-orientation (de Kam and de Haan, 1991). The Minister of Finance is in favour of privatization of the Public Employment Service, other members of the Cabinet favour decentralization. The new Minister of Social Affairs and Employment, Mr. Jan de Koning, operates with characteristic caution. The Wassenaar Accord of late 1982 and the regained social partnership in external adjustment must not be put in jeopardy; on the other hand, decentralization is in line with other developments in government organizations, firms, and industrial relations. In November 1983 he instructs the SER to consider the role of local government in its advice.[16] As he went along, Mr de Koning develops a preference for cooperation with the social partners on the one hand and regional implementation on the other. He departs from the idea of his predecessors, Mr. Albeda and Mr. den Uyl, that the PES should remain part of the Ministry. He wishes to clear the way for regional decentralization of labour market policy, but is not ready to integrate regional employment services with regional social security administration. He observes, in a matter-of-fact way, that there is no support from the employers and unions for regionalization in social security. His Junior Minister, Mr. Louw de Graaf, who is responsible for social security, does not agree. He is not in favour of a tripartite employment service, except under the condition that integration with social security is possible, the social partners run both domains in an integrated fashion, and the government retreats from provision into a supervisory role in both domains. These ideas begin to play a role in the 1990s, but in 1985 they were too far fetched.

In 1984, after four years of deliberation, the SER's Labour Market Council publishes an interim advice.[17] The Council argues that administrative involvement of the social partners in the area of labour market policy is consistent with the policy legacies and emphasis on self-regulation in other fields, in particular wage determination and social security. The SER expresses its surprise that the employment services, in a time of rapid expansion of temporary employment agencies, has remained a state monopoly and argues that 'the time has come that the institutional commitment of the social partners to the employment service should also be reflected in the choice for a tripartite structure of the service both at the central and regional level'. In 1985, when the final advice is published, the SER forms various tripartite working parties, with representation from the government, in order to prepare a new organization.

The central administration, as suggested by the SER, should have three tasks in the new structure: to create the conditions under which the PES structure will be able to mature; to stipulate the criteria of performance; and to develop the instruments and provisions which will be geared toward bolstering labour market allocation. The PES, in terms of policy content, should direct its attention to find ways to overcome the segmentation between internal and external labour markets. The differences between skilled and ablebodied workers on the one hand and a category of vulnerable workers on the other should be reduced and the PES should try to counter tendencies towards discrimination. In this context, specific policies of vocational training should be further developed and expanded, and methods should be found to address the mismatch between educational and labour market needs.

The report concludes that the role of the state in PES should be recast and be limited to coordination of labour market policy in overall social and economic policy. Central steering should be indicative rather intervening. Only if self-regulation demonstrably fails, should the government be allowed to step in with corrective measures. In further negotiations, the SER accommodates the minister's preference for tripartization along territorially decentralized lines and the sectoral dimension is played down. The Minister goes along with the advice and hopes that tripartism will 'condemn' the social partners and the government to greater 'interdependence' in the fight against unemployment. This could encourage more coherence in social and economic policy formation, with a strong focus on both supply and demand, undergirded with high levels of societal support, based on the heightened awareness of the unions and employers of the labour market consequences of their own policy choices. The social partners, in particular the employers, are the only ones who can rescue the PES from its bad image. In his Memorandum in reply to parliamentary questions, the Minister also argues that the involvement of so-cial partners will facilitate sectoral policies, in which collective agreements with the social partners can serve as a linkage with general policy objectives. He realizes that the new employment service, in order to succeed, needs a good mix between the objectives of effectiveness and justice which the social partners were able to provide. The unions had their own motives for accept-ing responsibility for the employment service. They want full employment and see the service as a tool to bring this objective nearer and they also per-ceive themselves as protectors of an equal distribution of employment and its fruits, and as defenders of a decent and fair level of social security. Hence the employment service should be accessible to all, free of charge. Employers have different reasons – they want an efficient service. Their decision to join in is very much determined by the bad experience with the old employment service, both at the local and central levels. They find the local offices inade-quate and the central service of the Ministry meddlesome. Moreover, in sev-eral central accords with the unions there had been employment targets (for example in 1984, 1986, and 1990), but institutional support has remained wanting. Now it was hoped that a direct link between labour market policies and industrial relations could be established and that both could be moved in the direction of greater flexibility. For this it was necessary to have a position of influence; experience in other European countries had already taught the same lesson.[18]

The Lubbers I cabinet accepts the basic ideas of the SER advice, and in the next cabinet Mr. Koning continues with the preparation of a new Employ-ment Services Bill. Much time is spent on defining the administrative, finan-cial and legal rules for a service, which is neither public nor private and whose authority is shared between the state and the social partners. The new Public Employment Service is to have a fully independent status under public law, governed by a tripartite board of administration. Privatization is therefore a misnomer, although the 4,300 employees of the services are no longer civil servants.

When the Bill is introduced in parliament in 1988, questions arise as to how the Minister thinks he can be held accountable for a service over which he has no final say. Parliament has severe misgivings about functional decen-tralization and giving up its prerogative of budgetary control, but as in the case of international treaties, there is no room for renegotiation. When parlia-ment wants to amend the Bill, De Koning's reply is, quite simply, that it is 'all or nothing at all'. The threat to drop the whole project is effective and in De-cember 1989 and July 1990 both houses of parliament give their final go ahead. The new Act replaces the Labour Exchange Act of 1930 and the 1965 regulation on temporary work agencies. On January 1st 1991 the new tripar-tite employment service is a fact.

The Employment Service Act recasts the institutional roles, structures and responsibilities in three important ways. First, the service will be governed on a tripartite basis, under public law. Second, the service will be territorially decentralized, not only in its implementation – as was the case, on paper at least, with the old service – but also in its policy formation. Third, labour exchange and job placement activities are no longer a monopoly of the state (Van Gestel, 1994). Other, private exchange agencies, and temporary job agencies can offer services of leasing of temporary staff, outplacement, headhunting, and so on; for some of these activities they need special permits from the central or regional governing bodies of the new service.

The new employment service organization is to operate on two levels, central and regional. The Central Employment Board (CBA) operates under an independent (non-voting) chairperson, the membership of the board is equally divided between the central employers' organizations, the union confederations, and the central government, each with three votes. Government representatives are drawn from the Ministries of Social Affairs and Employment, of Economic Affairs and of Education, Arts and Science. The Association of Dutch Municipalities (VNG) has a non-voting member on the board. The 28, from 1997 on 18 Regional Employment Boards (RBA's) have the same design, with representation from local government.

The CBA formulates the main lines of policy, and the RBAs are responsible for applying these guidelines regionally. The RBA's have a strong position, they are not just subsidiaries to the CBA. As a result, a significant part of national labour market policies and their implementation is determined by the central government in conjunction with municipalities and the social partners at the central and regional levels. This new Employment Service Organization is funded by a 'fixed' annual state subsidy of one billion guilders from the Ministry of Social Affairs and Employment. The Minister of Social Affairs and Employment has retained the authority of supervision, must approve the budget, and audits the financial accounts and administrative procedures of the service.

The law defines as the employment service's task the encouragement of 'an effective and equitable allocation of demand and supply of labour' (art. 3). The first objective implies transparency and efficient placement; the second requires extra attention to vulnerable groups in the labour market. The service will be reviewed after four years, the first time in 1995. For this first period its policy targets are determined in a multi-annual policy framework; to fill 75 percent of vacancies with unemployed persons and target groups; to significantly reduce the number of long-term unemployed; to reduce the unemployment rate amongst ethnic minorities; to reduce youth unemployment; to consolidate equal opportunities for women; and to swiftly rehabilitate people who are partially incapable of working.

In order to solve the image problem, the CBA decides to promote a socalled 'slipstream' strategy: to establish good contacts with employers by presenting duly qualified workers for as many vacancies as possible, and if that works, to try to place the less qualified and convince employers to recruit the hard-to-place unemployed. Placement figures suggest a flourishing enterprise. According to CBA figures each year more than 100,000 unemployed have been helped to get a job, which is some percentage points above the target. Of these, 30 percent have been jobless for longer than one year, which is below the target. According to its own statistics, the service accomplished in 1994 37 percent more placements than in 1990 and its market share in all registered job beginnings had risen from 18 percent in 1992 to 22 percent in 1994.

PERSISTENT INSTITUTIONAL FRAGILITY OF LABOUR MARKET POLICY INITIATIVES

In 1994 the new structure of the employment service was up for evaluation. The official review, written by a government appointed committee, chaired by former Minister of the Interior Van Dijk (CDA), was published in March 1995. It was wholly negative with respect to the performance and functioning of the new tripartite employment service organization. The committee argued that the CBA failed to take charge, that decentralization had gone too far, finances were poorly managed, and decision-making procedures were unclear, slow and cumbersome. The organization had undeniably gained more zest; and especially at the regional level, there was more labour market research, activity, visits to companies, regional networking, and job placement. The image of the PES among employers had improved considerably. But the final verdict remained negative: it had all been very costly and the policies with respect to the target groups of the young unemployed, the long-term unemployed and ethnic minorities had failed. The committee calls the slipstream method ineffective and accuses the representatives of employers and unions in the governing board of the CBA to have acted 'in the interest of their own members' rather than for the 'common good'. In addition, the committee finds that the Regional Employment Boards have become too sovereign and that each acts independently with its own rules and subsidies, obstructing transparency and control. Financial accountability of their operations is highly problematic.

The review committee was also critical with regard to the representative of the Minister of Social Affairs and Employment in the Central Board. In essence, this representative combined four important roles: that of co-manager, legislator, financier and supervisor. This particular combination of responsibilities lead to confusion and created friction and irritation on the part of the social partners, particularly when the Minister decides to cut the budget, something he repeatedly did in spite of the fixed dowry given in 1991.[19] Clearly, this had undermined the will to cooperate of the social partners and not stimulated 'public regarding' behaviour on their part. The Van Dijk committee ends its report with making a number of suggestions to change the 1991 Act. [20]

The government used the findings to propose a change in the legislation. It had already formed a negative judgment on the service and wanted to close the experiment with autonomy. The Ministry wanted a return to an organization under direct control and fully accountable to parliament, while leaving administrative tasks with the social partners. Mid 1994 the CBA, presenting its new policy plan for the future, just before the new 'purple coalition' took office, commits the political blunder to suggest that job-seekers who are too far removed from the formal labour market should (temporarily) be dealt with by other institutions such as municipal social services, social and psychiatric help services, drug counseling bureaus and so on. This caused a moral uproar. Newspaper headlines read: the CBA stops placement of vulnerable groups; the CBA wants to dump the 'socially weak'. All this happens a month before the new 'purple' coalition takes office. The prime minister designate, Mr. Kok, expresses indignation: this is the opposite of what he and the new cabinet stands for. The new 'jobs, jobs, and more jobs' strategy of the new government, in which the problems of social disintegration in larger cities, inactivity, welfare dependence, and crime were given highest priority, required more not less concentration of resources to be spent on the fight against long-term unemployment. A month later, seizing the first opportunity, the new Minister of Social Affairs and Employment, Mr. Ad Melkert (PvdA), deciding to reign in the CBA, announces a series of budget cuts, the preparation of a new law, and a whole series of 'job-creation plans' (so-called Melkertjobs) for vulnerable groups in the labour market. Late in 1994, the social partners and the Minister reach a truce, on the basis of which the employment service redefines its policy course.

The social partners are furious about the critique of the Van Dijk committee and complain that the experiment had never been given a fair chance, that the government had repeatedly violated agreements and plundered the finances (Van Hooff, 1996). They reject the accusation of self-interested 'rent-seeking' behaviour and threaten to withdraw their cooperation if the government goes ahead. Once again employers defend their cooperation in a tripartite setting on the grounds that it provides better knowledge of existing vacancies, helps to achieve the objection of prevention of unemployment, creates a link with sectoral policies, and helps to bring about a fruitful interaction through collective bargaining. Without a direct influence on the policy direction of the organization it is impossible to achieve these objectives. [21] The unions share this view and defend the 'slipstream' strategy with the argument that this truly is a 'win-win' solution.

However, they do not get what they want. The cabinet wants the money spent on groups that most urgently need it, the long-term unemployed and the ethnic minorities. Within the PvdA the lobby from the major cities, where most concentrations of vulnerable groups are found, is strong. The other partners of 'purple', the Liberal Party (VVD) and Democrats (D66), were unhappy about the corporatist experiment in the first place and shed no tears over its truncation. Heeding the advice of the Van Dijk review committee, the government changes the law once again. In terms of policy content, the task is narrowed down to having the PES concentrate on vulnerable groups in the labour market. The success of private job placement agencies feeds the suggestion that there is no need for an expensive public service with regard to labour market exchange and informational services for people with work. Temporary job agencies are a booming industry in the Netherlands and the most extensive in the OECD area.[22] The public employment service can therefore safely retreat and concentrate on vulnerable target groups. In addition to an agreed public budget, performance budget rating is introduced. For this purpose a 'phasing model', from category one of unemployed workers who should be able to find employment on their own to category four of people who have no chances on their own accord, is introduced. Social security agencies and municipalities receive grants to purchase training and placement services from the regional employment boards. With these financial incentives it is expected that the employment boards will concentrate their activities more on the 'hard-to-place' job seekers.

There are also changes in the governance structure. Government officials will no longer be members of the central board; their place will be taken by members appointed by the crown, similar to the model used for the Social Economic Council (SER). The central board will set out key policy avenues, while the general management is granted more freedom in the execution of policies. Consequently, the influence of the social partners is reduced. In the central board (CBA), the unanimity requirement is replaced by decision-making on the basis of simple majorities, hence removing the possibility of veto. The greater influence of the Minister finds its expression in three ways: prior consultation over policy objectives and targets, the possibility of repressive control by way of 'administrative orders' and a new method of financing. The annual budget is divided between a basic allowance and a performance-related part.

The 1996 Employment Services Act coheres with recent social security reform efforts. The regional employment boards are expected to develop close contact with sectoral and municipal social security administrations. These policy goals should be achieved through the commercialization of relations between municipalities and the PES and through the development of an integrated client oriented system of services, currently going under the name of Cooperation for Work and Income. The linkage between unemployment insurance, public assistance and labour market policy concerns is once again reestablished. Unemployment recipients are obliged to register with employment offices and actively seek to re-enter the labour market. Both the revision of the National Assistance Act (1996) and the new Social Security Organization Act (2000) are designed to enhance co-operation between municipalities, industrial insurance associations and the regional employment boards, but the reforms stop short of creating a 'one counter' service.[23]

ADDITIONAL EMPLOYMENT PROGRAMS

Since the early 1990s, Dutch governments have, in large part independent of the PES, taken further steps to redress the balance of active and passive policies: these include 'labour pools', the 'Youth Work Guarantee Plan', and the so-called Melkert-jobs, named after the current Minister of Social Affairs and Employment. The overall volume of these programs will have been doubled from 1.5 to 3 percent of total paid employment near the end of the cabinet's tenure. The majority of these additional employment measures are carried out by municipalities and partially financed by wage costs subsidies.

There are 21,500 long-term unemployed in subsidized 'labour pools' in the public sector, which were introduced in 1990 for long-term unemployed with little chances in the regular labour market. The program grants minimum-wage jobs in the public sector, primarily in municipalities. Most participants are expected to stay until retirement. The so-called 'route placement' program, also introduced in the early 1990s, is tailored to the needs of the long-term unemployed, offering a program of motivation, training or retraining, work experience and, finally, placement in the open labour market.

The 'Youth Work Guarantee Plan' was established in 1992 after various years of experimenting, and offers a combination of training and work experience to school-leavers up to the age of 23 who have not been able to find a job within six months and have less than one year previous work experience. The scheme provides for a minimum wage for a 32 hour week plus one day for extra schooling. In 1995 some 20,000 young people were offered a temporary work experience on this program. For the period up until 1998 it has been decided to raise the upper limits by one year annually. The program is administered by local authorities. Wages cannot be higher than 120 percent of the legal minimum (which decreases steeply with age for people under 23). In 1990 the central employers' and union organizations pledged 60,000 additional jobs with the objective to raise the employment share of ethnic minorities.[24] In October 1995 the pledge is renewed, considering that ethnic unemployment remains very high in spite of a faster employment growth.[25] Only half of all, mostly larger, firms employ non-native workers, whose share in the total labour force has risen to eleven percent. A special law requiring employers to register non-native workers and report annually on progress, has met with much resistance.

Minister Melkert has implemented a number of labor policy innovations geared towards the reintegration of the unskilled and low-paid workers in the labor process. He has significantly reduced employers' wage costs, through reductions in taxes and social security contributions, instigating a decline in the tax wedge for employer who hire long-term unemployed and other vulnerable workers (see Chapter Six). Policy measures which reduce gross labour costs for employers who hire long-term unemployed are particularly popular in the purple coalition. Wage subsidies are also given to employers hiring persons with a work handicap, who can claim subsidies for a period of four years. The reductions add up to as much as 25 percent of the annual wage. In 1996 the charges paid by employers for jobs at or near the minimum wage level were structurally lowered, so as to make simple labour cheaper for the employer. An employer hiring someone who has been out of work for a year or more, who will earn less than 130 percent of the minimum wage, does not have to pay any social security contributions for a four year period.[26]

Until 1998, 40,000 extra 32 hour-jobs will be created in the public sector for people who have been unemployed for longer than twelve months. These include watchman's jobs in hospitals and homes for the elderly and work in day-care centers. Additional Melkert-jobs will be created in large cities with serious social problems. In the private sector, a maximum of 20,000 extra temporary jobs will be created. They are financed through related savings in social security benefits and partly through a contribution from the government. Finally, the long-term unemployed who are truly unable to find paid employment, may perform unpaid activities and retain their benefit, so as to ensure that they do not become entirely alienated from the labor market. Some 20,000 such jobs will be created before 1998. Finally, in 1998 a novel policy instruments will be introduced which enable municipalities to subsidize work-experience places.[27] The PvdA and the Minister of Social Affairs and Employment have staked a lot of political capital on the success of these measures.

CONCLUSION

The crooked path of institutionalizing an active labour market policy commitment in the Netherlands must be understood against the background of developments in policy domains of external adjustment and domestic compensation. Compared with both domains, the labour market policy domain has remained underdeveloped and institutionally fragile. Two developments have combined to keep labour market policy off the policy agenda. First, for the first twenty years after the war Dutch labour market policy essentially revolved around the very stringent policy of corporatist wage restraint. There was little apparent need for additional policy measures geared towards raising the overall quality of Dutch labour supply. Postwar prosperity allowed the employment service to live on as a dormant monopoly. Second, when unemployment returned, additional plans of job creation were ventured, but relatively soon the policy priorities shifted towards domestic compensation,

Table 24: Additional employment programs

in thousands	1980	1985	1990	1992	1994	1996	1998*
subsidised employment	74	80	93	107	125	144	175
social job creation	74	80	82	85	87	81	82
Youth Work Guarantee Law (JWG)	–	–	7	6	18	25	0
Job Pools	–	–	4	16	20	23	0
Melkert I	–	–	–	–	–	11	40
Melkert II	–	–	–	–	–	4	–
WIW	–	–	–	–	–	–	53

Source: Ministry of Social Affairs and Employment; OECD, *Economic Surveys the Nether-lands 1996*, p. 41.
* estimated

consistent with the 'compensatory' bias in the Dutch welfare state. More-over, the highly centralized bureaucracy of the Dutch employment service was ill-suited for the fight against unemployment. Local employment offices were increasingly overburdened and attempts to re-fashion the local employ-ment offices failed. Loss of confidence, especially on the part of employers, in the performance of the employment service resulted in a major crisis of polit-ical credibility against the background of soaring unemployment.

The 1991 Employment Service Act is the product of a long period of dis-cussion and intricate decision-making procedures. Preparation began in 1980, if we discount the aborted early attempt at tripartization in 1969. The preference for a tripartite service, with involvement of the social partners, was not popular among the Ministers of the first Lubbers cabinet, but it was quietly supported by Mr. de Koning. The Minister of the Interior and the As-sociation of Dutch Municipalities advocated territorial decentralization of a public service, while the Minister of Finance championed privatization. The changes that were eventually made in subsequent phases of negotiations, re-flected a potpourri based on a combination of functional and territorial de-centralization, without a clear delineation of the status of the Ministry.

Immediately after its tripartite inception, the employment service was at-tacked from different angles. In the face of the inactivity crisis, the larger Dutch cities, where the problem of persistent unemployment is concentrat-ed, wanted further territorial decentralization. The 'social innovation' pro-gram championed by the Social Democrats in the third Lubbers government, meant to cut through bureaucratic red tape at the local level, gave further fuel to this preference. At the same time, temporary job agencies have grown in importance and give support to the idea that the labour market can organize itself, except where vulnerable groups are concerned. Another new school of thought maintains that a Public Employment Service should 'earn' its money; its existence and budget should be dependent upon the quality of the services it renders to clients, municipalities, and Industrial Insurance Associations, who should consequently have a greater choice in making use of these services. Competition in the labour exchange is again an option, in spite of the memories of the 1920s and 1930s and the obligation to maintain a public service in correspondence with the 1948 ILO convention.

While the demonopolization of placement and the tenuous combination of functional and regional decentralization, represented a major break in Dutch labor market policy, the high expectations in terms of performance were, however, not met. Output had increased, but there was a shift in policy focus: from an 'active' to an 'activating' labour market policy commitment. The link with social security reform had gained absolute priority. As a result, the fragile institutional arrangement of the 1991 employment service, reflecting a problem definition of the mid 1980s, is again up for grabs.

The corporatist design of the employment service was truncated before it could prove its 'good works'. It was unable to develop a prominent institutional position in Dutch social and economic policy making, because it lacked serious commitments from all interested parties, not only the Ministry of Social Affairs and Employment and the social partners. Parliament, the Ministry of Economic Affairs and the Ministry of Education, together with the Association of Dutch municipalities, have remained unconvinced supporters throughout the period of PES institution building. Institution building takes time, more than four years, and needs more enthusiastic support. Moreover, in institutional terms, the employment service reorganization may have been a bridge too far, as it involves a shift from a dormant state monopoly to an active, functionally tripartite, territorially decentralized and demonopoliszd organization (Van der van der Veen and Hemerijck, 1995).

Taking heed of the conclusions of the Van Dijk-commission, Minister Melkert's impulse was to seek alternative policies rather than restructure and patch-up the existing arrangement. Under the new Employment Service Act the scope of the employment service has once again been limited to a labour provision service for the weak. Going his own way, the Minister today relies on fiscal measures to subsidize low-paid employment at the bottom end of the labour market, rather than spending resources on employment measures, vocational education and training. Soon the 1967 critique of the OECD of the Dutch employment service will again be relevant.

Notes

1   Göran Therborn, 'Nederland en het falende arbeidsmarktbeleid', Utrecht, 20 December 1988, reprinted, with a collection of responses and interviews from politicians and policy makers, in P. Broert-jes, *Getto's in Nederland. Visies op armoede en werkloosheid,* Amsterdam: van Gennep, 1989, 23-36.

2   Hein Kroft, Godfried Engbersen, Kees Schuyt, and Frans van waarden, *Een tijd zonder werk. Een onderzoek naar de levenswereld van langduring werklozen,* Leyden: Stenfert Kroese, 1989; later published with Westview Press: G. Engbersen, H. Korft, K. Schuyt, and F. van waarden (1993), *Cultures of Unemployment: a comparative look at long-term unemployment and urban poverty.*

3   These quotes can be found on page 93, 44 and 57 in Broertjes, *Getto's in Nederland,* o.c.

4   Broertjes, Getto's in Nederland, o.c., p. 15.

5   'Topambtenaar veroordeelt arbeidsmarktbeleid overheid' (Top civil servant condemns public labour market policy), *De Volkskrant,* 21 December 1988.

6   WRR, *Activerend arbeidsmarktbeleid,* The Hague: SDU, 1987, Report to the government no. 33; and *Een werkend perspectief,* The Hague: SDU, 1990, Report to the government no. 38.

7   OECD, *Manpower and Social Policy in the Netherlands,* Paris, 1967.

8   'Gas geven en remmen tegelijk', in Broertjes, *Getto's in Holland,* o.c., 37-45.

9   Andeweg (1995: 208) calls this the 'hidden privatization of a pseudo-private sector' which may have been more important, in terms of money, than the quasi privatization of a few state monopolies such as the money services of the post office (Postbank), the state printing office, the public broadcasting company or the PTT. In all, together with smaller projects, privatization affected and estimated 125-150,000 civil servants; subsidies to the private sector were reduced from 2.7 percent of GDP in 1982 to less than 1 percent ten years later.

10   'The OECD Jobs Strategy: synopsis of the recommendations for the Netherlands' in: *Economic Survey for the Netherlands 1996,* Paris, Organisation for Economic Cooperation and Development, 72-3.

11   The 1948 Employment Convention of the ILO stipulates that each country shall have a service whose essential duty it is 'to ensure, in cooperation where necessary with other relevant public and private bodies, the best possible organization of the labour market as an integral part of the national programme for the achievement and maintenance of full employment and the development and use of productive resources.

12   'Recommendation of the Council on Manpower Policy as a Means for the Promotion of Economic Growth', Paris, 1964.

13   OECD, *Manpower and Social Policies in the Netherlands,* o.c.

14   The importance of the central direction increases. Total resources increase, but much have to be negotiated on a year by year basis. The total staff of the PES increases with 57 percent, from 2,300 in 1972 to 3,600 in 1982 (Maarse, 1984: 108).

15   see: WRR, *Activerend Arbeidsmarktbeleid*, The Hague: Staatsuitgeverij, 1987; reports to the government no. 33.

16   Letter from the Minister of Social Affairs and Employment of 22 November 1983.

17   Raad voor de Arbeidsmarkt, 'De rol van de sociale partners in het arbeidsvoorzieningenbeleid', The Hague: SER, 9 May 1984

18   RCO, *Ondernemingen en de Arbeidsvoorzieningswet*, Zoetermeer, September 1990.

19   Already in 1992, in contravention with promises given, but with parliamentary approval, the minister decided to cut the PES budget with 150 million guilders; in negotiations the cuts were reduced to 100 million. In 1994, the social partners, angry about repeated cuts in the budget and interventions from the Ministry , threatened to step down from the CBA. Until 1994 the government's subsidy was reduced three times.

20   Review committee Van Dijk, *Arbeidsvoorziening in perspectief; evaluatie arbeidsvooorzieningswet 1991-1994*, The Hague: SDU, March 1995.

21   J.W. Blankert, *Arbeidsvoorziening. Naast plichten ook rechten*, Zoetermeer: VNO/NCW, June 1995. Mr. Hans Blankert was chairman of the NCW in 1995. In 1996 he became the chairman of the combined VNO/NCW federation.

22   The number of hours supplied through these offices has more than tripled and currently adds up to three percent of the total.

23   In 1996, after the legal changes, there were 18 regional employment offices (RBAs), 19 industry insurance associations (IIAs) and 647 municipalities.

24   STAR, *Meer werk voor minderheden*, 14 November 1990.

25   Between 1990 and 1995 job growth among non-native workers was three times the national average.

26   *Wet vermindering afdracht loonbelasting en premies volksverzekering*, 1 January 1996.

27   *Wet Inschakeling Werkzoekenden* (WIW, 1998).

Conclusion

Some Lessons from the Dutch Experience

A T THE END OF THE TWENTIETH CENTURY there is much anxiety over the future of the welfare state in Europe. Critics point out that the European welfare state has accumulated a vast array of labour-market rigidities which impede flexible adjustment, block technological innovation and hamper necessary economic and employment growth (OECD *Jobs Study*, 1994). From this perspective, the recipe is to the scale down the ambitions of the welfare state. The Dutch experience analyzed in this book suggests that there is still considerable scope for these ambitions, despite the increasing constraints brought on by European integration, global competition, industrial restructuring, an ageing population and changing family relations. The Dutch case of negotiated social policy reform proves that modernization of the European welfare state is possible after all. This social invention, with its roots in the 19th century, will still be relevant – in an updated version – for the 21st century. That this has been possible in the Netherlands is significant, because the Dutch welfare state is a specimen of the Bismarckian, continental, corporatist, breadwinner, hence antiquated and compensatory welfare state regimes—the hardest to change of them all.

All European welfare states are confronted by demographic, social, economic and political changes which contradict the foundations upon which they were built and developed. While the architects of the postwar welfare state, like Beveridge, assumed stable families and properly functioning male labour markets in a Keynesian world of embedded liberalism, they could focus social policy innovation on measures for those who were no longer able to work, like the sick, the disabled, the widowed and the aged. This picture of economy and society no longer holds. Today's social and economic policies have to respond to the new rules of global competition, deal with the new shape of working life and answer for the new realities of double, one-and-a-half, and less-than-one-earned-income households, unstable family structures and the predicament of demographic ageing.

Welfare states differ. They have different histories and respond in various ways to the challenges of modernization. Successful policies, as a consequence, can never really serve as 'export commodities'. Mr. Ad Melkert, the Minister of Social Affairs and Employment, put it well in his opening address to the conference 'Social Policy and Economic Performance' in January 1997 in Amsterdam, held under the Dutch presidency of the European Union:

'There are no models of eternal bliss to copy'. The 'tulipmania' on the cover of this book and the very history of the Dutch Republic are reminders of the transcience of success. This sobering thought does not, however, imply that it is pointless to take stock of the successful reform efforts that have been undertaken. We can learn from them.

Understanding reform is crucial in a time of trial, uncertainty and policy experimentation. In our view, there are at least three reasons for taking the recent Dutch reform experience seriously. First of all, in terms of performance, the Dutch miracle of extraordinary job creation over the past decade represents a departure from the current unemployment malaise in the European Union. That is no small feat. Just as interesting, secondly, is the composition of the new Dutch labour market. The surge of part-time work, including larger numbers of men working in part-time jobs, the revolutionary increase of female participation and the rapid expansion of the service sector deserve special mention. The 'Dutch miracle' represents a case story of a welfare state which is adapting to the new realities of post-industrial working life and family relations. Both elements combined suggest, thirdly, that the continental welfare state can be reformed and that it can be done without a 'big bang'.

The continental welfare state model depends on high levels of employment. This is often seen as a weakness, especially in combination with the way of financing social security. The reliance on payroll taxes makes these welfare states particularly vulnerable to increases in unemployment, in whatever form, but especially if it takes the nasty form of long-term unemployment or inability. It raises social expenditures and reduces revenues at the same time. As a consequence, it then becomes necessary to either reduce benefits at a time when more persons become dependent upon them, or to raise payroll taxes at a time when firms are particularly sensitive to labour cost increases. Cost increases may be balanced by productivity increases and leave the competitive position of firms in the exposed sector unaffected, but they are likely to retard or prevent job growth in the domestic service sector job growth.

If this is true, the reverse may also hold. If wage moderation, after a first phase of boosting competitiveness in the exposed sector, can help to create more jobs in domestic services, slow down or lower the number of people depending on benefits and hence reduce the social wage component, allow governments to use the improved public finances to lower the tax and contribution wedge at or near the minimum and get more unskilled workers back into jobs, then the vicious circle of 'welfare without work' can be reversed. In our chapters about social security and labour market policies we have shown that this requires a number of extremely unpleasant decisions, with painful consequences for the people involved and high political risks for decision makers. It is therefore important that there is 'light at the end of the tunnel'. In other words, the 'jobs, jobs, and more jobs' strategy is vital, and the promise of these jobs has to be realistic when social programs, such as the disability program in the Netherlands, are drastically curtailed. In this sense, wage moderation, beginning with the 'change in policy and mentality' leading to the Wassenaar Accord of 1982, has been the foundation for the other changes documented in this study.

Successive changes in external adjustment and domestic compensation coincided with a general shift in the problem definition of the crisis of the Dutch welfare state at the turn of the decade. Dutch labour market policy priorities have made a U-turn. The overarching policy objective is no longer to keep overt unemployment down by channeling people into other programs. Instead, the Scandinavian preoccupation with maximizing the rate of labour force participation has become a number one priority. Instruments like the I/A ratio have translated this priority into a new norm for wage bargaining and a policy instrument for the government in its management of minimum wage and benefit adjustments. The 1993 'New Course' agenda, agreed upon between the central organizations of employers and unions, has also picked up the message:

> All proposals of parties in collective bargaining, for which this Agenda sets the priorities, should be tested on their possible effects on and their contributions to the reinforcement of the profitability and competitiveness of companies, as well as the increase in labour participation and employment.[1]

The commitment to high levels of participation became the core of social and economic policy of the Kok government. The 'jobs, jobs, and more jobs' slogan is implemented through support for wage and wage cost moderation by means of a reduction of social contributions for employers and tax incentives for the employed, in particular at or near the minimum wage. Special job programs are designed to further the participation of low-skilled workers, foreign nationals and people who have poor chances in the labour market. We have however shown that the institutionalization of 'a right to work' in public policy remains very problematic, especially in a country that historically lacks an active labour market commitment.

Finally, the paradigmatic shift in the world of work and the world at home implies a refocusing on achieving a new balance between flexibility and security, and between paid and unpaid work. Paid work will remain the main engine of social integration and economic independence and is likely to remain so for decades to come. The new policy priority of maximizing employment opportunities for everyone implies a shift away from full-time, lifetime jobs for men, towards more varied ways of combining paid employment, family responsibilities, education and leisure for both men and women at different stages of their lives. The post-industrial welfare state must actively promote that both men and women seek and find paid work, help households to harmonize work and family obligations, and train the population with the kinds of skills that the modern economy demands. In our view, the growth of one-and-half-income families is a positive trend because it reduces the household's narrow dependency on the family wage and job security of one breadwinner, and because such families are a better defence against child poverty. Initiatives for providing more flexibility in career and working hours, child rearing and care for the elderly should be at the heart of the modernization of the welfare state. The 'New Course' agenda and later agreements on part-time and flexible work patterns show that Dutch trade unions and, less surprisingly, Dutch employers have come out in support. It has brought the unions international acclaim, jobs and members.

A rough and ready comparison of recent social policy reform efforts in Europe reveals one critically important precondition for successful reform. Given the tremendous challenges of structural change that European welfare states today face, societal consensus is crucial for effective reform. In all welfare states there are many veto points and actors with the power to obstruct. A politics of imposition is likely to provoke conflicts which may retard or even reverse the process. Modernization of the welfare state, as discussed in this book, is a long-term process. It requires the construction of a political will and long-term commitments, built on norms of trust and networks of civic engagement, in order to overcome the inevitable opposition of groups who will lose. As the Dutch case reveals, opposition is most easily overcome when reform advocates can negotiate with strong, nationally organized, encompassing interest associations with the capacity and willingness to learn and take account of the interests of others. But corporatism is no *passepartout*; the 'problem solving style' of decision making which it can help produce, is better than its alternatives, but it is inherently unstable and fragile. Corporatism easily produces policy stalemates.

We have tried to show how through processes of 'puzzling' and 'powering' the stalemate was broken in three core domains of the welfare state (see Figure 13). In *Corporatism regained*, the chapter about industrial relations or 'external adjustment', we traced the central role of the concertation between highly co-ordinated organizations for the development and implementation of a successful and protracted strategy of external adjustment of the national economy – firms and workers – to a higher level of international competition. The institutional framework for a negotiated and concerted policy of wage moderation did not have to be invented but was regained from 'immobilism'. This took a considerable amount of time, a drastic signal of the market, especially the recession of 1981-3, and, on occasion, a well-designed 'shadow of hierarchy', for instance in the form of the contingent application of public protection to the private agreements concluded between trade unions and employers' organizations. We recall from our definition of corporatist governance that state support for private interest government is conditional upon substantive outcomes. In this case, the 'good works' required were lower wage scales for target groups of inexperienced and low-skilled workers. The general point is that the procedures and outcomes of corporatist decision making are not beyond criticism. In democracies, governments must answer, ultimately, to parliaments and voters. Strong corporatism needs a strong state.

Figure 12: Corporatist change in the Netherlands

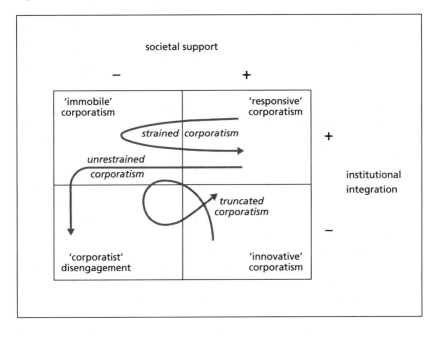

On the other hand a strong state does not mean that state actors can change the level of social and organizational integration as if they were operating a lever. Our two chapters on social policy, or 'domestic compensation', and on labour market policy, or 'social activation', make clear that states can be strong in one domain, and weak in another; moreover, they are hardly ever in a position to tell organized functional interest groups what to do.

The chapter on *Unrestrained Corporatism* confirms our thesis that corporatist institutions cannot by themselves sustain the benign economic and social outcomes, proposed in corporatist theory. Corporatism needs strong signals from the market; the less these signals are felt, as was the case in social policy provision until recently, the stronger must be the 'shadow of hierarchy'. Historical legacies had left behind a muddled organization of social security administration and implementation, in which many veto points did prevent change and 'rent seeking' behaviour was tolerated. In the domain of social security the state, not the trade union movement, was the learning organization. The initiative, in this case, was political and it is not insignificant that in the past fifteen years all major political parties, from right to left, shared at some stage in the government responsibility for welfare retrenchment. It should however be added that Corporatism Regained in the 1980s had laid the foundation for successful external adjustment and sustained job growth. It was exactly the economic recovery and rediscovery of a job-intensive growth path which created the political conditions for welfare reform. Put simply, without jobs welfare reforms would have been much harder to sell.

In *Truncated Corporatism,* our chapter about labour market policies, we discovered the limits of the state in another way. In contrast to the domains of social security and industrial relations, there was no policy tradition to build upon. Perversely, the successful policy of wage moderation after the war had given the impression that no active labour policy was needed; and in later years labour market policy had been subordinated to social policy concerns. A dormant state monopoly ran job placement offices which were shunned by employers and skilled workers, and overrun by the unemployed for which little could be done. The truncated experiment with a functionally and decentralized service shows how important long standing commitments, small numbers, clear responsibilities, and trust are, and of all of these there was too little. It may have been that the experiment with tripartization was heading straight towards 'immobilism', a form of institutionalization without societal and political support. On the other hand, the recent disengagement of the state leaves behind a very fragile construction, confused and hardly ready for the demanding tasks of an activating and active labour market. In this domain, it seems to us, it is not the state, but society that has learned—most changes have come from the altered patterns of behaviour of women, employers, husbands, trade unions, and many of these chances were unforeseen or the response to the failure or absence of public policies.

We have thus far avoided the expression 'polder model', a term which during the past year has become popular among the policy making elite and has been used as reference term in the national and international press. Our rejection of the term can serve as a summary of the key argument that we have tried to develop. Although the Dutch experience of the past fifteen years harbours a positive sum solution to the problem of the modernization of the welfare state, it does not add up to a model that can serve as a policy example for others to follow, like the Swedish model notoriously did for academics, journalists and policy makers in the 1970s. There has not at any point in time been a grand design, master plan or major political exchange from which subsequent policies have followed. The Dutch trajectory of adjustment and reform was paved with many contingencies, such as a major recession, a change in the balance of power between capital and labour, a spiralling crisis of inactivity, and changes in the political landscape. Most of the time, the availability of a dense and multi-tiered institutional infrastructure for a problem solving style of decision making proved an asset. But there is no uniform institutional format or a common 'polder model' across policy domains. On the contrary, the institutional orders and provision logics differ across the three domains of welfare state we have analyzed in this study and have required quite different processes of change and learning in the past fifteen years. Likewise, there is no constant 'Dutch culture' of consensual decision making, which only has just to be mobilized in times of international danger and crisis to the nation. The breaking of the political stalemate of corporatist immobility required hard-won changes and slow learning processes, and success was not assured. Neither was it always possible to break with policy deadlocks without a significant departure from the corporatist problem solving policy style. Finally, the notion of a 'polder model' suggests too much *virtù*, while many of the changes made were expedient, short-term responses to immediate crises. But as Macchiavelli already knew, policy learning cannot do without *fortuna*.

Note

1   Foundation of Labour, *A new Course*, The Hague, December 1993, p. 3.

Bibliography

Aarts L. and Ph. de Jong (1992), *Economic Aspects of Disability Behavior*, Amsterdam: North-Holland Publishing Company.

Aarts L. and Ph. de Jong (1996), *Curing the Dutch Disease*, Aldershot: Avebury.

Albeda, W. (1987), 'Loonvorming in de tijd van neergang tot beginnend herstel 1973-1987', in: A. Knoester (ed.), *Lessen uit het verleden. 125 jaar Vereniging voor de Staathuishoudkunde*, Leiden/Antwerpen: Stenfert Kroese, pp. 305-18.

Albeda, W. (1990), 'Werkloosheid', in: J.W. van Deth and S.C.P.M. Vis (eds.), *Politieke problemen*, Leiden: Stenfert Kroese, pp. 73-90.

Albeda, W. and W.J. Dercksen (1994), *Arbeidsverhoudingen in Nederland*, Alphen a/d Rijn: Samsom.

Allaart, P. (1988), *The Labour Market in Five Small European Countries*, Organisatie voor Strategisch Arbeidsmarktonderzoek, The Hague.

Andeweg, R.B. and G.A. Irwin (1993), *Dutch Government and Politics*, Basingstoke: MacMillan.

Andeweg, R.B. (1994), 'Privatization in the Netherlands: The result of a decade', in: V. Wright (ed.), *Privatization in Western Europe: Pressures, problems and paradoxes*, London: Pinter, pp. 198-214.

Axelrod, R. (1984), *The Evolution of Cooperation*, New York: Basic Books.

Baglioni, G. and C.J. Crouch (1990), *European Industrial Relations: the Challenge of Flexibility*, London: Sage.

Beaudry, P., and D. di Nardo (1991), 'The effect of implicit contract on the movement of wages over the business cycle; evidence from micro data', in: *Journal of Political Economy*, pp. 665-688.

Beer, P. de (1996), *Het onderste kwart. Werk en werkloosheid aan de onderkant van de arbeidsmarkt*, Rijswijk: Sociaal en Cultureel Planbureau.

Bekkum, R. van (1996a), *Tussen Vraag en Aanbod: Op zoek naar de identiteit van arbeidsvoorzieningsorganisatie*, The Hague: SDU.

Bekkum, R. van (1996b), 'Knutselen aan het organisatiemodel voor de arbeidsvoorziening', in: *Openbaar Bestuur*, no. 617, pp. 16-22.

Berger, S., and R. Dore (1996) (eds.), *National Diversity and Global Capitalism*, Ithaca NY: Cornell UP.

Betten, L. (1985) *The Incorporation of Fundamental Rights in the Legal Order of the European Communities with Special Reference to the Right to Strike*, The Hague: Martinus Nijhoff

Bottenburg, M. van (1995), *Aan den Arbeid! In de wandelgangen van de Stichting van de Arbeid, 1945-1995*, Amsterdam: Bert Bakker.

Bovenberg, L. (1997), 'Dutch Employment Growth: An analysis', in: *CPB Report*, 1997/2, pp. 16-24.

Boyer, R. (1988), *The Search for Labour Market Flexibility: The European economies in transition*, Oxford: Clarendon Press.

Braam, S. (1994), *De blinde vlek van Nederland. Rapportages over de onderkant van de arbeidsmarkt*, Amsterdam: Van Gennep.

Braun, D., (1988), *Der Niederlandische Weg in die Massenarbeitslosigkeit (1973-1981), Eine Politisch-Institutionelle Analyse*, Dissertation, Amsterdam.

Brink, M. van de, H.S. Gustafsson and W. Groot (1995), *Kinderopvang tussen markt en overheid*, Amsterdam: Welboom.

Broeder, C. den (1996), *Institutions At Work: Commitment and flexibility on the German and Dutch labour market*, CPB, The Hague.

Broertjes, P. (ed.) (1989), *Getto's in Nederland. Visies op armoede en werkloosheid*, Amsterdam: Van Gennep.

Bruno, M. and J. Sachs, (1985), *The Economics of Worldwide Stagflation*, Cambridge Mass: Harvard University Press.

Calmfors, L. and J. Driffill (1988), 'Bargaining Structure, Corporatism and Macroeconomic Performance', in: *Economic Policy*, April 1988, pp. 15-61.

Casey, B. (1983), 'Staatliche Maßnamen zur Förderung der Teilzeitarbeit: Erfahrungen in Belgien, Frankreich, Grossbrittannien, den Niederlanden und der Bundesrepublik Deutschland', in: *Mitteilungen aus der Arbeitsmarkt- und Berufsforschungen*, vol. 16 (1983), no. 4, pp. 416-7.

Catz, F. (1983), 'De vele slagen on de arbeidstijd', in: *Tijdschrift voor Politieke Economie*, vol. 7, no. 1, pp. 6-33.

Cawson, A. (1986), *Corporatism and Political Theory*, Oxford: Blackwell.

Conradi, H. (1982), *Teilzeitarbeit: Theorie, Realität, Realisierbarkeit*, München: Minerva Verlag.

Cox, R.H. (1993), *The Development of the Dutch Welfare State. From workers' to universal entitlement*, Pittsburgh: University of Pittsburgh Press.

Crouch, C. and A. Pizzorno (eds.) (1978), *The Resurgence of Class Conflict in Western Europe since 1968*, London: MacMillan.

Crouch, C. (1985), 'Conditions for Trade Union Wage Restraint', in: L.N. Lindberg and C.S. Maier (eds.), *The Politics of Inflation and Economic Stagnation*, Washington: Brookings Institute, pp. 103-39.

Crouch, C. (1986) 'Sharing Public Space: States and Organized Interests in Western Europe', in: J. Hall (ed), *States in Societies*, Oxford: Blackwell, pp. 179-180.

Crouch, C. (1993), *Industrial Relations and European State Traditions*, Oxford: Clarendon Press.

Crouch, C. (1994), 'Incomes Policies, Institutions and Markets: An overview of recent developments', in: Dore R., R. Boyer, and Z. Mars (eds.), *The Return to Incomes Policy*, London: Pinter, pp. 175-196.

Crouch, C. (1995a), 'Organized interests as resources or as constraint: rival logics of vocational training policy', in C. Crouch and F. Traxler (eds.), *Organized Industrial Relations in Europe: What Future?*, Aldershot: Avebury. pp. 287-308.

Crouch, C. (1995b), 'Reconstructing corporatism? Organized decentralization and other paradoxes', in C. Crouch and F. Traxler (eds.), *Organized Industrial Relations in Europe: What Future?*, Aldershot: Avebury. pp. 311-330.

Crouch, C. (1996), 'Revised Diversity. From the neo-liberal decade to beyond Maastricht', in: J. van Ruysseveldt and J. Visser (eds.), *Industrial Relations in Europe: Traditions and Transitions*, London: Sage, pp. 358-375.

Crouch, C., and F. Traxler (1995), *Organized Industrial Relations in Europe: What Future?*, Aldershot: Avebury.

Daalder, H. (1966), 'The Netherlands: Opposition in a segmented society', in: R.A. Dahl (ed.), *Political Opposition in Western Democracies*, New Haven: Yale University Press.

Dellen, H. van (1984), *Een nieuw elan, de marktsector van de jaren tachtig*, Deventer: Kluwer.

Delsen, L., and E. de Jong, 'Het wankele mirakel', *Economisch-Statistische Berichten*, 23 April 1997, pp. 324-7.

Dercksen, W.J. (1986), *Industrialisatiepolitiek rondom de Jaren Vijftig: een sociologisch-economische beleidsstudie*, Assen: Van Gorcum.

DIW (1996), *Employment and Social Policies under International Constraints*, The Hague: VUGA.

Doorn, J.A.A. van (1981), 'Corporatisme en technocratie – een verwaarloosde polariteit in de Nederlandse politiek', in: *Beleid en Maatschappij*, 8, pp. 134-149.

Douma, K. (1997), 'De bruine bonen van de flexibilisering', in: Tijdschrift voor Arbeidsvraagstukken, 13, 2, pp. 13-15

Elster, J. (1983), 'Is there (or should there be) a right to work?', in: A. Gutman (ed.), *Democracy and the Welfare State*, Princeton NJ: Princeton University Press, pp. 53-78.

Engbersen, G., H. Kroft, K. Schuyt, and F. van Waarden (1993), *Cultures of Unemployment: A comparative look at long-term unemployment and urban poverty*, Boulder Co.: Westview Press.

Engfer, U., K. Hinrichs, C. Offe and H. Wiesenthal (1983), 'Arbeitszeitsituation und Arbeitszeitverkürzung aus de Sicht de Beschäftigten', in: *Mitteilungen aus der Arbeitsmarkt- und Berufsforschung*, no. 16.

Esping-Andersen, G. (1990), *The Three Worlds of Welfare Capitalism*, Princeton: Princeton University Press.

Esping-Andersen, G. (1996a), 'After the Golden Age? Welfare State dilemmas in a global economy', in: G. Esping-Andersen (ed.), *Welfare States in Transition, National adaptations in global economies*, London: Sage, pp. 1-31.

Esping-Andersen, G. (1996b), 'Positive-Sum Solutions in a World of Trade-Offs?', in: Esping-Andersen (ed.), *Welfare States in Transition, National adaptations in global economies*, London: Sage, pp. 256-267.

Esping-Andersen, G. (1996c), 'Welfare States without Work: The Impasse of Labor Shedding and Familialism in Continental European Social Policy', in: G. Esping-Andersen (ed.), *Welfare States in Transition, National adaptations in global economies*, London: Sage.

Esping-Andersen, G. (1997), 'The Double Problem of Coordination in Contemporary Welfare States', lecture, delivered at high-level conference, *Social Policy and Economic Performance: Employment, Activating Welfare State and Economic Competitiveness*, 23-25 January, Amsterdam.

Fase, W.J.P.M. (1980), *Vijfendertig jaar loonbeleid in Nederland: terugblik en perspectief*, Alphen a/d Rijn: Samsom.

Flanagan, R., D.W. Soskice and L. Ulman (1983), *Unionism, Economic Stabilisation and Incomes Policies*, European experience, Washington D.C.: The Brookings Institute.

Flora, P. and J. Alber (1981), 'Modernization, Democratization, and the Development of Welfare States in Western Europe', in: P. Flora and A.J. Heidenheimer (eds.), *The Development of Welfare States in Europe and America*, New Brunswick: Transaction Books, pp. 37-80.

Flora, P. (1986), 'Introduction', in: P. Flora (ed.), *Growth to Limits: The Western European welfare state since World War II*, Berlin/New York: Walter de Gruyter, vol. 2, pp. XII-XXXVI.

Fortuyn, P. (1981), *Sociaal-economische Politiek in Nederland, 1945-1949*, Alphen a/d Rijn: Samsom.

Freeman, R. and L. Katz (1994), *Differences and Changes in Wage Structures*, Chicago: University of Chicago Press.

Freeman, R. and J. Medoff (1984), *What Do Unions Do?*, New York: Basic Books.

Freeman, R. J. Hartog and C. Teulings (1996), *Pulling The Plug: An analysis of mandatory extension in the Dutch system of labour relations*, The Hague: OSA-voorstudie W144.

Garrett, G. and P. Lange (1986), 'Performance in a Hostile World: Economic Growth in Capitalist Democracies 1974-80', in: *World Politics*, 38, no. 4, 517-45.

Genschel, P. (1997), 'The Dynamics of Inertia: Institutional Persistence and Institutional Change in Telecommunications and Health Care', in: *Governance. An International Journal of Policy and Administration*, no. 1., pp. 43-66.

Gestel, N.M. van (1994), *De Onzichtbare Overheid: Naar nieuwe vormen van sturing, het voorbeeld van de arbeidsvoorzieningswet*, Delft: Eburon.

Goldthorpe, J.H. (ed.) (1984), *Order and Conflict in Contemporary Capitalism*, Oxford: Clarendon Press.

Haas, A.W.A. de (1996), 'De Philips-cao's verklaard', *Economisch-Statistische Berichten*, 14-8-1996, pp. 664-69.

Hall, P.A. (1986), *Governing the Economy: The politics of State Intervention in Britain and France*, Oxford: Polity Press.

Hall, P.A. (1989), *The Political Power of Economic Ideas: Keynesianism across Nations*, Princeton: Princeton University Press.

Hall, P.A. (1992), 'The Movement from Keynesianism to Monetarism: Institutional analysis and British economic policy in the 1970s', in: S. Steinmo, K, Thelen, and F. Longstreth (eds), *Structuring Politics: Historical institutionalism in comparative analysis*, Cambridge: Cambridge University Press.

Hall, P.A. (1993), 'Policy Paradigms, Social Learning, and the State, The Case of economic policy-making in Britain', in: *Comparative Politics*, April, 1993, pp. 275-296.

Hall, P.A. and R.C.R. Taylor (1996), *Political Science and the Three New Institutionalisms*, MPIFG Discussion Paper 96/6, Max Planck Institute for the study of societies.

Hanf, K. and F.W. Scharpf (eds.) (1978), *Interorganizational Policy Making. Limits to coordination and central control*, London: Sage.

Hardin, R. (1968), 'The Tragedy of the Commons', in: *Science*, 1962, pp. 1243-48.

Hartog, J., and C. Teulings (1994), *Markets, Institutions and Wages*, Ministerie van Sociale Zaken en Werkgelegenheid, werkdocument 8, The Hague.

Hartog, J. and J.J.M. Theeuwes (1983), *De onstuitbare opkomst van de werkende gehuwde vrouw*, ESB, pp. 1152-7.

Heclo, H. (1974), *Modern Social Politics in Britain and Sweden: From relief to income maintenance*, New Haven: Yale University Press.

Heertje, A., and E. van der Wolk (1982), *Werkloosheid: verwording en verwachting. De economische crisis en haar slachtoffers*, Amsterdam: Keesing.

Heertum-Lemmen, A.H. and A.J.C.M. Wilthagen (1996), *De doorwerking van de aanbevelingen van de Stichting van de Arbeid*, The Hague: SDU.

Hemerijck, A.C. (1993), *The Historical Contingencies of Dutch Corporatism*, dissertation, Balliol College, Oxford.

Hemerijck, A.C. (1995a), 'Corporatist Immobility in the Netherlands', in: C. Crouch and F. Traxler (eds), *Organized Industrial Relations in Europe: What Future?*, Aldershot: Avebury, pp. 183-226.

Hemerijck, A.C. (1995b), 'De lange schaduw van de geleide loonpolitiek, 1968-1995', in: Rigter, D. et al, *Tussen Sociale Wil en Werkelijkheid: Een geschiedenis van het beleid van het Ministerie van Sociale Zaken*, The Hague: VUGA, pp. 313-354.

Hemerijck A.C. and R. Kloosterman (1995), 'Der Postindustrielle Umbau des korporatistischen Sozialstaats in den Niederlanden', in: W. Fricke (ed.), *Jahrbuch Arbeit und Technik 1995: Zukunft des Sozialstaates*, Bonn: Verlag J.H.W. Dietz, pp. 287-296.

Hemerijck, A.C. and R.J. van der Veen (1995), 'De Nederlandse verzorgingsstaat in perspectief: een tussenbalans', in: Rigter, D. et al., *Tussen Social Wil en Werkelijkheid: een geschiedenis van het Ministerie van Sociale Zaken*, The Hague: VUGA, pp. 293-311.

Hemerijck, A.C. and K. van Kersbergen (1997), 'A Miraculous Model? The New Politics of the Welfare State in the Netherlands, *Acta Politica* (forthcoming).

Hen, P.E. de (1980), *Actieve en re-actieve Industriepolitiek in Nederland: de overheid en de ontwikkeling van de Nederlandse industrie in de jaren dertig en tussen 1945 en 1950*, Amsterdam: De Arbeiderspers.

Heijden, P.F. van der (1993) 'Loonwet 1994: collectieve contractsvrijheid ingevroren, *Nederlands Juristenblad*, pp. 33-35.

Heijden, P.F. van der (1995) 'Ontslagrecht zonder ontslagvergunning', *Mededelingen van het Hugo Sinzheimer Instituut*, no. 10, pp. 1-16.

Hirschman, A.O. (1970), *Exit, Voice and Loyalty: Responses to decline in Firms, Organizations and States*, Cambridge, Mass.: Harvard University Press.

Hoefnagels, H. (1961), 'Nederland een sociaal paradijs?', in: *Sociologische Gids*, 8, 6, pp. 274-89.

Hofstra, N.A. and P.W. Nobelen (1993), *Toekomst van de overlegeconomie*, Assen: Van Gorcum.

Hooff, C. van (1996), *Bouwen aan vertrouwen: Een institutionele analyse van de rol van de overheid in de arbeidsvoorziening*, (honours thesis), University of Leiden, Department of Public Administration.

Hupe, P.L. (1992), *Om de kwaliteit van de macht: Het werkgelegenheidsplan van Minister Den Uyl in vijfvoud beschouwd*, Arnhem: Gouda Quint.

Immergut, E.M. (1992), *Health Politics, Interests and Institutions in Western Europe*, Cambridge: Cambridge University Press.

Kam, C.A. de, and J. de Haan (eds), *Terugtredende Overheid: Realiteit of retoriek? Een evaluatie van de grote operaties*, Schoonhoven: Academic Services.

Katzenstein, P.J. (ed.) (1978), *Between Power and Plenty: Foreign economic policies in advanced industrial states*, Madison: University of Wisconsin Press.

Katzenstein, P.J. (1985), *Small States in World Markets, Industrial policy in Europe*, Ithaca NY: Cornell University Press.

Kersbergen, K. van (1995), *Social Capitalism: A study of Christian Democracy and the Welfare State*, London/New York: Routledge.

King, D. (1995), *Actively seeking Work? The Politics of Unemployment and Welfare Policy in the United States and Great Britain*, Chicago: The University of Chicago Press.

Klandermans, P.G. and J. Visser (1995), *De vakbeweging na de welvaartsstaat*, Assen: Van Gorcum.

Klamer, A. (1990), *Verzuilde dromen. Veertig jaar SER*, Amsterdam: Bert Bakker.

Kleinknecht, A. (1996), *Is Labour Market Flexibility Harmful to Innovation?*, Discussion Paper TI 96-37/6, Tinbergen Instituut, Vrije Universiteit, Amsterdam.

Kloosterman and Elfring (1990), *Werken in Nederland*, Schoonhoven: Academic Service.

Knoester, A. (1987) (ed.), *Lessen uit het Verleden*, Nederlandse Vereniging voor Staatshuidhoudkunde, Leiden/Antwerpen: Stenfert Kroese.

Kohli, M, M. Rein, A. Guillemard, and H. van Gunsteren (eds) (1991), *Time for Retirement. Comparative Studies of Early Exit from the Labour Force*, Cambridge: Cambridge University Press.

Koole, R.A. (1995), *Politieke partijen in Nederland: Ontstaan en ontwikkeling van partijen en partijstelsel*, Utrecht: Het Spectrum.

Korpi, W. (1983), *The Democratic Class Struggle*, London: Routledge & Kegan Paul.

Krasner, S.D. (1984) 'Approaches to the State: Alternative Conceptions and Historical Dynamics', in: *Comparative Politics*, 1, pp. 223-46.

Krasner, S.D. (1988), 'Sovereignty: An Institutional Perspective', in: *Comparative Political Studies*, 21, pp. 66-94.

Kroft, H., G. Engbersen, K. Schuyt and F. van Waarden, *Een Tijd zonder Werk: Een onderzoek naar de levenswereld van langdurig werklozen*, Leiden: Stenfert Kroese.

Kruse, F.H.A.M (1987), 'Een partuur met perspectief: Sturing arbeidsmarkt door samenwerking overheid en sociale partners', in: A. Buitendam (ed.), *Arbeidsmarkt, arbeidsorganisatie, arbeidsverhoudingen*, Deventer: Kluwer, pp. 27-31.

Lange, P. and G. Garrett, (1985), 'The Politics of Growth: Strategic Interaction and Economic Performance in the Advanced Industrial Democracies', in: *The Journal of Politics*, 47/3, pp. 792-828.

Lash, S., and J. Urry (1987), *The End of Organized Capitalism*, Oxford: Polity Press.

Layard, R., S. Nickel and R. Jackman (1991), *Unemployment, Macroeconomic Performance and the Labour Market*, Oxford: Oxford UP.

Lehmbruch, G. and Schmitter, P.C. (1982), *Patterns of Corporatist Policy-Making*, Beverly Hills/London: Sage.

Lehmbruch, G. (1992), 'The Organization of Society, Administrative Strategies and Policy Networks', in: R. Czada, and A. Windhoff-Héritier, *Political Choice*, Frankfurt/Main: Campus.

Leijnse, F. (1985), *Bevordering van deeltijdarbeid: Een verkenning van de mogelijkheden voor stimuleringsbeleid van de overheid*, Instituut voor Toegepaste Sociologie, Nijmegen.

Lijphart, A. (1968), *The Politics of Accommodation: Pluralism and Democracy in the Netherlands*, Berkeley: University of California Press.

Lijphart, A., R. Rogowski and R. Kent Weaver (1993), 'Separation of Powers and Cleavage Management', in: R.K. Weaver and B.A. Rockman (eds.), *Do Institutions Matter? Government Capabilities in the United States and Abroad*, Washington D.C.: Brookings Institute.

Lindbeck, A. and D.J. Snower (1988), *The Insider-Outsider Theory of Employment and Unemployment*, Cambridge, Mass.: MIT Press.

Locke, R., T. Kochan and M. Piore (1995), *Employment Relations in a Changing World Economy*, Cambridge, Mass.: MIT Press.

Looise, J. (1989), The Recent Growth in Employees' Representation in the Netherlands: Defying the Times?', in: C.J. Lammers and G. Széll (eds.), *International Handbook of Participation in Organisations*, vol. 1: *Organisational Democracy, Taking Stock*, Oxford: Oxford University Press, pp. 268-284.

Maarse, J.A.M. (1984), 'Arbeidsmarktbeleid: enkele trends en effecten', in: *Sociologische Gids*, vol. 31, 1, pp. 96-120.

Maassen-van de Brink, H. (1994), *Female Labour Supply, Child Care and Marital Conflict*, Amsterdam: Amsterdam University Press.

Macchiavelli, N. (1970) *The Discourses*. B. Crick (ed.), Harmondsworth: Penguin.

Maddison, A. (1982), *Ontwikkelingsfasen van het kapitalisme*, Utrecht: Het Spectrum.

Mannoury, J. (1967), *Hoofdtrekken van de sociale verzekering*, Alphen a/d Rijn: Samsom.

Mannoury, J. (1970), *Kernpunten van de sociale politiek*, Groningen: Wolters-Noordhoff.

Mannoury, J. (1985), 'De ontwikkeling van de Nederlandse verzorgingsstaat', in: F.L. van Holthoorn (ed), *De Nederlandse samenleving sinds 1815: Wording en samenhang*, Assen: Van Gorcum, pp. 187-202.

March, J. and J.P. Olsen (1989), *Rediscovering Institutions: The Organizational Basis of Politics*, New York: Free Press.

Marin, B. (ed.), *Generalized Political Exchange, Antagonistic Cooperation and Integrated Policy Circuits*, Frankfurt a/Main, Boulder Co: Campus and Westview.

Marshall, T.H. (1963), 'Citizenship and Social Class', in: Marshall, T.H., *Sociology at the Crossroads and other Essays*, London: Heinemann, pp. 67-128.

Mayntz, R. and F.W. Scharpf (1975), *Policy-Making in the German Federal Bureaucracy*, Amsterdam: Elsevier.

Mayntz, R. and F.W. Scharpf (1995), 'Der Ansatz des akteurzentrierten Institutionalismus' in Mayntz R. and F.W. Scharpf (eds.), *Gesellschaftliche Selbstregelung und politische Steuerung*, Frankfurt/Main: Campus.

Meer, M. van der (1996), 'Belangenbehartiging onder druk. De langste bouwstaking na de Tweede Wereldoorlog' in: J. Visser (ed.), *De vakbeweging op de eeuwgrens*, Amsterdam: Amsterdam University Press, pp. 118-43.

Messing, F. (1988), 'Het economisch leven in Nederland 1945-1980', in: J.C. Boogman et al., *Geschiedenis van het Moderne Nederland. Politieke, economische en sociale ontwikkelingen*, Houten: De Haan.

Metze, M. (1990), *Intermediair rapport: Hoe flexibel is de BV Nederland?*, Utrecht: Het Spectrum.

Morée, M., (1991) 'Een illusie van economische zelfstandigheid', in: C. Bouw, J. van Hoof, P. de Jong, B. Kruithof and L. van der Maesen (ed.), *Macht en onbehagen: Veranderingen in de verhoudingen tussen vrouwen en mannen*, Amsterdam: SUA, pp. 101-14.

Naschold, F. and B. de Vroom (eds.) (1994), *Regulating Employment and Welfare: Company and national policies of labour force participation at the end of worklife in industrial societies*, Berlin/New York: Walter de Gruyter.

Nobelen, P.W.M. (1983), 'Nederland: Kwijnend corporatisme en stagnerende verzorgingsstaat', in: T. Akkermans and P.W.M. Nobelen (eds.), *Corporatisme en verzorgingsstaat*, Leiden: Stenfert Kroese, pp. 99-142.

Offe, C. (1981), 'The Attribution of Public Status to Interest Groups: Observations on the West German Case', in: S. Berger (ed.), *Organizing Interests in Western Europe: Pluralism, Corporatism, and the Transformation of Politics*, Cambridge: Cambridge University Press, pp. 123-158.

Olson, M. (1965), *The Logic of Collective Action: Public Goods and the Theory of Groups*, Cambridge Mass: Harvard University Press.

Olson, M. (1982), *The Rise and Decline of Nations: Economic Growth, Stagflation, and Social Rigidities*, New Haven: Yale University Press.

Panitch, L. (1986), *Working Class Politics in Crisis: Essays on Labour and the State*, London: Verso Books.

Pen, J. (1963), The Strange Adventures of Dutch Wage Policies, in: *British Journal of Industrial Relations*, 1, 3, pp. 318-30.

Pen, J. (1973), 'Trade Union Attitudes Toward Central Wage Policy: Remarks on the Dutch experience', in: A. Sturmthal and J.G. Scoville (eds.), *The International Labor Movement in Transition: Essays on America, Asia, Europe and South America*, Urbana Ill.: University of Illinois Press, pp. 259-82.

Peijpe, T. van (1985) *De ontwikkeling van het loonvormingsrecht*, Nijmegen: Ars Aequi Libri.

Pierson, P. (1994), *Dismantling the Welfare State? Reagan, Thatcher, and the politics of retrenchment*, Cambridge: Cambridge University Press.

Pierson, P. (1996), 'The New Politics of the Welfare State', *World Politics*, 48, 2, pp. 143-9.

Piore, M.J. and C.S. Sabel (1984), *The Second Industrial Divide, Possibilities for Prosperity*, New York: Basic Books.

Pizzorno, A. (1978), 'Political Exchange and Collective Identity in Industrial Conflict', in: C.J. Crouch and A. Pizzorno (eds.), *The Resurgence of Class Conflict in Western Europe since 1968*, vol.2, London: MacMillan, pp. 277-298.

Prins, R. (1991), 'Arbeidsongeschiktheid in internationaal perspectief', *Economisch-Statistische Berichten*, 16-1-1991, pp.64-67.

Putnam, R. (1993), *Making Democracy Work: Civic Traditions in Modern Italy*, Princeton: Princeton University Press.

Regini, M (1995), *Uncertain Boundaries, The Social and Political Construction of European Economies*, Cambridge: Cambridge University Press.

Reynaerts, W. (1985), 'Kantelende posities: Arbeidsverhoudingen in een keertijd', *in Bespiegelingen over de toekomst van de sociale partners*, OSA-voorstudie no. 4, The Hague.

Rigter, D.P., E.A.M. van den Bosch, R.J. van der Veen en A.C. Hemerijck (1995), *Tussen sociale wil en werkelijkheid: Een geschiedenis van het beleid van het Ministerie van Sociale Zaken*, The Hague: VUGA.

Rijswijck-Clerkx, L. van (1981), *Moeders, kinderen en kinderopvang*, Nijmegen: SUN.

Rinnooy Kan, A. (1993), 'De Nederlandse overlegeconomie en de jaren negentig: een kritische balans', in: N.A. Hofstra and P.W.M. Nobelen (eds.), *Toekomst van de Overlegeconomie*, Assen: Van Gorcum, 38-52.

Roebroek, J.M. and B. van Koten (1985), 'Sociaal-Economische Raad en sociale zekerheid', in: *Beleid en Maatschappij*, 7/11.

Rogers, J., and W. Streeck (1995), *Works Councils: Consultation, Representation, and Cooperation in Industrial Relations*, Chicago: University of Chicago Press.

Rojer, M. (1996a), 'De reparatie van de WAO-gat: Een dynamische analyse van de cao-onderhandelingen' in: Visser, J. (ed.), *De vakbeweging op de eeuwgrens*, Amsterdam: Amsterdam University Press, pp. 92-117.

Rojer, M. (1996b), *Cao-onderhandelingen: Een voorspelbaar, logisch en rationeel proces?*, Amsterdam: Thesis publishers.

Rood, M. (1991), *Staken in Nederland*, Schoonhoven: Academic Service.

Roorda, W.B. and E.H.W.M. Vogels (1997a), *Concurrerende arbeidsverhoudingen*, Werkdocument no. 33, Ministry of Social Affairs and Employment, The Hague.

Roorda, W.B., and E.H.W.M. Vogels (1997b), 'Arbeidsmarkt, bescherming en prestaties', *Economisch-Statistische Berichten*, 26 Maart, pp. 245-8.

Rooy, P. de (1979), *Werklozenzorg en werkloosheidsbestrijding 1917-1940: Landelijk en Amsterdams beleid*, Amsterdam: Van Gennep.

Rothstein, B. (1992), 'Labour Market Institutions and Working Class Strength', in: S. Steinmon, K. Thelen, and F. Longstreth (eds.), *Structuring Politics: Historical Institutionalism and Comparative Analysis*, Cambridge: Cambridge University Press, pp. 33-56.

Roubini, N. and J. Sachs (1988), *Government Spending and Budget Deficits in the Industrial Economies*, Paper presented at the Fall meeting of the Economic Policy Panel, Turin, Italy.

Ruysseveldt, J. van, and J. Visser (eds.) (1996), *Industrial Relations in Europe: Traditions and Transitions*, London: Sage.

Salverda, W. (1996), 'Is the Dutch Economy Really Short of Low-paid Jobs?', in: C.H.A. Verhaar (ed.), *On the Challenge of Unemployment in a Regional Europe*, Aldershot: Avebury, pp. 221-40.

Salverda, W. (1997) 'Verdringing en arbeidsmarktbeleid voor de onderkant', in: F. Bergman, J. Hartog, P. Hiemstra, R. Kloosterman, W. Salverda and J. Theeuwes (eds.), *Creëren van werk aan de onderkant*, Amsterdam: Welboom, pp. 55-74.

Scharpf, F. (1986), 'Policy Failure and Institutional Reform: Why should form follow function?', in: *International Social Science Journal*, 108/1986, pp. 179-189.

Scharpf, F.W. (1987), 'The Political Calculus of Inflation and Unemployment in Western Europe: A Game-Theoretical Interpretation', Working Paper, Harvard University, Center for European Studies.

Scharpf, F.W. (1988), 'The Joint-Decision Trap: Lessons from German Federalism and European Integration', In: *Public Administration*, 66, pp. 239-278.

Scharpf, F.W. (1989), 'Decision Rules, Decision Styles, and Policy Choices', in: *Journal of Theoretical Politics*, 1, pp. 149-176.

Scharpf, F.W. (1991), *Crisis and Choice in European Social Democracy*, Ithaca NY: Cornell University Press.

Scharpf, F.W. (1993), 'Coordination in Hierarchies and Networks', in: F.W. Scharpf (ed.), *Games in Hierarchies and Networks: Analytical and empirical approaches to the study of governance institutions*, Frankfurt a/Main and Boulder Co: Campus and Westview.

Scharpf, F.W. (1997), *Games Real Actors Play: Actor-Centered Institutionalism in Policy Research*, Boulder Co: Westview Press.

Schattschneider, E. (1960), *The Semi-Sovereign People*, New York: Holt, Rinehart and Winston.

Schmid, G. (1996), *The Dutch Employment Miracle? A comparison of employment systems in the Netherlands and Germany*, Discussion Paper FS 96 -206, Wissenschaftszentrum Berlin für Sozialforschung (WZB), Berlin.

Schmitter P.C. (1983), *Neo-Corporatism, Consensus, Governability, and Democracy in the Management of Crisis in Contemporary Advanced Industrial-Capitalist Societies*, European University Institute, Florence (unpublished paper).

Schmitter, P.C. (1989), 'Corporatism is dead! Long live corporatism!', in: *Government and Opposition*, The Andrew Sonfield Lectures (4) vol. 24, no 1., pp. 54-73.

Schmitter and Streeck, (1981), *The Organization of Business Interests. A research design to study the associative action of business in the advanced industrial societies of western Europe*, IIM Discussion papers, IIM/LMP 81-31, Wissenschaftszentrum Berlin.

Schmitter, P.C. and G. Lehmbruch (eds.) (1979), *Trends towards Corporatist Intermediation*, Londen/Beverly Hills: Sage.

Schutte, C.E.M. (1995) *Overzicht van het cao-recht*, Nijmegen: Ars Aequi Libri.

Skocpol, T. (1985), 'Bringing The State Back In: Strategies of analysis in current research', in: Evans, P.B., D. Reuschemeyer and T. Skocpol (eds), *Bringing the State Back In*, Cambridge: Cambridge University Press.

Skowronek, S. (1982), *Building a New American State: The Expansion of National Administrative Capacities, 1877-1920*, Cambridge, Cambridge University Press.

Smirzai, A. (1981), 'Matigingsbeleid en het dilemma van de gevangenen, in: *Economisch-Statistische Berichten*, 23 September, pp. 912-9.

Smit, E., K. Schilstra and J. Paauwe (1995), *Belangenbehartiging van werknemers: een toekomstverkenning*, The Hague: VUGA.

Sorge, A. and W. Streeck (1988), 'Industrial Relations and Technical Change: The Case for an Extended Perspective', in R. Hyman and W. Streeck (eds.), *New Technology and Industrial Relations*, Oxford: Blackwell.

Streeck, W. (1984), 'Neo-corporatist Industrial Relations and the Economic Crisis in Germany', in: Goldthorpe, J.H. (ed.), *Order and Conflict in Contemporary Capitalism*, Oxford: Clarendon Press.

Streeck, W. (1992), *Social Institutions and Economic Performance: Studies of Industrial Relations in Advanced Capitalist Economies*, London: Sage.

Streeck, W. (1995), 'Works Councils in Western Europe: From Consultation to Participation', in: J. Rogers and W. Streeck (eds.), *Works Councils. Consultation, representation, and cooperation in industrial relations* Chicago, Ill.: The University of Chicago Press, pp. 313-48.

Streeck, W. and P.C. Schmitter (1985), 'Community, Market, State – and Associations?, in: *European Sociological Review*, 1, 119-138.

Svensen, P. (1989), *Fair Shares: Unions, Pay, and Politics in Sweden and West Germany*, Ithaca NY: Cornell University Press.

SZW (1996), *De Nederlandse verzorgingsstaat in internationaal en economisch perspectief*, Ministry of Social Affairs and Employment, The Hague.

Teulings, C.N. (1996), *De plaats van de vakbeweging in de toekomst*, Amsterdam: Welboom.

Teulings, C., and J. Hartog (1997), *Corporatism and Competition*, Cambridge: Cambridge University Press (forthcoming).

Teulings, C. R.J. van der Veen and W. Trommel (1997), *Dilemma's van sociale zekerheid, een analyse van 10 jaar herziening van het stelsel van sociale zekerheid*, The Hague: VUGA (forthcoming).

Thelen K. and S. Steinmo (1992), 'Historical Institutionalism in Comparative Politics', in: S. Steinmo, K. Thelen and F. Lonstreth (eds.), *Structuring Politics: Historical Institutionalism in Comparative Analysis*, Cambridge: Cambridge University Press.

Therborn, G. (1986), *Why Some People Are More Unemployed Than Others*, London: Verso.

Therborn, G. (1989), 'Nederland en het falende arbeidsmarktheid', in: P. Broertjes, *Getto's in Neder-land. Visies op armoede naar de levenswereld van langdurig werklozen*, Amsterdam: Van Gennep, pp. 23-36.

Tijdens, K. and A. Goudswaard (1994), *Kantoorarbeid van vrouwen in de industrie*, Amsterdam: Welboom.

Tijdens, K, H. Maassen-van den Brink, W. Groot and M. Noom (1994), *Arbeid en zorg: Maatschappelijke effecten van strategieën van huishoudens om betaalde arbeid en zorg te combineren*, OSA, The Hague, W-124.

Tijdens, K. (1996), *Atypical jobs: Employers strategies and women's preferences. The case of working hours in Dutch banks*, paper IREC conference, Kopenhagen, September 1996.

Toren, J.P. van den (1996), *Achter gesloten deuren? CAO-overleg in de jaren negentig*, Amsterdam: Welboom.

Toirkens, J. (1988), *Schijn en werkelijkheid van het bezuinigingsbeleid 1975-1986*, Deventer: Kluwer.

Traxler, F. (1990), 'Political Exchange, Collective Action and Interest Governance. Towards a theory of the genesis of industrial relations and corporatism', in: B. Marin (ed.), *Generalized Political Exchange*, Frankfurt a/Main: Campus and Westview, pp. 37-67.

Traxler, F. (1995), 'Farewell to Labour Market Associations? Organized versus disorganized decentralization as a Map for Industrial Relations', in: C. Crouch and F. Traxler (eds.), *Organized Industrial Relations in Europe: What future?*, Avebury: Aldershot, pp. 3-19.

Traxler, F. (1996), 'Collective Bargaining and Industrial Change: A case of Disorganisation? A Comparative Analysis of Eighteen OECD Countries', in: *European Sociological Review*, 12, 3, pp. 271-87.

Tsebelis, G. (1990), *Nested Games: Rational Choice in Comparative Politics*, Berkeley: University of California Press.

Ulman, L. and R.J. Flanagan (1971), *Wage Restraint: A Study of Income Policies in Western Europe*, Berkeley: University of California Press.

Veen, R.J. van der (1995), 'Van Bescherming naar stimulering: De herziening van de social zekerheid 1968-1995', in: Rigter, D., et al., *Tussen sociale wil en werkelijkheid: Een geschiedenis van het beleid van het Ministerie van Sociale Zaken*, The Hague: VUGA, pp. 359-390.

Veen, R.J van der, J. Burger and A.C. Hemerijck (1995), 'De demonopolisering van de Nederlandse arbeidsvoorziening tussen 1965 en 1995', in: Rigter et al., *Tussen sociale wil en werkelijkheid: Een geschiedenis van het beleid van het Ministerie van Sociale Zaken*, The Hague: VUGA, pp. 391-407.

Veen, R.J. van der, and A.C. Hemerijck, 'Continuïteit en verandering: de herziening van de Nederlandse verzorgingsstaat' (1995), in: Rigter, D., et al., *Tussen sociale wil en werkelijkheid: Een geschiedenis van het beleid van het Ministerie van Sociale Zaken*, The Hague: VUGA, pp. 409-423.

Veldkamp, G.J.M. (1968), *Sociale triptiek: Verantwoording en achtergronden van een beleid*, The Hague: Staatsuitgeverij.

Venema, P.M., A. Faas and J.A. Samadhan (1996), *Arbeidsvoorwaardenontwikkeling in 1995*, SZW, Labour inspectorate, The Hague.

Visser, J. (1989), 'New Working Time Arrangements in the Netherlands', in: A. Gladstone, R. Lansbury, J. Stieber, T. Treu and M. Weiss (eds.), *Current Issues in Labour Relations: An international perspective*, Berlin and New York: De Gruyter, pp. 229-50.

Visser, J. (1990a), *In Search of Inclusive Unionism*, Deventer and Boston: Kluwer.

Visser, J. (1990b), 'Continuity and Change in Dutch Industrial Relations', in: G. Baglioni and C. Crouch, *European Industrial Relations: The challenge of Flexibility*, London: Sage, pp. 199-240.

Visser, J. (1992), 'The Netherlands, The End of an Era and the End of a System', in: R. Hyman and A. Ferner (eds.), *Industrial Relations in the New Europe*, Oxford: Basil Backwell, 1st ed., pp. 323-356.

Visser, J. (1995), 'The Netherlands: From Paternalism to Representation', in: J. Rogers and W. Streeck (eds), *Works Councils: Consultation, Representation, and Cooperation in Industrial Relations,* Chicago: Chicago University Press, pp. 79-114.

Visser, J. (1997), *Two Cheers for Corporatism, One for the Market: Industrial Relations, Unions, Wages, and Labour Markets in the Netherlands,* Max Planck Institute for the Study of Societies (Cologne), Department of Sociology/Cologne, University of Amsterdam, forthcoming in: *British Journal of Industrial Relations.*

Voorden, W. van (1975), *Institutionalisering en arbeidsmarktbeleid,* Alphen a/d Rijn: Samsom.

Voorden, W. van (1980), 'Het beklemde sociaal-economische beleid van het kabinet van Agt', in: *Civis Mundi,* no. 5, September, pp. 195-201.

Vording, H. (1993), *Koppelingen in de social zekerheid 1957 1992. Van wetten en praktische bezwaren,* Amsterdam: Thesis Publishers.

Waarden, F. van, (1985), 'Regulering en belangenorganisaties van ondernemers', in: F. van Holthoorn (ed), *De Nederlandse samenleving sinds 1815: Wording en Samenhang,* Assen: Van Gorcum, pp. 227-60.

Wassenberg, A.F.P. (1982) 'Neo-Corporatism and the Quest for Control: The Cuckoo Game', in: G. Lehmbruch and P.C. Schmitter (eds.), *Patterns of Corporatist Policy-Making,* Beverly Hills: Sage, 83-108

Weaver. R.K., and B.A. Rockman (eds.), *Do Institutions Matter? Government Capabilities in the United States and Abroad,* Washinton D.C.: Brookings Institute.

Weaver, R.K. (1987), 'The Politics of Blame Avoidance', in: *Journal of Public Policy,* vol. 6, no. 4, pp. 371-398.

Weber, Max (1985, [1922]) *Wirtschaft und Gesellschaft,* Tübingen: J.C. Mohr, fifth revised ed.

Weick, K.E. (1976) 'Educational Organisations as Loosely Coupled Systems', *Administrative Science Quarterly,* 21: 1-20

Weir, M. (1992), *Politics and Jobs: The Boundaries of Employment Policy in the United States,* Princeton: Princeton University Press.

Wellink, A.H.E.M. (1987), 'De ontwikkeling in de jaren zeventig en tachtig en enkele daaruit te trekken lessen', in: A. Knoester (ed.), *Lessen uit het verleden: 125 jaar Vereniging voor de Staathuishoud-kunde,* Leiden/Antwerpen: Stenfert Kroese, pp. 333-66.

Wijnbergen, S. van (1996), 'Institutionele aspecten van de arbeidsmarktproblematiek in Nederland', in: OSA, *Preadviezen over institutionele aspecten van de arbeidsmarkt,* The Hague, werkdocument W139, pp. 31-56.

Windmuller, J.P. (1969), *Labor Relations in the Netherlands,* Ithaca NY: Cornell University Press.

Wolinetz, S. (1989a), *The Strange Adventures of Dutch Tripartitism in the 1970s and 1980s,* Harvard, Cambridge, Mass., (unpublished paper).

Wolinetz, S.B. (1989b), 'Socio-economic Bargaining in the Netherlands: Redefining the Post-war Policy Coalition', in: *West European Politics: Politics in the Netherlands, How Much Change?,* special issue, London, vol. 12 no. 1, 79-98.

Wolff, P. de and W. Driehuis (1980), 'A Description of Post War Economic Developments and Economic Policy in the Netherlands', in: R.T. Griffiths (ed.), *The Economy and Politics of the Netherlands since 1945,* The Hague: Martinus Nijhoff, pp. 12-60.

Zanden, J.L. van and R.T. Griffiths (1989), *Economische geschiedenis van Nederland in de 20e eeuw,* Utrecht: Het Spectrum.

Index